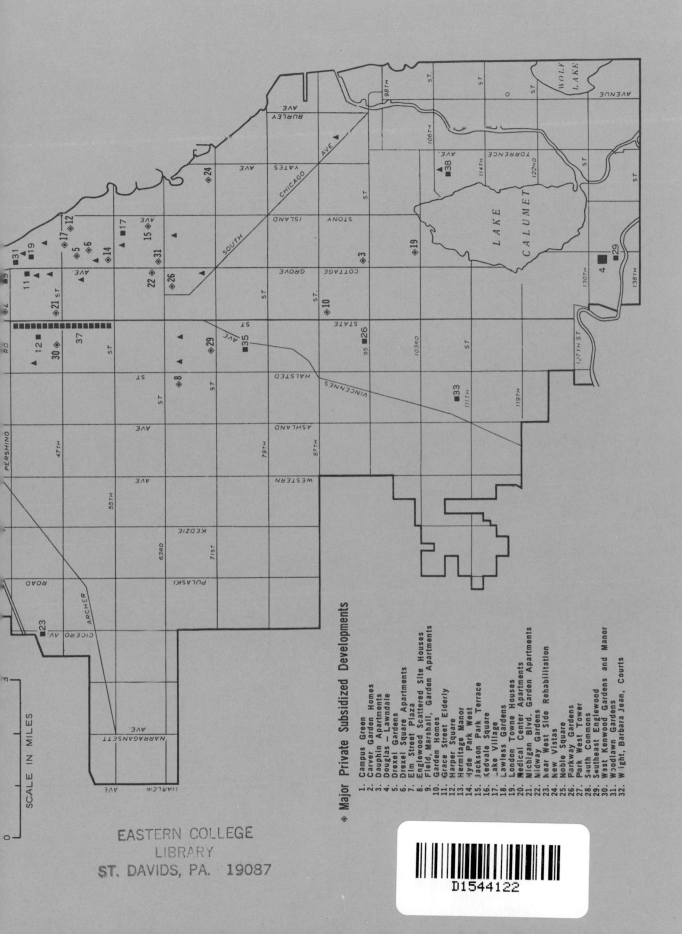

◇ **Major Private Subsidized Developments**

1. Campus Green
2. Carver Garden Homes
3. Dauphin Apartments
4. Douglas — Lawndale
5. Drexel Gardens
6. Drexel Square Apartments
7. Elm Street Plaza
8. Englewood Scattered Site Houses
9. Field, Marshall, Garden Apartments
10. Garden Homes
11. Grace Street Elderly
12. Harper Square
13. Hermitage Manor
14. Hyde Park West
15. Jackson Park Terrace
16. Kedvale Square
17. Lake Village
18. Lawless Gardens
19. London Towne Houses
20. Medical Center Apartments
21. Michigan Blvd. Garden Apartments
22. Midway Gardens
23. Near West Side Rehabilitation
24. New Vistas
25. Noble Square
26. Parkway Gardens
27. Park West Tower
28. South Commons
29. Southeast Englewood
30. West Kenwood Gardens and Manor
31. Woodlawn Gardens
32. Wight, Barbara Jean, Courts

The Poorhouse

Subsidized Housing in Chicago, 1895–1976
by Devereux Bowly, Jr.

SOUTHERN ILLINOIS UNIVERSITY PRESS

Carbondale and Edwardsville

FEFFER & SIMONS, INC.

London and Amsterdam

This book was written under a grant from the
Graham Foundation for Advanced Studies in the Fine Arts

Library of Congress Cataloging in Publication Data

Bowly, Devereux, 1942–
  The poorhouse.

  Includes bibliographical references and index.
  1. Public housing—Illinois—Chicago—History.
I. Title.
HD7304.C4B68 1978   301.5'4   77-28271
ISBN 0-8093-0831-2

To Professor Carl W. Condit, whose books and lectures
encouraged my interest in the history of the city

Contents

List of Illustrations

Preface

Although untold billions of dollars have been spent in this country over the last half century on subsidized housing, it is a subject that has received too little attention. The various programs have come and gone with inadequate evaluation of their social and economic impact. In the next few years major decisions will have to be made about the direction of housing in America. Future programs can only be planned intelligently in the context of achievements and failures of past programs.

Chicago makes an ideal subject for a case study of subsidized housing. Incorporated in 1833, it is one of the youngest of the major cities, its entire development having occurred during the post–Industrial Revolution period. It has long been an innovator in the technology of building, and is unexcelled in the quality of its architectural design, yet its experience with subsidized housing has, on the whole, been a negative one. This raises serious questions as to the very nature of subsidized housing, whether or not we should have it, and if so in what form.

The basic scope of the book is limited to the City of Chicago, and to multi-family developments. The matter of subsidized single family houses is a large subject deserving of its own study. A major focus of attention here will be housing constructed by governmental agencies, or with public grants. Projects with subsidized mortgages and rents will be considered, as will housing constructed as private philanthropic endeavors.

Devereux Bowly, Jr.

Chicago, Illinois
February 6, 1978

The Poorhouse

1 Philanthropic Housing Projects

Subsidized housing was originally the work of individual philanthropists. Between 1895 and 1930 four projects, all of imagination and high quality, were built in Chicago: Francisco Terrace, Garden Homes, Marshall Field Garden Apartments, and Michigan Boulevard Garden Apartments.

Francisco Terrace

The first subsidized housing in Chicago, Francisco Terrace, was a forty-four-unit "model tenement" which stood until 1974 at 255 North Francisco Avenue, three and one-half miles west of the Loop. Designed in 1895 by Frank Lloyd Wright, then a twenty-six-year-old little-known architect, it is a classic in the history of low-income housing.[1] The most important aspect of Francisco Terrace was the way it was laid out. It filled the perimeter of its mid-block rectangular site, completely enclosing a courtyard in the center. Constructed of brick, with terra cotta cornice and trim, it was only two stories tall, and had a tunnellike passageway connecting the street to the courtyard.

All of the apartments faced the courtyard, except on the street side of the building where there was a double row of apartments, the front ones of which opened to the sidewalk. The four corners of the courtyard contained semienclosed stair towers for access to a wooden gallery onto which the second floor apartments opened. By having no hallways, but rather the apartments open directly to the outside, Wright created the feeling of a tiny village built around a square. This is in stark contrast to later buildings, many of which have the apartments opening to long, depressing hallways. Francisco Terrace was built to a human scale, a characteristic all but lost in later low-income housing. It was small enough so that people knew their neighbors, and a feeling of community could exist.

The developer of the building was Edward Waller. He lived in suburban River Forest, across from a notable house Wright had designed in 1893 for the William Winslow family. Waller was interested in architecture, being a close friend of Daniel Burnham, and being the longtime manager of the famous Rookery Building, designed by Burnham and Root, and remodeled by Wright. He became quite close to Wright, and it was in Waller's home that Burnham offered to send Wright to Paris and Rome for six years to study. Wright, who did not want to study classical architecture, rejected the offer.[2] Waller budgeted $25,000 for Francisco Terrace. The subsidy for the project came from the fact that Waller planned from the first to earn only a 3 percent return on his investment.[3] For comparison purposes one need only consider the company town of Pullman, built by George Pullman south of Chicago in 1880. Although the town was planned as a model community, to house the workers of Pullman's Palace Car Company, a 6 percent return on investments in the rental properties was expected.[4]

Francisco Terrace, Chicago's first subsidized housing, was designed by Frank Lloyd Wright in 1895—Courtesy Oak Park Public Library, Oak Park, Illinois

The apartments of Francisco Terrace, which originally rented for twelve dollars a month, were small and occupied mostly by newly-weds of modest means. This led some people to call the building "Honeymoon Flats." Edward Waller died in 1931, and shortly there-after the neighborhood and building changed from white to black occupancy. The building and land were subdivided and sold off as twenty-two separate parcels, each containing two apartments, one on top of the other. The original central heating plant was abandoned in favor of individual units. The Depression, World War II, a lack of unified ownership, and the general decline of the West Side all took their toll on the building. By 1971 it was very dilapidated,

Francisco Terrace courtyard. By having the apartments open directly to the outside rather than onto the hallways, Wright created the feeling of a tiny village.—Courtesy Oak Park Public Library, Oak Park, Illinois

only partially occupied, and the subject of a demolition suit brought
by the City of Chicago. Though there was an effort to get someone
to rehabilitate the building, it was torn down in 1974.

The plan and concept of Francisco Terrace were so good that in
late 1976 they were being replicated. At the time of demolition
architect Benjamin Weese and realtor John Baird financed the re-
moval and storage of the terra cotta decoration of the building. After
considering several sites for the rebuilding of Francisco Terrace,
they settled on one at Lake Street and Euclid Avenue in Oak Park.
The building is being constructed of new materials, except for the
terra cotta. The exterior will be nearly the same as the original, but
the interior is to contain seventeen two- and three-story condominium town houses. The project is a fitting postscript to the life
of Frank Lloyd Wright, who was living in Oak Park when he designed Francisco Terrace, and where about thirty of his houses still
stand. It is also a tribute to the quality of the original design of the
development.

*Unidentified Chicago alley about 1915.—Courtesy of Chicago Historical
Society*

Garden Homes

The first large-scale subsidized housing project in Chicago, the Garden Homes, was built in 1919 by Benjamin J. Rosenthal. He had gotten his start in the millinery business, but later became a real estate developer. In 1912 he built the nineteen-story North American Building at 36 South State Street, still a major shop and showroom building. Rosenthal's interest was not limited to business, but included social and charitable activities. In addition to being a member of the Chicago Board of Education he served as chairman of a committee to find employment for men living in the Municipal Lodging House of Chicago. He also headed committees to encourage employment of the crippled and black women. In a book he wrote in 1919 he asked the questions: "Can a workman be efficient if he is crowded in a badly lighted, unclean house in a congested neighborhood? Can he be happy if he is obliged to occupy living rooms that are unfit for human habitation?"[5]

The answers for Rosenthal were no. He believed that private businesses, or even government, should develop and sell houses to workmen, and that home ownership would increase their efficiency and make them more responsible. His interest in housing for the masses was not shared by most businessmen of the time. For example, Daniel Burnham's famous *Plan of Chicago*, published in 1909 by the Commercial Club, contained but a few sentences dealing with the problems of slum housing.[6]

Rosenthal, who had traveled to England to see the garden cities there, purchased for his experiment in Chicago six square blocks of land bounded by 87th Street, 89th Street, Indiana Avenue, and State Street. The forty-acre site is bisected by 88th Street, and divided by Wabash and Michigan avenues. He subdivided the land into 175 residential lots, 30 feet wide, and from about 162 to 200 feet in length. The generous depth of the lots, by city standards, was to encourage gardening and landscaping.[7] The architect chosen to carry out Rosenthal's scheme was Charles Frost, who had been involved in the design of well-known buildings including the Chicago and Northwestern Railway Station, and the Northern Trust Company Building. He designed 133 detached houses, and 21 double, or party-wall, houses. The detached houses are of brick, two stories high, with full basements and concrete foundations. Their outside dimensions are approximately 22 by 25 feet. The first floor contains a living room, kitchen, and dinette, and there are three bedrooms and a bath upstairs.

The houses are basically the same, except there are seven slightly different exterior designs to provide variety. On each block front there are one, two, or three double houses. These are covered with stucco, and are of simplier lines with sharply sloping roofs, somewhat reminiscent of English cottages. Because of the unity of scale, the mixture of single and double houses, and the facade design variations, the overall effect is quite handsome when compared to later moderate-income housing. The houses were sold, at cost, to working families for $5,700, with Rosenthal taking back mortgages. He and his manager spent three or four afternoons a week personally inspecting the present apartments of prospective buyers. Though most of the houses were quickly sold, problems did develop. The location was somewhat remote from the built-up areas of the city and major transportation facilities. Some of the mortgages had to be foreclosed for nonpayment and the units rented.

The Depression certainly didn't help the Garden Homes. After Rosenthal's death in 1936, his foundation and his estate continued

The first large-scale subsidized housing project in Chicago, the Garden Homes, was built in 1919 by Benjamin J. Rosenthal.—Photograph by Devereux Bowly, Jr.

to deal with many of the properties, buying back some at tax sales. As late as 1940, records indicate they still had an interest in about two dozen of the houses, but eventually all were sold. Market values of the houses went up and down through the years. By the late 1920s houses were sold for $8,500, but a decade later some were in poor condition and valued at only $3,350.[8]

On the western edge of the development, along State Street (which now faces the Dan Ryan Expressway), and the northern edge, on 87th Street, "business lots" were located. Only in recent years have they been developed, with a few shops, but mostly with housing. By the mid-1970s the Garden Homes themselves were still in good condition, considering that they had been built more than fifty-five years before, along economic construction lines. Some had been altered, and some had not been well maintained, but the overall scheme was still intact and quite a pleasant contrast to most

Garden Homes, double house.—Photograph by Devereux Bowly, Jr.

later subdivisions. The houses have sold in recent years for about
$25,000.[9] Ultimately, the Garden Homes have to be viewed as a
failure from the standpoint of Rosenthal's dream that they would
demonstrate that moderate-income housing could be developed at a
profit. They were built and survived the early years only because of
his continuing subsidy.

During the decade of the 1920s there was unprecedented apartment construction in Chicago. In that ten-year period 227,786 new
apartment units were built, 36,875 in 1927 alone.[10] Despite this
incredible level of activity, which has never even been approached
since, there were no experiments in Chicago with subsidized housing projects until the end of the decade, when two projects were
built almost simultaneously, the Michigan Boulevard Garden
Apartments and the Marshall Field Garden Apartments. Although
one was intended for black tenancy and one white, the two projects
are very similar in their concept and design. There is no evidence,
however, that there was any collaboration or even communication
between their developers or architects.

Michigan Boulevard Garden Apartments

The Michigan Boulevard Garden Apartments were built by Julius
Rosenwald, probably the greatest philanthropist Chicago has seen.
He was born in Springfield, Illinois, in 1862. At an early age he
became a merchant in New York City, and later Chicago. In 1895 he
bought a one-quarter interest in Sears, Roebuck and Company for
$37,500. Twenty-five years later, due to the phenomenal growth of
the mail-order business, Sears stock had a par value of $105 million,
with Rosenwald and his family owning about 40 percent of it.

Progressive in his business practices, Rosenwald installed the
money-back guarantee for Sears's customers, and one of the first
profit-sharing plans for its employees. Over the years he became extremely active in social causes, first through Jewish charities, and
later through nonsectarian ones. He was an admirer of Jane Addams,
and a longtime board member of Hull House. He was also on the
Board of Trustees of the University of Chicago, although he himself
had not completed high school. His contributions to that institution
alone were over $4 million. He founded the Museum of Science and
Industry, ultimately giving it about $7 million. His greatest contri-
butions, however, were to black causes.

Rosenwald was very impressed with Booker T. Washington's
autobiography, *Up From Slavery*. He became a close associate of Dr.
Washington, and a trustee of the Tuskegee Institute, which Washington headed. Rosenwald was a major supporter of the NAACP,

Chicago Urban League, Frederick Douglass Center, and Wendell Phillips Settlement. He contributed to the construction of YMCA and YWCA buildings for blacks in Chicago and fifteen other cities, and endowed the black Provident Hospital in Chicago. He became concerned about the lack of educational opportunities for black children in the South. Only 20 percent of those in Alabama, for example, attended school. In 1912 Rosenwald and Dr. Washington started a program of building small rural schoolhouses for black children. By the time of his death in 1932, Rosenwald had assisted in the construction of 5,357 public schools, shops, and teachers' houses in 833 counties in fifteen southern states. He contributed over $4.4 million toward the total cost of $28.4 million, or about 15 percent. The rest came from local tax funds (64 percent), funds raised by local blacks (17 percent), and local whites (4 percent).[11]

Rosenwald visited Vienna in 1926 and paid great attention to the municipal housing projects there. In 1928 his son-in-law, Alfred K. Stern, took charge of his plan for a black housing project in Chicago. At that time there was an almost complete lack of sound housing

Michigan Boulevard Garden Apartments, architect's perspective. These apartments were built by Julius Rosenwald in 1929.—Photograph by Kaufmann & Fabry Co., courtesy of Mort Kaplan Public Relations.

occupied by blacks. In addition to addressing that specific problem, Rosenwald wanted to demonstrate, as did other philanthropists who developed housing, that private investment could be attracted to such projects. The location chosen for the Michigan Boulevard Garden Apartments was the block bounded by 47th Street, Michigan Avenue, 46th Street, and Wabash Avenue, except the northeast corner of the block where an existing building remained. The site is

Consisting of a massive five-story walk-up building enclosing a central landscaped court, the Michigan Boulevard Garden Apartments contains 421 flats.—Photograph by Mildred Mead, courtesy of Chicago Historical Society.

little more than a mile from the Hyde Park–Kenwood neighborhood and the University of Chicago. Rosenwald had built a house there in 1903, but later moved to the suburb of Ravinia, now a part of Highland Park. The site was in the long, but then relatively narrow, South Side black ghetto. There was a great black migration from the South to Chicago during World War I, because the wartime labor shortage had for the first time opened up large numbers of jobs for blacks. Though the black population of Chicago increased from only 44,103 in 1910 to 233,903 in 1930, it still constituted only 6.9 percent of the population in that year.[12]

The Michigan Boulevard Garden Apartments consist of a massive five-story walk-up building, enclosing a central landscaped court, with its back to the four surrounding streets. It has the feeling of a college campus quadrangle. The construction is brick, with simple terra cotta doorways for the eight street entrances to the courtyard. The architect was Ernest Grunsfeld, Jr. Best known for designing the

Interior of a flat at the Michigan Boulevard Garden Apartments.—Courtesy of Mort Kaplan Public Relations.

Adler Planetarium, he also participated in the design of later housing projects. The development has 421 apartments, and there are fourteen stores along the 47th Street side of the property. Four of these were initially black owned, and among the others were a Sears, a Walgreen, and an A & P Store. Originally there were two nursery schools and recreational activities under the direction of Marion Stern, Rosenwald's daughter, and Mrs. Alfred S. Alschuler, an expert in early childhood education.

Rosenwald invested $2.7 million in the project, but only 2.4 percent was earned on the investment during the first seven years. This is not enough, of course, to attract private capital.[13] The rents when the building opened in 1929 averaged $42.13, $50.73, and $58.09 for the three, four, and five room apartments respectively. Bonus certificates of two to three dollars per month were issued for good housekeeping. The tenants were not in the poverty category; they included service workers, post office employees, teachers, and even a handful of doctors and lawyers.

Marshall Field Garden Apartments

The 628-unit Marshall Field Garden Apartments was, at the time of its construction in 1929 and 1930, the largest moderate-income housing development in the country. The developer was the Estate of Marshall Field, the famous Chicago merchant, under the direction of his grandson, Marshall Field III. The locátion was in a run-down Italian neighborhood, on the North Side, little more than two miles from the Loop. The Field estate purchased in sixty-five separate parcels land covering the two-square-block area bounded by Sedgwick Street, Evergreen Avenue, Hudson Avenue, and Blackhawk Street, at a cost of $1.2 million. This was done without the power of eminent domain, but only at a cost three times the original estimate. The city vacated Connors Street, from Sedgwick to Hudson, and sold it to the estate for fifty cents per square foot, and two alleys were sold for twenty-five cents per square foot. The site was selected, after an intensive survey, in consultation with Edith Abbott, dean of the School of Social Service Administration, at the University of Chicago. The experiment aimed not only at providing housing at a reasonable cost, but providing a catalyst for spread of renewal to the surrounding area.

The prototypes for the Marshall Field Garden Apartments were earlier and smaller developments in New York City by the Metropolitan Life Insurance Company, and by John D. Rockefeller, Jr. Marshall Field III was presumably familiar with them, since he lived in New York, although he visited Chicago regularly to tend to family business interests. Unlike his grandfather, he was a liberal. He founded the *Chicago Sun* (now the *Chicago Sun-Times*) as an alternative to the *Chicago Tribune*; he was a friend and supporter of the controversial community organizer Saul Alinsky, and was closely associated with Roosevelt University, which in its early years was considered by some a radical institution.

The architect in charge of the buildings was Andrew J. Thomas of New York, designer of the Rockefeller Homes. His associate architect was Ernest R. Graham, of the giant Chicago firm of Graham,

Exterior entrance to the Marshall Field Garden Apartments. At the time of construction in 1929–30, this project was the largest moderate-income development in the country.—Photograph by Devereux Bowly, Jr.

Anderson, Probst, and White. Plans for the project were announced in 1927, with press reports quoting officials of the Marshall Field estate as saying it was hoped to be only the first of two, three, or four such projects. The complex consists of ten interconnected buildings, four and five stories tall. They are located along the exterior of the site and surround the garden court that runs the length of the property and comprises over half its area. The exterior, and the interior public hallways, are of common brick. The walls are load bearing, with concrete floor slabs and steel columns.[14] The design is very simple, save for the carved limestone doorways and repeated terra cotta decorative eagles at the roof level. Twenty stores are located on the ground floor of the buildings along Sedgwick Street.

Except for the absence of elevators, which is surprising in four and five story structures, the buildings contain many amenities. The rooms are comparatively large; for example, some of the living rooms are eleven by sixteen feet, and dining rooms eleven by fourteen feet. All rooms have outside light and cross ventilation. Twenty-four-hour heat was originally provided by a heating plant located a block east of the buildings, to insulate them from the noise and smoke. There was a handicraft workroom, tenant auditorium and social room for parties and meetings, and a fully equipped free laundry room. There were children's playgrounds and a garage for 288 cars. The maintenance staff included three engineers, four men to fire the boilers, three gardeners, eleven janitors, an electrician, plumber, carpenter, and plasterer.

The most famous feature of the development, however, was the Marshall Field School for Children. It was a progressive demonstration school, up to the fourth grade level, run by the Pestalozzi Froebel Teachers College.[15] The school was subsidized by the Field estate, so the cost to working mothers was less than hiring a baby sitter. The tenants had their own newspaper, theater group, and numerous clubs. In retrospect it appears that all of these facilities caused the Marshall Field Garden Apartments to be too self-contained. The project really never became a part of the community in which it was located. The belief that the complex would generate private renewal and redevelopment of adjacent properties proved unfounded, and the Marshall Field estate built no additional moderate-income housing projects.

An early rental brochure stated that the apartments were designed to meet the needs of "everyone—teachers, business women, bachelors, young married couples and family groups."[16] The buildings quickly developed the reputation, however, as being for young professional couples, just beginning their families, who would move to the North Shore after a few years. Although the apartments were 100 percent rented, with a waiting list, because of the Depression rents were lowered more than 18 percent in 1933. The three-and-one-half-room apartments went from $48 to $35, the four-room ones from $42 to $34, the five-room ones from $53 to $45, and the six-room units from $63 to $55.

Even though financial reports were not made public, it is clear the project never lived up to the expectations of Marshall Field III. His biographer, Stephen Becker, states that it was not built as "an experiment in avant-garde social philosophy," but rather to demonstrate "that economic building techniques and slow amortization could make low-rent housing profitable."[17] He states that because of high

Marshall Field Garden Apartments courtyard. The complex consists of ten interconnected buildings, four and five stories tall.—Photograph by Devereux Bowly, Jr.

real estate taxes, among other costs, Field got only a 1 or 2 percent return. The buildings, which had cost $6.25 million in 1930, were sold in 1942 for $1.75 million to Louis Barkhausen, a businessman, and attorney Randolph Bohrer. They renamed the project the Town and Garden Apartments, and in 1954 they in turn sold them to realtor Arthur Rubloff and others for an undisclosed price. Through these changes in ownership the quality of the management and services remained high. In 1960 the development was sold still again, this time to a group of eastern investors, for $4.2 million, about one-third of its then estimated replacement cost of $12 million. This sale signaled the beginning of a period of decline, and later rehabilitation of the development.

The four early philanthropic housing projects in Chicago had two things in common. Unlike most of the later subsidized housing they were well designed, pleasant places to live. They also all failed to live up to the financial expectations of their developers. They demonstrated it was not possible to build sufficient housing for the low-income population of Chicago, unless it were done by governmental bodies, or at least with governmental subsidy. They heralded the way for the first public housing projects.

2 Early Public Housing

The end of the decade of the 1920s brought the United States into its most severe economic depression. Apartment construction in Chicago virtually came to a standstill. In the worst year, 1933, only 21 apartment units were built.[1] Due to the lack of construction, and the large migration to Chicago before, during, and after World War I, there was a severe shortage of housing, especially for low-income families. From 1930 to 1938 there were 18,221 dwelling units demolished in Chicago, and only 7,619 new ones constructed, leaving a deficit of 10,602. The city had an increase of 60,517 families during the eight-year period. It has been estimated that it would have taken 150,000 additional units of housing for low-income families to eliminate the shortage.[2]

The shortage of housing was aggravated by two additional factors, poverty and existing slum conditions. During the mid-1930s about a third of the families in Chicago had incomes below $1,000 a year.[3] This placed them in a position where there was almost no chance of securing decent housing on the private market. Large areas in Chicago, especially in the inner city, were occupied by dilapidated housing, much of it little more than wooden shacks. Efforts to improve housing through zoning ordinances, building code inspection, and enforcement had not met with notable success, and to the extent that these attempts had caused buildings to be maintained or improved, they had also priced them out of reach of poor families.

The Depression caused the already severe housing problems of poor people in Chicago to take on crisis proportions by 1931. In that year a number of eviction disturbances occurred, where bailiffs serving eviction notices encountered hostility and had to summon the police. The most tragic incident took place in August 1931, after two bailiffs had moved the possessions of a destitute South Side black family out on the street. A crowd of 2,000 gathered and moved the family back into the building. The police were called, three members of the crowd were shot and killed, three policemen and a crowd member were seriously injured. The next day the *Chicago Tribune* said there would be a policy of "firmness in dealing with communistic eviction disorders."[4]

Private social agencies helped some poor families to pay their rents, but many families had to give up their apartments and move in with friends or relatives. The inability of many tenants to pay rent meant that landlords did not have funds to maintain their buildings, and the housing supply deteriorated. Because of the Depression, and the restrictions on building during World War II, the period from 1930 through 1945 was the most disastrous in the history of the city's housing supply. In fact, it can be argued that Chicago housing never fully recovered from that period.

When Franklin D. Roosevelt was elected president in 1932, many of his New Deal programs to provide employment and remedy social problems were quickly adopted. Public housing was launched in 1933 with the establishment of the Housing Division of the Public Works Administration (PWA), which in 1935 was consolidated into the Works Progress Administration (WPA). PWA built, at a cost of $134 million, fifty-one demonstration projects, three in Chicago. They were the Jane Addams Houses, Julia C. Lathrop Homes, and Trumbull Park Homes, on the West, North, and Far South sides of the city, respectively. Although the three projects were built by PWA, they were managed from the first by the Chicago Housing Authority (CHA). Under the CHA's contract with the United States Housing Authority (USHA), CHA kept enough of the rental income for administrative and operating expenses, and paid a specified amount to USHA as a reserve for repairs and replacements. Eventually CHA got actual title to the projects.

The Chicago Housing Authority was incorporated in 1937. It is not an agency of the City of Chicago, although its commissioners are appointed by the mayor, and it has to submit an annual report to him. It is a municipal not-for-profit corporation, created pursuant to state statute, and operating within the boundaries of the City of Chicago. CHA has no taxing power, and receives no annual appropriation from the city. It has a dual purpose: 1) to provide decent, safe and sanitary housing to poor families and individuals who live in substandard dwellings and cannot get adequate housing in the private housing market, and 2) to remove slums and blighted areas. Its policies are developed by the five unpaid commissioners, and are carried out by a professional staff, headed by the executive director, in the early years called the executive secretary.

The PWA projects were the first governmentally subsidized housing in Chicago, and thus they represented official realization that neither private enterprises nor private philanthropy could adequately house poor people. The movement of government into this area of activity was controversial to many people, but was made more palatable by the designation of the initial developments as "demonstration" projects, built during a time of national economic emergency, in part to create jobs.

To the social reformers public housing was a giant step forward, long overdue. One of the best known of them was Edith Abbott, who lived for more than eighteen years at Hull House, and wrote the book *The Tenements of Chicago: 1908–1935*, published in 1936. In it she talks of the open space, trees, gardens, and playgrounds, the fireproof and sanitary construction of the Jane Addams Houses, then in the planning stage.[5] She surprisingly neglects, however, consideration of the long-term sociological implications of the concept of public housing.

Jane Addams Houses

The largest of the PWA projects, with 1,027 units, is the Jane Addams Houses, located on a twenty-four-acre site bounded by Cabrini Street, Roosevelt Road, Racine Avenue, and Loomis Street. The site is two miles west of the Loop, and about one-half mile west of Hull House, the area in between having in recent years been occupied by the University of Illinois at Chicago Circle. Jane Addams never saw the project named for her. She died in 1935, the buildings were not occupied until January 1938. The PWA projects in Chicago were designed by large temporary associations of architects, brought

Buildings to be torn down on Grenshaw west from Loomis, 1934, to clear the site for the construction of the Jane Addams Houses.—Courtesy of Chicago Historical Society.

together specifically for each project, presumably to fulfill the ob-
ligation of providing maximum employment. The architects for the
Jane Addams House were: John Armstrong, Melville Chatton,
Ernest Grunsfeld, Jr., Frederick Hodgdon, John Holabird, Ralph
Huszagh, Elmer Jensen, Philip Maher, John Merrill, and Chester
Wolcott.

The Jane Addams Houses consist of thirty-two buildings, mostly
three- and four-story apartment buildings, with some two-story row
houses. The design of the project is devoid of any real architectural
distinction. The buildings are constructed of brick, with no architectural detail work, and merely a tile coping at the roof line. The project does have some redeeming features, however, at least when
compared to many of the later ones. As with all early public housing, it was built to a human scale, in keeping with the low-rise na-

*Courtyard of Jane Addams Houses with WPA statues, 1951. This largest of
the PWA projects, with 1,027 units, was completed in 1938.—Photograph
by Mildred Mead, courtesy of Chicago Historical Society*

ture of the neighborhood. Only 28 percent of the land area is covered with buildings, the rest is landscaped and play areas.

The site consisted of property formerly belonging to the Jewish Peoples Institute, and adjacent slums. Unlike the buildings it replaced, the Jane Addams structures are fireproof and well constructed. Designed for at least a sixty-year life-span, the buildings have concrete floors covered with asphalt tile. Partitions include two-inches of solid plaster between rooms, with hollow tile walls between apartments. The windows are metal framed casement units.

Julia C. Lathrop Homes

The opening of the Julia C. Lathrop Homes came shortly after the Jane Addams project. Though its 925 units makes it slightly smaller

Kitchen in a Jane Addams Houses apartment.—Courtesy of Chicago Housing Authority

than Jane Addams, its land area of 35.3 acres is 50 percent larger, and thus only 17.6 percent of the land area is covered by buildings. The site, four miles north of the Loop, is adjacent to the North Branch of the Chicago River, on either side of Diversey Parkway. The eastern boundary is Clybourn Avenue (north of Diversey) and Damen Avenue (south of Diversey). It is in a semi-industrial neighborhood, and was vacant before the project was built. The architects again were a

Aerial view of Julia C. Lathrop Homes. Though its 925 units make it slightly smaller than the Jane Addams project, its land area is 50 percent larger and only 17.6 percent of the land is covered with buildings.
—Courtesy of Chicago Historical Society

temporary association, here headed by Robert DeGolyer. A number of well-known architects were included in the group of fifteen men working for DeGolyer: Hugh Garden, Hubert Burnham, Vernon Watson, Thomas Tallmadge, Israel Loewenberg, Max Loewenberg, E. E. Roberts, Elmer Roberts, Roy Christiansen, Everett Quinn, Charles White, Bertram Weber, Edwin Clark, Earnest Mayo, and Peter Mao.

Like Jane Addams, the Julia Lathrop project is composed of three- and four-story apartment buildings, and two-story row houses. The architecture, however, is slightly less severe than the Addams project. To give variety, some of the buildings are dark red brick, some brown brick; there are handsome brick arches connecting some of the buildings, and there are limestone cornices and limestone trim around the doorways. As with most public housing developments, there is a central heating plant to serve all the buildings. On the

The Lathrop project has some buildings of dark red brick, some brown; and there are handsome brick arches connecting some of the buildings and limestone cornices and trim around the doorways.—Courtesy of Chicago Housing Authority

corner of Diversey and Clybourn there is a small administration building for the project.

Because of the extreme shortage of housing, and the low wage levels during the Depression, the tenants in the initial projects were not the hard-core poverty families that we associate with public housing today. Although every family had to have an income low enough to meet the CHA standards, a survey of tenants at the Lathrop Homes found about as many skilled craftsmen and foremen as there were unskilled service workers or laborers.[6] In the early years at Lathrop there existed a system of adult education classes in arts, crafts, homemaking, dressmaking, and millinery.

Trumbull Park Homes

The third of the PWA projects, also opening in early 1938, was the Trumbull Park Homes. With 426 units it is less than half the size of the other two projects. It was built on vacant land at 105th Street and Oglesby Avenue, in the Southeast Side industrial area, only three blocks from the Wisconsin Steel Works. The architecture of

Bedroom in a Julia C. Lathrop Homes Apartment.—Courtesy of Chicago Housing Authority

the two-story row houses and four-story apartment buildings is very similar to the Jane Addams Houses. In fact, the five architects of the Trumbull Park Homes, John Armstrong, Ernest Grunsfeld, Jr., John Holabird, Elmcr Jensen, and Philip Maher, were all involved in the design of the other project. The low-density design (here only 19 percent of the land is covered with buildings) fits in better in this low-density neighborhood than it would have in the teeming Near West Side location of the Jane Addams Houses, and the moderate size of the Trumbull Park project, only twenty-one acres, is more manageable and humane than the Addams project. Unfortunately, this lesson was lost on CHA, as it developed mammoth sites and expanded others over the years.

The contract CHA had with the United States Housing Authority provided that any surplus of funds received, more than needed for operating expenses and the reserve for repairs and replacements, went to USHA. There was thus an incentive to keep rents as low as possible, so there would be no surplus to turn over to the federal agency. CHA was so successful in keeping down expenses that in

Aerial view of Trumbull Park Homes. With 426 apartments, this third of the PWA projects is less than half the size of the Addams and Lathrop developments.—Courtesy of Chicago Historical Society

January 1940 they were able to reduce the rents up to 16 percent at the Jane Addams and Julia Lathrop projects, and up to 7 percent at Trumbull Park. At that time CHA set its rents according to apartment size, but not according to family size or income. After the rent reduction, the rent for a three-room apartment at Addams and Lathrop went from $23.70 to $20.55, and a four-room unit at Trumbull Park from $27.35 to $26.25. These rents included utilities. CHA felt it was to the tenant's advantage not to have individual utility meters, since electricity and natural gas are less expensive per unit when purchased in quantity.

The early record of rent payment by the tenants was amazing. In 1941 CHA reported only one-third of 1 percent of rents unpaid. In 1940 CHA tenants paid a total of $629,145 in rents, or an average of

Consisting of two-story row houses and four-story apartment buildings, the Trumbull Park Homes project is similar to the Addams Houses, but because of its moderate size more manageable and humane. —Courtesy of Chicago Housing Authority

about $260 annually per apartment. It was estimated that the federal subsidy, by charging no interest on its investment in the project, and not getting repayment of the amount invested (other than the repair and replacement payments) amounted to $540,000 or $224 per unit.[7] Thus the federal subsidy was almost equal to the rental income. The figures do not take into account another, but indirect, subsidy of public housing. The city and other local governmental bodies also subsidize public housing to the extent that CHA does not pay real estate taxes on its properties. This was a controversial aspect of early public housing, in that it placed an additional burden on the other taxpayers. CHA did agree to pay a "service charge in lieu of taxes" of 5 percent of the shelter rent (rent excluding the portion for utilities) for schools and other services received by the tenants. Although this amount is only a fraction of what a private landlord would have to pay in real estate taxes for comparable buildings, it is usually more than the amount of real estate taxes that were actually being collected on the land prior to being used for public housing, when it was vacant or occupied by blighted structures.

Ida B. Wells Homes

The last of the prewar public housing projects was the Ida B. Wells Homes, the site for which was selected by the PWA in 1934. Racial segregation in housing was the federal policy at that date.[8] Called the Neighborhood Composition Rule, it was formulated by Secretary of the Interior Harold Ickes, and provided that a housing project would not be permitted to alter the racial character of its neighborhood.[9] Since the Lathrop Homes and Trumbull Park Homes were in white areas, they were rented to exclusively white tenants. CHA admitted twenty-six black families to the Jane Addams Houses, because that number of black families had lived on the site before redevelopment. After the threat of a lawsuit, the number of black families was raised to sixty, but they were largely segregated in one section of the project.

The Ida B. Wells project was built for exclusively black tenants. The site had been selected by the PWA after consultation with the State Housing Board, the Chicago Plan Commission, a committee of prominent Negro leaders, and consultants from the University of Chicago. It was the forty-seven acre tract bounded by Martin Luther King, Jr., Drive (then called South Parkway), Pershing Road (39th Street), Cottage Grove Avenue, and 37th Street. Although acquisition of the land began in 1934, it proceeded so slowly that the PWA housing program ended before the site was cleared. The United States Housing Act of 1937 transferred the responsibility for the construction of public housing from the federal government to local agencies.

Upon taking over the public housing program in 1938, the new Chicago Housing Authority became involved in a double controversy with the Wells site. The black community was understandably bitter about the fact that although it suffered from the worst housing conditions, it had gotten virtually no public housing. In fact, demolition of the tenements on the Ida B. Wells site caused additional overcrowding in the black community, and increased activity on the part of white neighborhoods to the south in adding restrictive racial covenants to property deeds. The site was opposed by white property owners to the east and south who wanted it shifted half a mile west to the Rock Island Railroad tracks (at Federal Street) along the western boundary of the black ghetto. A suit by the whites failed in court, but considerably delayed acquisition of the land. Feelings became so strained that some people feared a repetition of the massive Chicago race riots of 1919.

The project was finally pushed by CHA, under the provisions of the 1937 act. CHA financed the construction by the sale of its own notes, backed by the federal guaranty of both principal and interest. The architect in charge of the project for CHA was Alfred Shaw, of Shaw, Naess, and Murphy; and in association with three other firms: Thielbar and Fugard; Nimmons, Carr, and Wright; Metz and

Mass meeting protesting repeated delays on site of Ida B. Wells Homes shortly before construction began.—Courtesy of Chicago Housing Authority

Gunderson. Rather than having its own architectural staff, CHA
hired architects in private practice, and also used general contractors
to build its projects. Shaw's first task was to revise the original PWA
plans to reduce streets running through the project, increase child
play areas, and cut down the number of apartment buildings in favor
of more row houses.

Although it is much larger than any of the PWA projects, the
Wells project is superior to them in some respects. Next to King

*Alley near site of Ida B. Wells Homes, 1951.—Photograph by Mildred
Mead, courtesy of Chicago Historical Society*

Drive, on the western edge of the site, there are four-story apartment buildings, placed diagonally to the street. Their height is in the same scale as the other buildings along King Drive, which is part of the landscaped boulevard system in Chicago. To the east of the four-story buildings, in the center of the property, are playgrounds and athletic fields owned by the Chicago Park District. This was the first housing project in Chicago that incorporated a city park with it. On the eastern side of the site are three-story apartment buildings and two-story row houses. Some of each have peaked roofs, with slate shingles, and all have copper canopies over the doorways. The overall effect is pleasant, and the location is a good one, being only a few blocks from Burnham Park and Lake Michigan. On the south edge of the site, along Pershing Road is the large Ida B. Wells Community Center, central heating plant, and management office.

The Ida B. Wells Homes consist of 1,662 units (868 apartments and 794 row houses and garden apartments) in 124 residential buildings. Its 24 percent land coverage is slightly higher than the average of the PWA projects, but the cost per unit was much less. It was only $5,045, as compared with $5,645 for Lathrop Homes, $5,736 for Trumbull Park Homes and $6,351 for Addams Houses. The Wells project opened in early 1941 and on May 7, 1941, was visited by Mrs. Eleanor Roosevelt. She was presented with a rose by a ten-year-old girl, who won the Ida B. Wells clean-up campaign. The project had 18,000 applications for apartments, or more than 10 for each unit. This proportion was comparable to the 28,000 applications received for the 2,414 units in the three PWA projects. Even the large number of applications received for the projects did not fully reflect the housing shortage that existed, especially for black families. While the white population of Chicago had increased from 2,185,283 to 3,258,528 from 1910 to 1930, the black population increased during the same period from 44,103 to 236,305. A 1938 CHA study found that about two-thirds of the units occupied by blacks in Chicago lacked the complete facilities of central heating, gas, electricity, unshared kitchen, and private bath.[10] The sterotype of black housing during this period was the kitchenette apartment. Thousands of large old homes and apartments in ghetto areas of Chicago were cut up into smaller units, where a different family would occupy each room, which had a kitchenette installed in it. A single bathroom would often be shared by several families.

The apartments at the Ida B. Wells Homes are larger than those of the PWA projects. Almost two-thirds of the total are four-room apartments, where the PWA buildings have a preponderance of three-room apartments. The rents at Ida B. Wells, however, were

slightly lower than the other projects. The average annual income of
families who initially moved into Ida B. Wells was only $767.28,
which also was lower than those of the PWA projects. One fifth of
the families who moved into Wells had no furniture, having
previously lived in furnished rooms. The Metropolitan Housing
Council (later renamed the Metropolitan Housing and Planning
Council), a private citizens' group, collected old furniture for these
families, and a WPA shop was set up to repair it.

Under CHA rules the maximum income a family could have to be
admitted to Ida B. Wells, for a four-room apartment, was $1,049 per
year. This was lower than the PWA projects. For example, it was
about $100 lower than the limitation at the Jane Addams Houses.
The standards were based upon a provision in the United States
Housing Act that excluded new tenants with an annual income
more than five times the annual rent. For the PWA projects CHA
accepted no families on direct relief, although WPA families were
accepted, and some families went on relief after they became tenants in the projects. At Ida B. Wells the policy was changed, and 17
percent of the early tenants received relief, as well as 23.5 percent

Dedication parade for the opening of the Ida B. Wells Homes, 1941.—
Courtesy of Chicago Housing Authority

who got WPA payments. An early endeavor of the tenants at Wells was a "Get off and keep off the WPA and Relief" club. This group gathered job vacancy listings and made them available to project residents. In the early years CHA accepted only "complete families" with children, except for a small quota of elderly couples for its two-room apartments. An elaborate investigation was made of CHA applicants that included: 1) an office interview by a social worker,

While larger than any of the PWA projects, the Ida B. Wells Homes are superior in some respects. Some of the buildings have peaked roofs with slate shingles, and all have copper canopies over the doorways. There are playgrounds and athletic fields in a city park incorporated within the project.—Courtesy of Chicago Housing Authority

2) employment verification, 3) check for a police record, 4) home visit by an investigator, and 5) scoring on a CHA formula giving preference to applicants in substandard apartments with insufficient income to get good housing on the private market.

The initial four public housing projects in Chicago were important in and of themselves, and because they set the tone for the public housing which came later. The precedent they set, not really to be broken for thirty years, was that public housing was to be stark, each building like the one next door, except for some variations in height, and each project clearly isolated from the surrounding community. The decision was made from the beginning that emphasis would be placed on housing that was well constructed, easy to maintain, but architecturally undistinguished. In part the form that public housing took was dictated by economics. The investment in the four initial projects was just under $23 million, for 4,076 units, or about $5,589 per unit. This was about 20 percent below the average cost of private residential construction in the area.

3 Chicago Housing Authority: The War Years

World War II brought major new responsibilities to the Chicago Housing Authority: providing housing for war workers, and later providing housing for returning veterans. The census of 1940 showed that 55,157 residential units in Chicago were overcrowded, using the standard of having more than 1.5 persons per room, and that 206,103 units had either no private bath, or the units were in need of major repairs.[1] Employment and wages increased during the war period, but the housing supply did not, because of wartime restrictions on construction, and because of rent control. The Federal Emergency Price Control Act of 1942 imposed rent control on Chicago and other "defense-rental areas," with high concentrations of war-industry workers. Rent control has the effect of perpetuating a housing shortage, because it removes incentives for new construction or renovation of housing. Also, because of artificially low rent levels, it encourages tenants to stay in large apartments when they might otherwise move to smaller ones, for example when their children leave home.[2]

With the attack on Pearl Harbor on December 7, 1941, the country mobilized for war. The Chicago area, being the major steel and industrial center of the country, had a tremendous in-migration of war-industry workers. Within a short time war production doubled, and the city faced its most severe housing shortage. Wages were pushed up, but the War Manpower Commission and the Office of Price Administration ordered that CHA stop evicting families whose income had risen above the normal CHA limits.[3] CHA was allowed to charge these "excess income" families higher rents. This was the first experience CHA had with different rents for identical apartments.

By federal ruling no new public housing could be constructed unless it was for war-industry workers. Projects that were planned, however, could proceed if they were in areas with a shortage of war-worker housing, and if it was agreed they would house war workers. CHA proceeded with four projects: Cabrini, Lawndale

Gardens, Bridgeport, and Brooks. Sites had already been selected for these as low-income projects. They were built under the terms of the 1937 housing act, but without the $1,200 maximum limitation of income for admission. It was planned from the beginning that these developments would be changed to low-income occupancy at the end of the war. A special set of eligibility standards was established for the war-industry-worker projects. They provided that: 1) the wage earner had to be employed in essential war work, 2) in-migrant war workers were to be given preference, since they had the least chance of finding housing, 3) the wage earner's family had to have at least one child and 4) the family's income at entrance could not exceed $2,000, though their income could go above that level after they were tenants.

Frances Cabrini Homes

The planning and land acquisition for the Cabrini Homes had started before the war. The development was originally projected at 920 units, for the site bounded by Chicago Avenue, Larrabee Street, Division Street, and Hudson Avenue, on the Near North Side, adjacent to the Montgomery Ward headquarters and mail order warehouses. Because of difficulty in acquiring the property, the project was reduced to 586 units on sixteen acres by making its northern boundary Oak rather than Division Street, and by moving its western boundary one-half block east.

Before redevelopment, the area was an infamous slum. Of the buildings on the site, 70 percent were over fifty-five years old, and 50 percent were of frame construction. Of the 683 units on the site, 443 had no bathtubs, 480 had no hot water, and 515 were heated only by stoves. Forty-three toilets were shared by two families each, there were twenty-nine yard toilets and ten "under sidewalk" toilets. Only half of the properties could be purchased by negotiation; the rest had to be acquired under CHA's condemnation power, which was a lengthy procedure. Actual construction of the Cabrini Homes took place in 1941 and 1942, and the first families moved in on August 1, 1942. Because the project opened so early in the war, it did not house exclusively war-industry-worker families, but also some low-income families. The total development cost was $6,333 per unit, comparatively high because of the difficulty in acquiring the site, and the cost of demolishing the buildings. Also, the units averaged 4.41 rooms each, which was larger than any of the earlier public housing in Chicago.

The architects were another group assembled for the job: Henry Holsman, George Burmeister, Maurice Rissman, Ernest Grunsfeld,

Jr., L. R. Solomon, G. M. Jones, K. M. Vitzhum, I. S. Loewenberg, and Frank McNally. Their design was for a total of fifty-five two- and three-story buildings. The three-story buildings are on the perimeter of the site. Facing outward are the entrances of stairways going up to duplex row houses on the second and third floors. On the first floor, really an English basement, are garden apartments entered from the opposite sides of the building with front doors facing the interior of the project. The interior land area is depressed approximately four feet from the street level. On this lower level are groups of two-story row houses. The rows and rows of houses are very regimental in appearance, giving the impression of army barracks. Since each unit has its own outside entrance there are no public hallways. The tenants have small yards; this was the first CHA project where residents had to provide their own refrigerators. Each unit was built with a separate heating plant. The purpose of the project design was

Consisting of two- and three-story buildings, the rows and rows of houses in the Frances Cabrini Homes, built in 1941–42, are regimental in appearance, almost like army barracks.—Photograph by Mildred Mead, courtesy of Chicago Historical Society

to keep CHA maintenance costs to an absolute minimum. In later years more projects were built adjacent to the Cabrini Homes, so they are now a small part of the vast Cabrini-Green complex, which has over 3,500 units and 15,000 residents.

Lawndale Gardens

The first CHA experiment with a small-scale public housing development was Lawndale Gardens, which opened in December

Lawndale Gardens, the first Chicago Housing Authority experiment with small-scale public housing, opened in December 1942. Covering six and one-half acres, the four long lines of two-story row houses contain 128 units.—Courtesy of Chicago Housing Authority

1942. It covers a mere six and one-half acres, about two city blocks, has 128 units, and is located at 25th Street and California Boulevard. All of the units are located in four long lines of two-story row houses. The architects were Eric Hall and Frank McNally. The design is virtually identical to that of the two-story row houses of the Cabrini Homes. This leads to the almost inescapable conclusion that the extreme pressure to keep costs to a minimum, and other requirements which federal agencies and CHA imposed upon the architects it hired during this period, were so specific that it made little difference who actually designed each project. The architecture of the Lawndale Gardens is somewhat compensated for by its small size. Even though all the buildings are identical, there are few enough of them so that some sense of individuality can be maintained by the residents. The site chosen for the project, however, leaves something to be desired. It was vacant before the project was built, and is in a largely industrial neighborhood, immediately north of the giant International Harvester manufacturing complex (now demolished), and just across from the Criminal Courts Building and County Jail.

Because wages rose considerably during the war, CHA made a major change in its procedures by abandoning flat rent schedules. Families whose income went above CHA limits simply could not find other housing, so as of November 1, 1942, a system of graded rents was adopted at the Addams, Lathrop, and Trumbull Park Projects. By early 1943 it had been extended to all CHA units. Under the system rent was determined by family income and size, within certain limits. The formula sought to have all tenants spend approximately the same proportions of their income for rent.

Bridgeport Homes

The other small development CHA built during the war was Bridgeport Homes, which opened in May of 1943. It was designed by the firm of Burnham and Hammond and is architecturally very similar to Lawndale Gardens. Its 141 units are all two-story row houses, grouped in eighteen buildings. It differs in one major respect from Lawndale Gardens: its site. Instead of being located in a low-density industrial area, this project is in the established neighborhood of Bridgeport.

The site runs from the alley west of Halsted Street, three-quarters of a block west to Lituanica Avenue, and from 31st Street to 32nd Street (31st Place abuts the site to the west). The Bridgeport Homes are thus not exposed to Halsted Street, the commercial center of the area, but do face the three surrounding streets. These are all residential streets, with bungalows, frame houses, and walk-up apartments, in the same scale as the public housing. Because of its small size and location in a residential neighborhood, this was the only project from the period not immediately identifiable, to a casual observer, as public housing. The history of public housing in Chicago would have been different if all the units had been built in small projects, integrated into residential communities.

The other small development that the Chicago Housing Authority built during the war was Bridgeport Homes, which opened in May 1943. Its 141 units are all two-story row houses grouped in eighteen buildings. —Photograph by Devereux Bowly, Jr.

Robert H. Brooks Homes

A major development built during this period, opening March 30, 1943, was the Robert H. Brooks Homes. Located in the area bounded by Roosevelt Road, Racine Avenue, 14th Street, and Loomis Street, the eight-square-block site is across the street from the Jane Addams Houses, and extends that complex four blocks further south. It thus set the precedent, when CHA was less than six years old, not only of building large projects, but of greatly expanding existing projects. Designed by the same architects as the Cabrini Homes, all of the 834 units are in two-story row houses. A community center and city park were included in the project. In clearing the land 865 units were demolished, making a net loss to the city of 31 units. The Brooks Homes did nothing, therefore, to reduce the housing shortage, but

The Robert H. Brooks Homes (with the high-rise Grace Abbott Homes in the background) opened on March 30, 1943. All 834 units are in two-story row houses. Built across the street from the Jane Addams Houses, this project set the precedent not only of building large projects but of greatly expanding existing ones.—Courtesy of Chicago Housing Authority

did replace terribly blighted housing. CHA's research indicated that one-fourth of the buildings demolished were from the Civil War period, 1860–65, and before redevelopment the area had nine times as many fires as other sections of the city of similar size.[4]

Under pressure from blacks and the federal government, which had somewhat liberalized its racial policies during World War II, the Chicago Housing Authority began to seek sites that would provide the basis for racially integrated projects, under the Neighborhood Composition Rule. It was planned that Cabrini Homes would be 80 percent white and 20 percent black, and that Brooks Homes would be 80 percent black and 20 percent white, in each case reflecting the racial composition of the area the projects were in. In Brooks CHA was unable to find sufficient whites who were willing to move in,

Kitchen of a Robert H. Brooks Homes apartment.—Photograph by Mildred Mead, courtesy of Chicago Historical Society

and stay in the project, and it became all-black. At Cabrini the 20
percent black quota was relaxed, and by 1949 it was the only permanent project that was well integrated, with a 40 percent black population.[5]

Altgeld Gardens

One of the greatest needs of war-worker housing was for black
workers in the Far South Side–Lake Calumet industrial area. The
response of the federal government and CHA was Altgeld Gardens,
the most self-contained and comprehensive public housing project
ever constructed in Chicago. The site chosen was an immense 157-
acre vacant tract, at 130th Street and Ellis Avenue. It was developed
and managed by CHA in conjunction with the National Housing
Agency and the Federal Public Housing Authority. Ownership was
originally held by the federal government, but went to CHA in 1956.

*Elizabeth Wood, executive secretary of the Chicago Housing Authority, at
the dedication of Altgeld Gardens, August 26, 1945. Constructed on an
immense 157-acre site, this project is the most self-contained and comprehensive public housing project ever constructed in Chicago.—Courtesy of
Chicago Housing Authority*

Initially the federal agencies were planning the construction of
1,500 temporary units, but by pointing out the long-range postwar
need for housing, CHA was able to persuade them to finance a permanent development instead. Construction of Altgeld Gardens
started in November 1943, and was completed less than two years
later, at a cost of $9.5 million. The architects were the firm of Naess
and Murphy. The houses, like the CHA prototype of the period, are
constructed of common brick, with concrete canopies over the front
doors. Their roofs, however, are sloping and were originally covered
with slate shingles, which have been replaced with asphalt ones.

*Aerial view of Altgeld Gardens. Because this 1,500-unit project was built
on the edge of the city, far from substantial residential areas, provision had
to be made for many community facilities, such as a public library, nursery
school, auditorium, and clubhouse. A shopping center, church, and schools
were also provided.—Courtesy of Chicago Housing Authority*

Each house has a front lawn and rear yard, tended by the tenants. The interior walls are four-inch plastered tile; the floors are five-inch concrete slabs, with ground terrazzo finish. The good condition of the project today, more than thirty years after it was built, demonstrates that the construction was not only fireproof, but of a high standard. The remoteness of the site, and the overall physical surroundings have something of the feeling of the New Towns located around London.

The project was designed with 1,500 units, divided into 162 groups of two-story row houses. There are 100 units of 3½ rooms, 600 of 4½ rooms, 600 5½ rooms and 200 with 6½ rooms. The units are thus larger, on the average, than earlier CHA projects, and were occupied by larger families. Of the 7,000 original tenants, only 3,000 were adults. Those under nineteen made up 61 percent of the popu-

The row houses at Altgeld Gardens are constructed of common brick, with concrete canopies over the front doors. The roofs were originally covered with slate shingles. Each house has a front lawn and a rear yard, tended by the tenants.—Courtesy of Chicago Housing Authority

lation of the development, whereas that age group only made up 27
percent of the population of the city as a whole.[6] The population
of Altgeld Gardens thus anticipated the current pattern of family
public housing, a preponderance of the residents being children.

Because the project was built on the edge of the city, far from any
substantial residential areas, and without mass transit except for
limited bus service, provision had to be made for many community
facilities. They included a Board of Health station, public library,
six-room nursery school for 240 children ages two to five, auditorium, clubrooms, and teen-agers' lounge. The Chicago Board of
Education built four one-story school buildings for elementary and
high school classes. Included in the center of the development was a
shopping center, privately developed on land sold by the federal
government. It originally contained a cooperatively owned food
store, drug and variety stores, doctors' offices, beauty and barber
shops, and a tavern. There are also the standard features of public
housing developments: playgrounds, a community center, and city
park. In 1950 an interdenominational church was built, under spon-
sorship of the Church Federation of Greater Chicago.

The total cost per unit at Altgeld Gardens was $6,385, several
hundred dollars higher than other projects built by CHA during the
same period. The reason for the high cost was the large size of the
units, and the facilities that had to be built. The land itself was very
inexpensive, only $57 per unit as compared with the sites obtained
by slum clearance, such as Brooks which cost $917 per unit, or
Cabrini which cost $1,238 per unit. Rents originally ranged from
$16 to $51 per month, and were pegged at about one-fifth of the
family's income, with family size also taken into consideration. For
example, a family of three with an income of $1,500 paid $30 per
month rent, while a family of four, with the same income, paid only
$27 per month for the same size unit. Because the project was built
for war-industry workers, there were no maximum income limits
imposed upon the initial tenants. From a public policy standpoint,
construction of Altgeld Gardens was very questionable. It reinforced
and extended the precedent, set by the earlier Ida B. Wells and
Brooks projects, of government action to segregate Chicago's black
population, in this case in an isolated location far from the established residential sections of the city.

West Chesterfield Homes

An absolutely unique project in the history of CHA was West
Chesterfield Homes. During December 1943 the National Housing
Agency assigned to the Federal Public Housing Authority, and its

agent the Chicago Housing Authority, the job of constructing a group of temporary housing units for black occupancy. The CHA commissioners were again reluctant to build merely temporary units so they convinced the federal agencies to authorize the construction of 250 permanent units, to be sold to families at the end of the war. They were constructed under provisions of the Lanham Act, and paid full real estate taxes. Actual ownership of the houses was held by the United States Public Housing Authority, who leased them to CHA, which in turn rented them to the individual tenants.

By August 1945 all the units were occupied by families of war workers, who paid a flat rent of $45 per month. In December of 1945 CHA increased the admission upper income limits for the low-income projects from a flat $1,200 to $1,500 for families of four or less, and $1,650 for families of five or more. At West Chesterfield, by contrast, a *minimum* annual income was required as a condition of

West Chesterfield Homes. Unique in the history of the Chicago Housing Authority, these homes built during World War II were planned to be sold to the tenants. This occurred in 1949.—Courtesy of Chicago Housing Authority

renting a unit, so that the families would be in a position to buy the houses, and in fact this occurred in 1949. That year the Federal Housing and Home Finance Authority, through the Public Housing Administration sold the houses individually, with the federal government providing the mortgages. All of the units of West Chesterfield are five-room, two-story houses, built in pairs. They are located on scattered sites, in what was at the time of construction a partially built-up area, running for several blocks west of Martin Luther King, Jr., Drive, at 92nd Street.

The West Chesterfield houses are quite different from other public housing. They are located on full city lots, so that each has a large rear yard. They are all adjacent to the street, most perpendicular, but some parallel to it. They have full basements. Although the houses are basically the same design, variety was introduced by an extra one-story room extension on the side of some of them. Designed by the firm of Loebl and Schlossman, the architecture of the West Chesterfield Homes is not nearly as severe as contemporary CHA projects. The houses even have "picture windows," a popular feature of single family housing during the 1950's. The design is not as good as Benjamin Rosenthal's Garden Homes, built twenty-five years earlier at a nearby location, but the West Chesterfield Homes appear to have been more substantially constructed. They are today in very good condition, including handsome landscaping. The owners of many of the houses have added rooms and garages. The houses fit well in their community, and in fact are larger and of better construction than many of the newer, privately developed houses in the area.

Veterans' Temporary Housing

Once the war ended, the housing imperative shifted from providing places for war-workers' families to live, to accommodating returning veterans and their families. The Chicago City Council voted in November 1945 to appropriate $1 million to provide the first group of temporary housing for veterans. The next month another $1 million was voted. It was decided, for reasons of economy and speed, that the housing would be placed on vacant property owned by the city, the Chicago Park District, the Board of Education, and the Cook County Forest Preserve District. Twenty-two sites were selected for the housing. There were six sites on the South Side, three additional ones on the Southeast Side, five sites on the Far North Side, and eight on the Northwest Side. Unlike the permanent housing controlled by CHA, the sites for most of the veterans' temporary houses were not in the inner city but in outlying middle class neighborhoods of single-family houses. By the end of 1945 arrangements had been made for the transfer to Chicago of 3,400 units of housing, of four types, including: 1) "demountables," prefabricated factory-built houses, 2) "temporaries," plywood houses built on the sites, 3) trailers, and 4) Quonset huts. The housing was obtained from the federal government and had formerly been used near war-production centers, such as Oak Ridge, Tennessee.

The first units were occupied in December 1945, and by June 30, 1947, there were 2,123 units occupied, and another 1,000 scheduled for completion by October 1. There were 25,000 applications for the 3,233 units eventually put in use. The city ultimately contributed $2.1 million, and the Federal Public Housing Authority $4,432,883, plus reimbursement to Chicago of $1,475,000. The rents charged were from $22 to $41 per month. The housing was livable, except for the 991 trailers, which had only cold running water. The residents of those units often had to go a block for toilet and laundry facilities. Originally the temporary housing was to be used only until July 1949, but that date was extended, and in 1951 there were 2,300 of the units still in use. The phasing out of the temporary housing was slow, because of the difficulty in relocating the veterans, but was finally completed in 1955.

To accommodate returning veterans, the Chicago City Council voted in November and December, 1945, to appropriate $2 million for temporary housing to be erected on vacant land owned by the city, the Chicago Park District, the Board of Education, and the Cook County Forest Preserve District. Some of this housing, as shown, consisted of plywood houses built on the site.—Courtesy of Chicago Housing Authority

The temporary housing brought CHA to its first massive racial integration confrontations. In 1946 CHA changed its integration policy to set the Neighborhood Composition Rule aside and to bring blacks, who accounted for 20 percent of the veterans needing housing, into the temporary projects in white areas. The decision was not surprising in light of the leadership of CHA. The chairman of the Board of Commissioners from 1943 to 1950 was Robert Taylor, a black man. He was appointed to the CHA board in 1938, and elected vice-chairman the following year. He had studied architecture at Howard University, graduated from the University of Illinois, and taken courses in business and economics at Northwestern University. He was secretary-treasurer of the Illinois Federal Savings and Loan Association, which encouraged black home ownership. His occupation was that of manager of Julius Rosenwald's Michigan Boulevard Garden Apartments, a post he held from 1927 until 1957.

The executive secretary of CHA, from its founding in 1937, was Elizabeth Wood, a progressive woman with a broad background. Born in Japan, the daughter of a lay missionary, she grew up in Bloomington, Illinois. She got her bachelor's and master's degrees in English literature at the University of Michigan, and taught at Vassar College. She did graduate work at the University of Chicago, was

Metal barracks used as veterans' housing.—Courtesy of Chicago Housing Authority

the director of publicity for the Home Modernization Bureau, was a caseworker with United Charities of Chicago, headed the staff of the Metropolitan Housing Council, and was executive secretary of the State Housing Board.

Mayor Edward J. Kelly, of the so-called Kelly-Nash Democratic machine, supported the integration idea, but suggested an informal 10 percent black quota. It was decided to work aggressively for integration of only the larger temporary projects, those of over 150 units. Taylor and the CHA staff carefully selected the black families to be integrated, and the first project opened without incident. Trouble developed, however, at the second project, Airport Homes, a 185-unit development located near Midway Airport. A group of fifty-nine white veterans from the area moved as squatters into the units that CHA was holding for black families being screened. It is believed politicians from the area were behind the maneuvers, to embarrass Mayor Kelly in the coming elections.[7] The squatters finally left when court action was threatened. After the first black families moved into the project, a crowd gathered, and 400 policemen had to be assigned to the area to keep order. After two weeks the black families left because of pressure from the community. CHA was unable to find other blacks willing to move into the project, and it remained white.

The next major confrontation occurred at the Fernwood Park site, also located on the Southwest Side. Miss Wood had angered the area residents at a public meeting in May 1947, when she said both

Trailers used as veterans' housing.—Courtesy of Chicago Housing Authority

blacks and whites would be welcomed to the project. On August 13,
fifty-two families moved in, 8 percent of whom were black. Despite
considerable "orientation" efforts in the area to avoid trouble, a
crowd immediately gathered which grew to 5,000 people. The crowd
returned the next night, and several acts of violence occurred. It was
two weeks before the police contingent could be reduced from 1,000
to 700, and six months before the black families were safely established in the project.[8] Between the Airport and Fernwood riots, Martin Kennelly was elected mayor in the spring of 1947. He was a
businessman, who was put up by the Democrats as a reform candi-
date when Kelly decided not to run again because of a scandal caused
by corruption in the school system. Unlike Mayor Kelly, however,
who had publicly supported CHA in its integration efforts, Kennelly
refused to do so. By the time twenty temporary projects were completed, eleven of them were racially integrated. Fourteen percent of
the occupants were nonwhite, 12 percent black. Residents of the Far
Northwest Side neighborhood of Edison Park sued to block a project
in their area, but the court held that restrictive covenants could not
apply to a government body like the Board of Education, which in
this case leased the land to CHA for one dollar a year.

Quonset huts veterans' housing. Two families lived in each building.
—Courtesy of Chicago Housing Authority

Wentworth Gardens

In addition to Altgeld Gardens, the Federal Public Housing Authority owned a project planned for war workers which it had CHA operate—Wentworth Gardens. It is located on the four-square-block area bounded by 37th Street, Wentworth Avenue (now adjacent at that point to the Dan Ryan Expressway), Pershing Road, and Princeton Avenue. Like Altgeld Gardens it was built for black occupancy. Construction started in 1945, and when the war ended later that year it was decided to use it upon completion for low-rent housing, though CHA did not get actual ownership of the project until 1956. The site, in a predominantly industrial area, required the demolition of twenty structures, including the baseball park where the White Sox played until 1910. The project has 422 units in thirty-seven buildings. The buildings are two-story row houses with a cluster of three-story apartment buildings in the center. The architecture is similar to other CHA developments of the period, except for the use of vertical panels of glass brick above the front doors of the apartment buildings to light the stairways.

Crowd waiting on first day that applications were accepted for Wentworth Gardens.—Courtesy of Chicago Housing Authority

The architects were Loebl and Schlossman (which became Loebl, Schlossman, and Bennett in 1946). Just after completing Wentworth Gardens the firm designed for a private developer the complete suburb of Park Forest, thirty miles south of downtown Chicago. The design of Wentworth Gardens was a disappointing repetition of earlier public housing in Chicago. There was the gridiron layout of buildings, each identical to the one next door. The density of only twenty-one families per acre was lower than any of the earlier projects, except Altgeld Gardens and West Chesterfield. The cost per unit was $6,950 including the community building and outdoor recreation space. At the time of completion in 1947, the population was 856 adults and 1,454 children.

Wentworth Gardens, completed in 1947, repeated the design of earlier public housing in Chicago, except the density of only twenty-one families per acre was lower than most of the earlier projects.—Courtesy of Chicago Housing Authority

After the war CHA went back to its original job of eradicating slums and providing housing for low-income families. The projects were all changed to low-income tenancy, as vacancies occurred. CHA's turnover in 1946, in the permanent projects, was only 440 families, or 6 percent of the total. In the eight-year history of the three PWA projects, almost 70 percent of the original tenants had moved on to private housing, but the proportion was much smaller in the all-black Ida B. Wells project. By 1946 CHA was getting to be big business. It had a total staff of 449 people—295 maintenance workers and janitors and 154 administrative and clerical personnel. It received 99 percent of its operating income from rents, with the average rent being $32.90. In 1947 a new rent schedule was adopted which provided that the maximum income a family could have to gain entrance to a CHA unit was $2,150. By that time CHA had over 11,000 units of housing—7,644 permanent low-income units, about 3,200 temporary veterans' units, and the 250 West Chesterfield Homes. In the short period of one decade CHA had established a good record in regard to efficiency of construction and maintenance. The question of integration, however, remained largely unresolved, as did the larger question of the advisability of publicly created enclaves exclusively for poor people.

Interior of a Wentworth Gardens Apartment.—Courtesy of Chicago Housing Authority

4 Chicago Housing Authority: The Middle Years

During the period after World War II the Chicago Housing Authority was given new opportunities to fulfill the mandate of providing housing for the poor, and at the same time faced new challenges. For the first time it was free of the constraints of operating under emergency federal programs created to deal with the special problems caused by the Depression and the war. It had to come to grips, however, with the difficult problems of what type housing should be built, on what sites, and how the plans could be carried out in light of existing political realities in Chicago. In the postwar era the significant housing construction in the Chicago area occurred in the suburbs, not in the city. In 1947 only 5,968 new homes and apartment units were constructed in Chicago, whereas 24,744 units were built in the metropolitan area outside of Chicago. By 1956 the Chicago total had risen to only 13,625, but the suburbs built 48,632 units that year.[1]

The postwar construction in Chicago's suburban areas did much to alleviate the housing shortage of the middle class, but not of the poor, except to the extent that middle-class housing "trickled down" to them. It also signaled the loss of a great deal of the middle-class population of the city, a trend that has continued in Chicago and most large American cities through the mid-1970s. The exodus from the city was financed in great part by the federal government, through Veterans Administration (VA) and Federal Housing Administration (FHA) guaranteed mortgages. There is no proof, however, that the same thing would not have occurred if the federal mortgage guarantees had not been available. In fact, this postwar pattern of housing construction was not new to Chicago. Traditionally most new housing had been built on the periphery of the built sections of the city. By the 1950s much of the land in the city was filled up, so large-scale residential construction had to spill over into the suburbs.

Of profound importance to Chicago, which by the end of World War II had acquired a substantial black population, was the 1948

United States Supreme Court decision making restrictive covenants unenforceable. The purpose of the covenants, which were common on residential deeds in Chicago, was to preclude the property from ever being sold to blacks. In the case of *Shelly v. Kraemer*,[2] the court held that neighbors could not bring suit to restrain a black purchaser of property covered by the covenant, because such use of the courts would be state action to deprive the black of equal protection of the laws, and the right to own property, guaranteed by the Fourteenth Amendment to the Constitution. The decision did not ban private discrimination in selling real estate, but it did cripple restrictive covenants by prohibiting their enforcement in court.

The *Shelly v. Kraemer* decision was helpful in making more housing available to blacks in Chicago. Between 1940 and 1950 the black population increased from 8 percent to 13.5 percent. This increase represented a geographical area of about five square miles of housing going from white to black occupancy, including 60 census tracts. By 1950, 285 of the city's 935 census tracts had 1 percent or more units occupied by nonwhite residents. The increased black population did not, however, bring stable integrated neighborhoods. From the period of World War I on, the black population of Chicago lived in clearly defined South Side, and later West Side, ghettos. These ghettos enlarged as adjacent neighborhoods "changed" on a block by block basis.

The Chicago Real Estate Board from an early date supported restrictions on black residential movement. It encouraged the establishment of neighborhood "improvement" associations, which were organized in Chicago, and elsewhere, to keep blacks out of their areas. In 1917 the board appointed a committee to study the problem of how to house the expanding black population in Chicago. The committee's report provided, in part: "Inasmuch as more territory must be provided, it is desired in the interest of all, that each block shall be filled solidly and that further expansion shall be confined to contiguous blocks, and that the present method of obtaining a single building in scattered blocks, be discontinued."[3]

During the postwar period CHA conducted two fairly extensive studies to provide it with information for future action. The first was done in 1946, and was called *The Slum: Is Rehabilitation Possible?* For detailed analysis they picked a large block, in the Near South Side black ghetto, bounded by 35th and 37th streets, Vernon and Rhodes avenues. Almost half of the seventy-eight residential buildings on the block had been constructed before 1885, and practically all of the remainder before 1895. The buildings, which were two and three stories tall and made of brick and stone, had been constructed for large, well-to-do families. CHA found that 70 percent of the units lacked private bath, private toilet, or both. Almost 30 percent of the families shared kitchens, and less than half of the apartments had both hot and cold running water. Half of the apartments had loose or missing plaster, and sagging floors or ceilings. Only 59 percent of the buildings had central heating, and three-quarters of the units were in need of major repairs. The conclusion reached, after a one-year study, was that the buildings could be rehabilitated, but that CHA could provide housing in new buildings at lower rents than in rehabilitated ones.

The other study involved the livability of existing CHA apartments.[4] The eighty-eight tenants surveyed had several complaints in common. The bedrooms were too small; many were about nine by twelve feet, though in one project some were as small as seven feet four inches by eleven feet. The closet space in most apartments was inadequate, and residents missed closet and kitchen doors, which had been omitted to cut costs. The tenants didn't like the concrete floors, most of which did not even have asphalt tile on them. The tenants of one project complained about unpainted concrete ceilings, which had rust marks from the metal forms used in construction. The occupants also did not like the fact that the walls of most of the units were painted a drab tan, and said they would prefer to have the bedrooms in different colors than the living room, and the kitchen a lighter color than tan (CHA policy called for repainting interiors every four years). The tenants in the apartments which were based upon "open planning" did not like it, because there was no separation between the kitchen and living room of the apartment. Surprisingly, the study did not even touch upon the exterior architecture and planning of CHA projects.

During this same period CHA's chief of statistics published two articles purporting to show that CHA residents had a lower tuberculosis mortality rate, fewer fires, slightly better school attendance records, and a lower infant mortality rate than slum dwellers.[5] Neither study, however, addressed itself to the possibility that these differences could be due to the self-selection of people who applied for CHA apartments during that period, and the selection process and criteria used by CHA itself to choose its tenants. The studies had no control groups for comparison with CHA tenants. The fact is that serious research, even from that period, indicated that the hoped for improvements in social welfare of families in public housing did not occur.[6]

CHA Redevelopment Project No. 1

CHA took on the job of clearing slums for a private development in 1946, when Michael Reese Hospital needed land for expansion. The four-square-block area involved was adjacent to the hospital, at 29th and Ellis. The hospital advanced CHA $675,000 and agreed to pay the full cost of the land assembly, relocation services, and CHA overhead. Unlike most later urban renewal projects there was no "write down" by selling the land for less than it cost the public agency. By 1948 CHA has acquired 77 percent of the ninety-five parcels of land, and had successfully resisted a suit challenging its right to acquire property in a blighted area for the sole purpose of removing the buildings on it, but not to provide housing.

With the Michael Reese Project, CHA considered it was killing two birds with one stone. It was providing an expansion site for a

Slum housing in the 3100 block of Giles Avenue near Michael Reese Hospital, 1951.—Photograph by Mildred Mead, courtesy of Chicago Historical Society

hospital and clearing slums at no cost to the taxpayers.' This conclusion demonstrates that CHA's two functions, slum clearance and
construction of low-income housing, do not necessarily go hand in
hand. Here the project reduced the housing supply, albeit slum
housing, available to poor people. The Michael Reese expansion was
part of the largest urban renewal area in Chicago. The Near South
Side project also involved, over a period of years, construction of the
Lake Meadows, Prairie Shores, and South Commons private housing
developments, expansion of the Illinois Institute of Technology and
Mercy Hospital, and construction of the Ida B. Wells Homes, Dearborn Homes, and several later CHA developments.

   In 1947 the city produced a slum clearance and relocation program
which was the beginning of large-scale urban renewal in Chicago.
The Chicago Land Clearance Commission was established to pur-

*Home at 3129 South Dearborn Street, 1951. The site is now part of the
campus of the Illinois Institute of Technology, adjacent to Dearborn
Homes.—Photograph by Mildred Mead, courtesy of Chicago Historical Society*

chase slum property, and resell it to private developers and institutions. Their first job was to acquire the property for massive Lake Meadows, initially 2,033 units on 100 acres, developed by the New York Life Insurance Company. It displaced over 3,600 families, about a quarter of whom moved into CHA apartments. Lake Meadows was the initial experiment in Chicago involving the construction of large-scale, racially integrated, private housing for middle- and upper-income families.

Interior of slum at 533 East 36th Place, in the Near South Side Urban renewal area, 1950.—Photograph by Mildred Mead, courtesy of Chicago Historical Society

Dearborn Homes

The site for Dearborn Homes was considered for public housing before the war, then considered for war-worker housing, but temporarily shelved when the war ended. It is the area immediately north of the Illinois Institute of Technology campus, running from 27th to 30th streets, and from State Street two blocks west to the Rock Island Railroad tracks. After the war it was finally decided to proceed with this development, whose importance lies in the fact that it was the first CHA project using elevator buildings, and it thus set the precedent for most of the subsequent public housing constructed in Chicago.

The project got off to a slow start because of the difficulty of relocating the residents of the buildings to be demolished. CHA set up a special relocation program for them, as something of a demonstration project to point out the need for a well staffed permanent relocation service.[8] When CHA started buying the land in 1946 there were 158 vacant parcels, 9 small commercial structures, 6 single family homes, 91 small and large apartment buildings, and 6 occupied shacks. There were a total of 406 units, including 190 for single men in the Douglas Hotel at 2908 South State Street. Almost all of the buildings were in very bad condition. Only 14 units were owner occupied.

In March of 1948 there remained 148 families, with 662 people, one-third of them children, excluding occupants of the men's hotel. CHA established a relocation office on the site, and special priorities were given to the people to be relocated into existing CHA projects. The normal admission income limits were temporarily raised 25 percent for those families, and the local autonomy of project managers in the matter of tenant selection was suspended in favor of a centralized selection office. Although CHA had brought court eviction suits against each of the families to be displaced, all of them relocated without having to be put out of their homes pursuant to court order.

The 800-unit Dearborn Homes was designed by Loebl, Schlossman, and Bennett as sixteen elevator buildings, six and nine stories in height. The total cost of the development, including land and all administrative costs, was about $9.8 million. Because the project was built in the period after war housing, but before the major postwar programs got underway, the money was obtained from city, state, and federal funds. There were federally guaranteed forty-year bonds issued for $5.4 million, state appropriations of $2,117,000, and $2,292,000 obtained from a city bond issue. It is the only CHA project ever built with such three-way financing.

By the use of elevator buildings, land coverage was reduced to 10 percent of the site. The justification CHA used for going to the elevator buildings was the high cost of land obtained by slum clearance, and to provide more space for children to play. Neither rationale withstands analysis. The cost of this project, just under $12,000 per unit, was more than twice as much per unit as the Ida B. Wells Homes. The Wells project, which has larger apartments than the Dearborn Homes, was built only eight years earlier on a slum-cleared site a few blocks away. High-rise buildings have extra con-

Lobby of Douglas Hotel, 2908 South State Street. This structure, which provided 190 housing units for single men, was among the buildings removed for construction of the Dearborn Homes.—Courtesy of Chicago Housing Authority

struction and maintenance costs, not found in smaller ones. Elevators are one such cost, and construction of Dearborn Homes required that 3,000 piles had to be sunk, to depths of sixteen to thirty feet, to support the buildings.

The 90 percent open land is not perceptibly more advantageous to children than the 75 or 80 percent open land that would have been available if the same number of apartments had been put in low-rise buildings, especially when balanced against the problems of elevator living for children. The more likely explanation of the CHA use of elevator buildings is that the staff and commissioners got caught up in the high-rise apartment fascination of the period, and failed to recognize that housing which may be quite acceptable for single people or childless couples may not be at all desirable for poor families with several small children.

Dearborn Homes, which was completed in 1950, was supposed to be an experimental project. Other than the use of elevator buildings the only thing innovative about it were special children's play

Architect's perspective of Dearborn Homes, the first high-rise Chicago Housing Authority project. Completed in 1950, the project consists of sixteen elevator buildings, six and nine stories in height.—Courtesy of Chicago Housing Authority

spaces, really enlarged tenant hallways, on each floor. The buildings
have a cruciform plan, and display the same lackluster architecture
as most of the earlier CHA projects. The one thing that can be said
in favor of the project is that the six- and nine-story buildings are not
tall enough to be completely overwhelming, as the later high-rise
projects are. The concept of Dearborn Homes clearly reflects the
influence of Le Corbusier, the Swiss-born architect who published a
number of plans in the 1920s and 1930s, especially *Ville Radieuses*
(1935), showing high-rise buildings in a parklike setting.

Elizabeth Wood made a speech before the American Public Works
Association in 1945 that demonstrated a great deal about her philos-

*Dearborn Homes was supposed to be an experimental project, but other
than the use of elevator buildings the only innovation was the special
children's play spaces, really enlarged tenant hallways, on each floor.
—Courtesy of Chicago Housing Authority*

ophy of planning, and in fact the prevailing views at the time. She
said that planning for the rebuilding of the city, by public and private redevelopment, should be "bold and comprehensive" or the
results would be a "series of small projects, islands in a wilderness of
slums beaten down by smoke, noise and fumes." She advocated
neighborhoods that would "compare favorably with the suburbs,"
and relocation of streets and public transit to create superblocks
averaging an immense eighty acres.[9] Sixteen years later Miss Wood
continued to discuss using superblocks of high-rise public housing
buildings to establish "a new kind of urban residential neighborhood," to "compete with the suburbs for social desirability, especially for families with children." She summed up her feelings as
follows: "To abandon the large-scale planning that lies behind projects is to abandon one of the most important innovations in city
development."[10]

Relocation Projects

At an early date it became obvious that urban renewal and public
projects in Chicago were going to displace thousands of residents,
most of whom were poor, black, and would have special problems
obtaining housing elsewhere. One study estimated that 16,199 families and single persons would be displaced by the Congress Street
(now Eisenhower) Expressway, New York Life project (Lake Meadows), West Side Medical Center expansion, Illinois Institute of
Technology expansion, elimination of "alley dwellings," and relocation for new or expanded CHA projects.[11] The response of the city
and state to the lack of low-income housing in general, and the need
for relocation housing, was a significant group of eight developments. The developments, sometimes called the "Court" projects to
differentiate them from other CHA projects, are: Racine Courts,
Leclaire Courts, Harrison Courts, Maplewood Courts, Ogden
Courts, Archer Courts, Loomis Courts and Prairie Avenue Courts.

In 1947 the state legislature appropriated funds for slum clearance
and relocation. These had to be matched by funds from voter-
approved bond issues of the municipality. These two sources provided a total of $18,333,000 for the special city-state program in
Chicago. Unlike the federal program, the building costs in these
projects were paid outright, not borrowed. The eight projects provided new housing for 1,500 families, half of whom were relocated
from sites being redeveloped. According to the agreement between
CHA and the city, the payments in lieu of real estate taxes were set
at 10 percent of shelter rents, the same figure CHA was then paying
for its other projects. The contract for the relocation projects also

provided that CHA would pay any surplus of rents over expenses, up
to a maximum equal to what full real estate taxes on the properties
would be. Because of low maintenance costs in the early years of the
projects' operation, CHA paid $190,000, an amount equal to full real
estate taxes, for the year 1953.

The relocation projects were unique because CHA had a relatively
free hand in their development, at least as far as the budgets would
permit. They were not constrained by federal guidelines or bureaucracy. CHA attempted to select the best architects they could get to
design the projects. Notwithstanding Elizabeth Wood's talk about
massive developments, all of those projects are small, averaging less
than 200 units each, and all except Leclaire Courts are on small
pieces of land. The size of the projects resulted more from the dic-
tates of the City Council than from CHA's preferences.

The original sites chosen by CHA for the relocation housing were
large parcels of vacant land in outlying areas of the city. CHA did
not have the last word on the sites, however. In 1948 an Illinois
statute was enacted providing that in cities of 500,000 or more persons, the city council had to approve each site selected for public
housing by the local housing authority.[12] Because of the 500,000
population requirement, the law only applied to Chicago, of course.
The sites selected by CHA proved unacceptable to Mayor Kennelly
and the City Council. A crowd of 5,000 people gathered to protest
one proposed site. A new group of sites was ultimately chosen, most
of which were in slum areas, adjacent to railroads, factories, and
expressways. Only four were vacant, the rest required at least some
residential demolition. Five of the sites were in white areas, and to
get the aldermen to go along with them, Robert Taylor had to agree
to an informal quota in those projects, limiting black occupancy to
10 percent. Although Miss Wood did not think the quota was proper,
she did think it might serve the course of public housing by reassur-
ing the aldermen.[13]

Racine Courts and Leclaire Courts

Racine Courts was built on an 8.1 acre triangular site east of
Racine Avenue, between 108th and 110th streets. It was constructed
in 1949 and 1950, under plans drawn by Perkins and Will. It has only
121 units, making it the smallest project built by CHA between its
founding and 1961. Located in a middle-class residential area, it is
one of the best projects ever constructed by CHA. The buildings of
Racine Courts are two-story row houses with full basements. They
are built in twenty-seven clusters, most placed diagonally to Racine
Avenue. They have copper trim at the roofs, and wooden canopies

above the front doors. They were the largest units CHA had constructed to that date, averaging six rooms each, and all having a minimum of three bedrooms. They were also the most expensive CHA had constructed; the total construction and development cost was $14,204 per unit. The project is generously landscaped, and in all respects comparable to private subdivisions of the period.

Racine Courts, constructed in 1949–50, has only 121 units, making it the smallest Chicago Housing Authority project built until 1961. The buildings are two-story row houses comparable to housing in private subdivisions of the time.—Courtesy of Chicago Housing Authority

Leclaire Courts, which also opened in 1950, is basically a larger version of Racine Courts. It is located west of Cicero Avenue, between 42nd and 44th streets. The two-story row houses here have horizontal siding over the top floor of the units. The roofs slope from the outside of the houses toward the center, to interior downspouts. The architects were the firm of Friedman, Alschuler, and Sincere, in association with Ernest Grunsfeld, Jr. The project has 316 units, but they average only five rooms, and cost less than $10,000 per unit. The location of Leclaire Courts is in a heavy-industry area, just off a major truck route. Like Racine Courts it was built on vacant land, but in this case on a relatively large 24 acre site. The site was expanded in 1954 when the federally financed 300-unit Leclaire Courts Extension was constructed, carrying the project south to 45th Street. The extension, designed by Naess and Murphy, is also made up of two-story row houses, here with conventional pitched roofs sloping outward, but without the siding. Especially in its expanded state, the project is so big that it has an institutional feeling, more like Altgeld Gardens than Racine Courts.

Both the Racine and Leclaire projects were originally leased on a flat rent schedule which CHA wanted to compare with the graded

Leclaire Courts, opened in 1950, is basically a larger version of Racine Courts.—Courtesy of Chicago Housing Authority

rent schedule used in the other projects. The rent was $30 a month, regardless of the size of the family or the unit, and the tenants paid their own utility bills. If family income went above the eligibility limit, the rent was increased, until the family could find private housing, to between $50 and $103 a month, depending on the family's income. The experiment was reported to be popular with the tenants, who had rent arrearages of less than one-half of 1 percent. In a 1957 magazine interview Elizabeth Wood advocated revising public housing procedures so that families are not evicted when their income goes above the eligibility level.[14]

Elevator Building Relocation Projects

The other five relocation projects, which opened between late 1950 and 1952, were all elevator buildings, on small inner-city sites. They are very similar to one another, having from 126 to 148 units

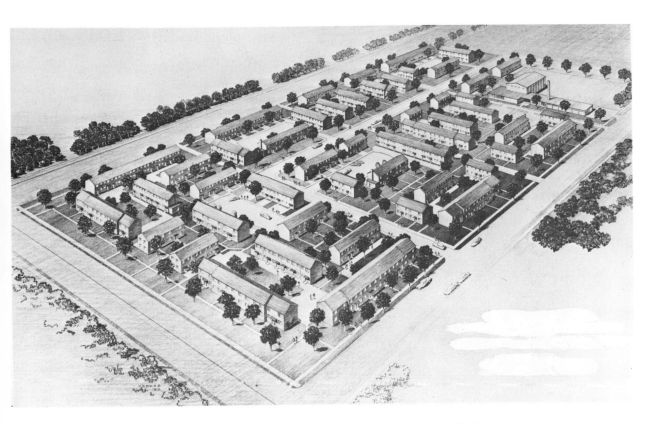

Architect's perspective of Leclaire Courts Extension, which was constructed in 1954. The extension, as is the adjacent Leclaire Courts, is made up of two-story row houses. —Courtesy of Chicago Housing Authority

on two to five acres. The first one was Harrison Courts, located just south of the Eisenhower Expressway at Harrison Street and Sacramento Boulevard. It was designed by Pace Associates, and is composed of three buildings, seven stories tall. The apartments are one-third efficiency units, one-third with one bedroom, and one-third two-bedroom units. They were designed to house aged couples without children, and also single persons, childless couples, or those with only one child. A new "feature" of the buildings was the use of unplastered concrete block interior walls. For economy reasons this became an almost universal feature of later CHA buildings. The next project is called Maplewood Courts. It also faces the Eisenhower Expressway but is located north of it at Van Buren and Maplewood. This project, designed by Harvey Peck, has two buildings, again seven stories. The Maplewood Courts buildings have a cruciform plan, whereas the Harrison Courts structures are each

Harrison Courts, composed of three buildings seven stories tall, was designed to house single persons, childless couples, those with only one child, or aged couples.—Courtesy of Chicago Housing Authority

composed of two overlapping parallel rectangles. The remaining projects have the same format, two buildings, each seven stories in height.

The third of the elevator projects is Ogden Courts, designed by Skidmore, Owings, and Merrill and also located on the West Side, at Ogden and Fairfield across from Mt. Sinai Hospital. Ogden's were the first CHA buildings to have their concrete frames left exposed. The buildings have good proportions, and red brick infill, a pleasant relief from the omnipresent common brick of virtually all the earlier projects. Another feature introduced in these buildings is that the apartments open to an eight-foot-wide fenced outdoor gallery. This type of gallery became a common element of CHA high-rise housing for the next decade.

Archer Courts, at 23rd Street and Archer Avenue, near Chinatown, was designed by Everett F. Quinn and Alfred Mell. It also has

Ogden Courts, designed by Skidmore, Owings, and Merrill, were the first Chicago Housing Authority buildings to have their concrete frames exposed.—Photographs by Devereux Bowly, Jr.

an exposed concrete frame and fenced galleries. Here the buildings
are very long, and only twenty-one feet deep. They thus have merely
a single span, and no interior columns nor girders in the ceilings.
The three-bedroom apartments are located in a row-house-like ar-
rangement on the bottom two floors, complete with private front
and rear entrances on opposite sides of the buildings. The galleries
on the upper floors are cantilevered out from the buildings.

The final project in this group, and visually the most interesting is
the Loomis Courts designed by Loewenberg and Loewenberg, and
Harry Weese and John Van der Muelen. The location is at Loomis
Boulevard and 14th Place, adjacent to the Robert Brooks Homes. It
was cited in 1951, as one of the ten best new publicly financed
housing projects in the nation, by a committee of architects appointed by the National Association of Housing Officials.[15] The
buildings each have two wings, at an obtuse angle to one another.
The wings have galleries on opposite sides that connect where the

*Loomis Courts were cited in 1951 by a committee of architects appointed
by the National Association of Housing Officials as one of the ten best new
publicly financed housing projects in the nation.—Courtesy of Chicago
Housing Authority*

wings come together, and at which point there is a common elevator
to serve both. The living and bedrooms have windows on the opposite side of the buildings than the galleries. On the gallery side the
kitchens and bathrooms have windows set high in the walls to provide privacy. The site plan has winding paths that pass through the
buildings at the point of the elevator lobbies.[16]

Prairie Avenue Courts

Architecturally the best of the city-state relocation developments
is Prairie Avenue Courts, located between King Drive and Prairie
Avenue, running south from 26th Street. It was designed by George

*Prairie Avenue Courts, designed by Keck and Keck, unlike most public
housing, contains different size buildings, to accommodate a variety of
families. The elevator buildings were built in 1951–52. The adjacent slums
were demolished and new two-story buildings constructed and the project
completed in the mid-1950s. —Photograph by Hedrich-Blessing, courtesy
of George Fred Keck–William Keck*

Fred Keck and William Keck. Because of the relocation problems of
the residents of the densely populated site, it was decided to build it
in stages. By doing this some of the displaced tenants could be re-
housed on the site as the first buildings were completed. Unlike
most public housing, Prairie Avenue Courts contains different size
buildings, to accommodate a variety of families.

*High-rise Prairie Avenue Courts building. This shows the typical exposed
concrete frame and gallery construction of the period.—Courtesy of
Chicago Housing Authority*

The first stage, which is composed of elevator buildings, contained 274 units, and was constructed in 1951 and 1952. The adjacent slum buildings were then demolished, and the new two-story buildings were constructed. When the project was completed in the mid-1950s it contained 343 units in thirteen buildings. There is a fourteen-story building, three buildings of seven stories, three apartment blocks of two stories, and six groups of row houses. The elevator buildings have exposed concrete frames and galleries, and the best proportions of any of the CHA high-rise buildings. The site plan is good, particularly in the way the different building heights relate to one another. The project, which in 1957 won a citation of merit from the Chicago chapter of the American Institute of Architects, represents the ultimate in CHA's efforts to give some degree of freedom to competent architects. Although there was no way to know it at the time, it pretty much offered the swan song of good architecture on CHA projects.

5 Chicago Housing Authority: Years of Turmoil

The major construction of public housing in Chicago after World War II was not the city-state financial relocation projects but federally financed ones. Although planning started for these projects in the late 1940s, the first one was not completed and occupied until 1953. The federal Housing Act of 1949 provided for the most comprehensive federal aid to housing to that date. Title I of the act set up a system of federally funded, but mostly privately developed, urban renewal of blighted areas. Title III amended the Housing Act of 1937 by authorizing loans and subsidies for a national program of approximately 810,000 units of low-rent housing, to be constructed by local housing authorities over a period of six years, on slum and vacant sites.

In anticipation of the federal legislation, CHA conducted studies to ascertain how serious the housing shortage was for poor families in Chicago. A preliminary study,[1] conducted in 1949, concluded that there were 1,178,000 families requiring housing, and only 906,000 standard units available, leaving a deficit of 272,000 units. The deficit was broken down as 95,000 "doubled-up" families, 144,000 units in blighted housing needing replacement, and 33,000 units needed for a normal vacancy reserve. A more comprehensive study, conducted a year later making use of census material, concluded that the 272,000 deficit figure was too low, and the true shortage was 292,000.[2]

The greatest need was in Chicago's black population, which had grown from 277,731 in 1940 to 492,265 in 1950. Although only about 14 percent of the 1950 Chicago population was black, almost half of the needed 292,000 units were for non-whites. At this time CHA had a waiting list which included 15,000 black families. The average income of black families in Chicago was only $2,900, compared to $4,000 for whites. During 1950 a total of 488 families moved out of CHA housing because of excess income, and more than 40 eviction suits were being filed each month against the 1,460 excess-income families who remained as of June 30, 1951.

By this time a clear change could be seen in the average CHA tenant family. When public housing began in the 1930s, it was to a considerable extent a program to provide decent housing for basically working-class families who were in difficult economic circumstances because of the Depression. Later it served those who were unable to find housing because of war shortages. The "up and out" theory was that as tenants' incomes rose above the maximum eligibility limits, they would then move to private housing. This turnover would make a large number of units regularly available for new applicants. By 1950, however, 27 percent of CHA families received public aid, and about one-third had one parent missing from the home. CHA was becoming the landlord for hard-core poverty families, who had suffered from long-term deprivation and discrimination.

Site Location Controversy

In July 1949 CHA produced an ambitious proposal for federally financed housing under the 1949 act which called for building a total of 40,000 units, during a six-year period, of which 15,000 would be on vacant land, mostly on the outskirts of the city. In November it submitted sites for the first 10,000 units to the City Council. The federal government had allocated 21,000 units for Chicago for the first two years, more than for any other city. The tremendous controversy that followed, concerning the sites for the new housing, so damaged CHA that it never fully recovered. The events were the subject of front-page newspaper coverage for months, and an in-depth study and book by Martin Meyerson and Edward C. Banfield (both then professors at the University of Chicago) called *Politics, Planning, and the Public Interest: The Case of Public Housing in Chicago*.[3]

In the early years of CHA's existence Mayor Kelly, for whatever his motives, had protected it from gross political interference. Elizabeth Wood was allowed to fill positions without regard to political affiliation and was insulated from the City Council. When Mayor Kennelly was elected in 1947 this all changed. He was not sympathetic to either public housing or racial integration and was furthermore a weak mayor without much influence over the City Council. Most of the aldermen were hostile toward CHA because it would not dispense its jobs on a patronage basis, and more importantly to them, because it provided the possibility of bringing blacks into their wards. It was for this reason that in 1948 Alderman William J. Lancaster, chairman of the Housing Committee, had gotten the state legislature to enact the statute giving the City Council power to approve each site proposed by CHA.[4]

During October 1949 Robert Taylor went to Mayor Kennelly and asked him to send the list of proposed sites, that CHA had drawn up for the first 10,000 units under the 1949 act, to the City Council with his strong endorsement. The mayor sent the list of seven sites to the aldermen in November, but with no endorsement, other than to say it was an important matter that deserved prompt attention. It soon became obvious that the aldermen didn't like the sites proposed, because too many of them were in outlying white neighborhoods. This left Taylor and the CHA board with two choices. They could come to a private compromise with the aldermen involving more slum clearance sites and fewer vacant sites in the white neighborhoods, or they could fight the battle with the City Council in public. They chose the latter course.

In February 1950 the City Council held a series of hearings that went on for four days and were attended by hundreds of people who strongly opposed the sites. The anti-public-housing forces were led by neighborhood groups, mostly from the Southwest and Far South sides of the city, who chartered buses to bring their members to the hearings. Among the most active of the groups was the Southwest Neighborhood Council which hired a lawyer to lead the opposition. Another was the Southtown Planning Association, which as one of its projects encouraged blacks to move out of the Englewood area where it operated to Robbins, an all-black suburb just south of Chicago. The third major opposition group, called the Taxpayers' Action Committee, had organized homeowners and businesses in the Roseland area to resist racial change.

After the hearings were over the City Council Housing Committee recommended approval of only two sites, both slum-clearance extensions of existing projects. They refused to recommend the remainder of the sites in the package, and then delegated the site selection problem to a subcommittee of nine aldermen. In March the subcommittee made tours of forty sites that had been proposed by one source or another. The subcommittee came up with its own list of thirteen sites, some of which were ridiculous, such as one in the path of a planned expressway. CHA then proposed a new package of sites, including some of the vacant sites from its first list. The new package, in fact, had two-thirds of its units on vacant-land sites. Kennelly refused to take any position on it. Alderman John J. Duffy, chairman of the Finance Committee, and Alderman Lancaster called an informal meeting of a few of the most influential of the fifty aldermen, and worked out what came to be referred to as the Duffy-Lancaster compromise. It provided for only 2,000 units on vacant land, and over 10,000 on slum-clearance sites. It had eight slum sites, all in black ghettos, and seven small vacant sites to accommodate from 300 to 588 units each. The Duffy-Lancaster proposal would dispalce 12,465 families, virtually all of the black, and provide a net addition to the housing supply of a mere forty-seven units.[5] It was a curious compromise proposal from the standpoint of the white aldermen. Since it would do almost nothing to alleviate the shortage of housing for black families, it would force the expanding black population into white neighborhoods—the very thing the white aldermen opposed. It would have been more logical from their standpoint to propose vacant inner-city sites, for example obsolete railroad yards, that would have created a large net addition to the housing stock available to blacks.

A great deal of pressure was put on Taylor and the other CHA commissioners to accept the Duffy-Lancaster compromise proposal. It was becoming obvious by this stage in the controversy that CHA had overestimated the influence of its liberal supporters and greatly underestimated the opposition. The *Sun-Times*, which was still being published by Marshall Field III, and had strongly supported CHA during the early stages of the controversy, endorsed the Duffy-Lancaster compromise. As negotiations proceeded, variations of it were put forward by Ralph H. Burke, a consulting engineer, who although in private practice did a great deal of work for the city, and had been called into this matter by Kennelly. By June 1950 the stalemate had lasted eight months, and there was some feeling that the City Council might not approve any new public housing at all.

CHA received less support than it expected from the United States Public Housing Administration, which was fearful of losing the entire Chicago program. Efforts to get President Truman to intervene in the situation were unsuccessful. Finally on June 16 the CHA commissioners voted to go along with the Duffy-Lancaster plan, as modified by Burke. The only commissioner voting against the compromise was Claude A. Benjamin. Robert Taylor resigned from the board in November 1950, three months after the City Council acted on the compromise. Benjamin was not reappointed by Mayor Kennelly when his term expired.

The sites finally agreed to numbered thirteen, of which seven were in the heart of the city on slum-clearance sites. They were planned for 8,000 to 11,500 units, and located as follows: 1) Cermak Road and State Street (site for Ickes Homes), 2) 35th and State Street (site for Stateway Gardens), 3) Lake Street, from Ashland to Damen (site for Henry Horner Homes), 4) Madison and Western (site for Rockwell Gardens), 5) Cabrini Extension, 6) Addams-Brooks Extension (Abbott Homes), and 7) Ida B. Wells Extension. The other six sites were all on vacant land. One was in the inner-city at Oakwood and Lake Park (site for Olander Homes) and the other five in outlying sections of the city. They were 1) Bryn Mawr and Kedzie, on the far north side (this site was never developed as public housing), 2) Altgeld Gardens Extension (Philip Murray Homes), 3) Leclaire Extension, 4) Trumbull Park Extension (never built), and 5) 95th and Wentworth (Lowden Homes). All of the eight inner-city sites were ultimately developed, but of the five sites in outlying areas, only three were built upon, and two of them were extensions of existing projects.

Trumbull Park Disturbances

The summer of 1953 brought CHA into a massive racial confrontation. Although reminiscent of the riots which had occurred six years earlier in connection with integration of veteran's temporary housing, these were more prolonged. In 1953 CHA, even though publicly it professed to be nondiscriminatory, still had four all-white projects which included Lathrop Homes, Lawndale Gardens, and the Trumbull Park Homes. On March 26, 1952, an Argentine woman with four children moved into Trumbull Park, and the next night six of her windows were broken. Three days later she moved out. On July 30, 1953, the Donald Howard family integrated the project without CHA realizing what was happening. Mrs. Howard and the two children had applied for the apartment; because they had very light skin, the CHA interviewer had not recognized them as blacks. Mr. Howard, who was a postal worker, had not been present at the interview. At this time Trumbull Park, because of its remote location, was one of only two CHA projects handling their own leasing rather than using the central CHA office.

By August 5, word had spread through the area that a black family had moved into the project. A crowd gathered, and that evening and the next paving bricks and stones were thrown at the Howards' apartment, even though extra police had been brought in. The windows of the management office were broken and a sulphur stink bomb thrown into it. By August 9, the crowd was estimated at 1,000 to 2,000 people, and repeated acts of violence were aimed at the Howards' apartment. In the next few days cars driven by blacks on nearby Torrence Avenue were stoned, as was a bus with black passengers. At least thirty cars were damaged, and one tipped over. An empty apartment in the project was damaged when gasoline was thrown in and ignited.

Rioters were arrested every day, twenty-two on August 11 alone, all for disorderly conduct. Elizabeth Wood cut short her annual vac-

ation and returned to Chicago. The police in the area, who at times
numbered 750, closed down the local taverns for a few days to try
and quell the riots but to no avail. On August 18 the NAACP filed
suit in the federal court in Chicago, alleging that CHA had discrimi-
nated against thirteen different applicants at the four projects. The
suit also alleged that CHA had secret agreements with neighborhood groups in the areas of four projects to keep blacks out.

Two tenants of the Trumbull Park Homes who had been involved
in the riots were served by CHA with termination of lease notices,
and all tenants were informed that similar action would be taken if
they joined in the riots. Observers believed that most of the rioters
lived in the neighborhood surrounding the project. On August 26 the
CHA commissioners voted to integrate all projects, and on October
13 three additional black families moved into Trumbull Park under
police protection. About forty women and children threw rocks and
tomatoes at them, and four of the women were arrested. Emil Pa-
cini, the local alderman, demanded Elizabeth Wood's resignation for
"fomenting racial trouble in the city." Alderman DuBois said the
CHA had radicals in control, and that Miss Wood was a "pinkee."[6]
Mayor Kennelly remained silent, except to appoint a Committee to
Study Racial Tension in Public Housing Projects.

On January 20, 1954, CHA served Mr. Howard with a thirty-day
eviction notice, claiming that the family had gained admission on
the basis of misrepresentation. It was alleged that Mrs. Howard had
taken a job as a telephone operator shortly before the family had
moved into the project and failed to report that fact to CHA. Her
salary when added to her husband's put them over the CHA admission income limit. The *Southtown Economist* newspaper estimated
that by the end of January the salaries of police assigned to the
project over the previous five and one-half months had cost the city
$2 million. In February large numbers of aerial bombs were being
exploded at the project, one of which broke five windows in the
Howards' apartment. In its March 1, 1954, edition *Time* magazine
had a large story on the riots, titled the "Seven Months War." On
March 19 the Chicago Negro Chamber of Commerce led a march of
about 350 people on City Hall, to complain that the police had not
exerted their full effort to protect the black residents of Trumbull
Park. By April 1, things had quieted down somewhat, and the
number of black families in the project had increased to ten.

In early April Mr. Howard was accused of firing a gun, after being
harrassed by white teen-agers. In August he was convicted of disorderly conduct in regard to the incident. On April 10 the *Chicago
Daily News* had an article saying the disturbances at the projects

were being encouraged by the South Deering Improvement Association, the National Citizens Protective Association, and to a lesser extent by the White Circle League. The warm weather of the spring of 1954 brought an increased number of incidents of violence. On May 3 the Howard family moved out of the project, complaining through their attorneys that the "officials of the City of Chicago, beginning with Mayor Kennelly, had consistently refused or failed to maintain law and order" at the project.[7] By the end of June there were fifteen black families in the project, and acts of violence were still occurring almost daily. On July 4, 1954, Eric Sevareid devoted his entire half-hour CBS network television show, "American Week," to the situation at Trumbull Park. Later that month 400 policemen were needed to protect a group of black tenants and their friends who were playing baseball in the park adjacent to the project. Almost 1,000 policemen were on duty during one twenty-four hour period, and sixteen arrests were made for assault, inciting to riot, and unlawful assembly. By September there were twenty black families at Trumbull Park, and their children had enrolled in the local schools, largely without incident.

By the end of the winter of 1954–55 the situation had calmed down somewhat, although the worst racial strife Chicago had suffered since the race riots of 1919 was by no means coming to an end. The project then had twenty-eight black families, or about 6 percent of the total. Sporadic acts of violence continued during the summer of 1955. For the twenty-two month period from August 7, 1953, through May 28, 1955, 202 adults and 87 juveniles were arrested. Most of those arrested were charged with disorderly conduct and fined five or ten dollars. One person was sent to jail for ten days after being convicted of aggravated assault and battery; another was put on one year court supervision for rioting and unlawful assembly, and several persons were put on six months probation.[8]

As a by-product of the rioting a tavern near the project which served blacks was destroyed by fire.[9] The Committee on Racial Tensions, appointed by Mayor Kennelly to look into the situation, issued its eight-page report on January 15, 1954.[10] After sketching the history of black migration to and residence in Chicago, the report recommended that future move-ins of black families to all-white public housing projects be preceded by an educational program for project residents. It also recommended an auxiliary emergency police force to deal with racial disturbances, and that the City Council enact a resolution against racial discrimination in public housing. The committee further recommended maintenance of building codes in "transition" areas, and securing assurances from the real estate and financial community that normal credit resources would remain available as long as property in the area was well maintained, regardless of its racial composition.

In June 1956 a new thirty-four-year-old minister was assigned to the South Deering Methodist Church. He integrated the congregation with black families from Trumbull Park Homes. Not only were windows in his nearby apartment smashed, and his car damaged, but during early 1957 aerial torpedo bombs were exploded outside the church during Sunday services. In fact, as late as March 1957, aerial bombs were still exploding almost nightly at the project, and the police still had a special fifty-man detail assigned there. As of that date only twenty-five black families remained, down from a high of thirty-one who had lived in the project at one point in 1955. During 1954 twenty-four black families had moved in, but the number fell to nine in 1955, and six in 1956. During the first three months of 1957 only one black family was admitted. Selection of the blacks and timing of move-ins remained a top level CHA administrative decision.[11]

Termination of Elizabeth Wood

During the Trumbull Park disturbances Elizabeth Wood left the Chicago Housing Authority. With Robert Taylor and Claude Benjamin no longer on the Board of Commissioners, her position was so tenuous that she could not withstand the double pressure of the site location and Trumbull Park controversies. Her difficulties with the politicians had started years before. Although she reached an accommodation with Mayor Kelly, she never did so with Mayor Kennelly or with most of the aldermen. Her beliefs were too liberal for them, and her refusal to compromise on issues such as patronage was considered arrogant. Miss Wood felt that an internal campaign had been going on for some time to undermine her position. Among other things, for a year before the trouble occurred she had been getting conflicting directives, from different sources, as to when and how to permit blacks to move into Trumbull Park Homes.[12]

In April 1954 CHA had commissioned a study, to be done by the firm of Griffenhagen and Associates, on CHA's structure and operation. At their meeting on August 23 the CHA commissioners gave Miss Wood a copy of the report, and told her that a new position of executive director had been established, and filled by a retired army lieutenant-general named William B. Kean. He was a graduate of West Point and a veteran of both world wars and Korea. The rationale for bringing him in was that management and business considerations had overridden the "social aspects" of CHA operations. It had become a $100 million corporation, collecting more than $500,000 per month in rent. It was the largest landlord in Chicago, with 12,000 units and another 8,000 under development. When Miss Wood charged publicly that she was being superseded because of her efforts to eliminate discrimination in CHA housing, she was discharged.

The Emergency Committee on the Chicago Housing Authority, made up of liberal supporters of Miss Wood, was formed and requested the State Housing Board to investigate the situation. The group had a testimonial meeting on her behalf, at the 8th Street Theatre, on October 28, 1954, before she went to New York and became a consultant to the Citizens Housing and Planning Council. Mayor Kennelly was dumped by the regular Democratic organization in 1955, and defeated in the Democratic primary election by Richard J. Daley. General Kean stayed at his new job only three years, resigning in 1957. The firing of Elizabeth Wood not only signaled the change in power of CHA from liberals to conservatives, but the end of an almost-twenty-year period where public housing was viewed as a vehicle for social change. In many respects the public housing movement was a successor to other social experiments such as the settlement-house movement. During the 1930s and 1940s reformers saw it as a major solution to the urban problems of slums, crime, and even as a way to lift people out of poverty. The controversy surrounding the termination of Elizabeth Wood obscured the more profound fact that public housing never was the hoped-for catalyst for profound social change. The expectations that it would perform that function were probably unrealistic from the start.

The transfer of control from Elizabeth Wood to William Kean brought with it a change in the informal racial quotas maintained by the Wood administration at several projects, in an attempt to promote and maintain racial integration. For example, when Leclaire Courts was constructed there was a secret understanding with the City Council that black tenants would be limited to 20 percent of the total, and they were until 1955. The system was not continued by General Kean, however, when first twenty and later thirty units formerly occupied by white families were rented to black families, rather than being held vacant until a sufficient number of white families applied to maintain the quota.[13] Subsequently, the entire project changed to black occupancy.

Low-Rise Projects

The ongoing activities of CHA did not stop, of course, during the Trumbull Park controversy and the termination of Elizabeth Wood. From 1953 through 1956 seven new projects or extensions of existing projects opened, only two of which were made up of low-rise buildings. The first was the Philip Murray Homes, a 500-unit addition to Altgeld Gardens completed in 1954. The two-story row houses, designed by Naess and Murphy, were similar to, if somewhat simpler than, the adjacent houses of Altgeld Gardens. The Murray project also included additions and alterations to the Altgeld community buildings.

Philip Murray Homes, a 500-unit addition to Altgeld Gardens, was completed in 1954. The two-story row houses are similar to, but somewhat simpler than, the Altgeld housing.—Photograph by Devereux Bowly, Jr.

The other low-rise development was the Governor Frank O. Lowden Homes at 95th and Wentworth. This was also a development of
two-story row houses, but here a small one. Part of the ten-acre tract
CHA acquired for the project had been purchased in 1940 by two
speculators for $2,500 and subdivided into lots, thirty-six of which
were sold on contract at prices ranging from $450 to $2,500. The lots
were of little value to those who bought them because of the lack of
streets in the subdivision. By the time CHA bought up the land,
almost all parcels had a market value lower than the delinquent real
estate taxes and penalties owed on them.

The Lowden site had originally been scheduled for 300 units, as
part of the 1950 package approved by the City Council. CHA
planned three buildings of seven stories containing 195 units, plus
nine groups of two-story row houses. The City Council, at the re-
quest of the local alderman, refused to enact the rezoning required
for the scheme. After some delays, CHA and the architect of the
project, Sydney H. Morris, settled on 128 row houses in eighteen
clusters. The design of the houses is similar to those of the Leclaire
Courts Extension and Philip Murray Homes. The Lowden project
adjoins a private rental development called Princeton Park Homes.

*Governor Frank O. Lowden Homes. This project consists of 128 row houses
in eighteen clusters and adjoins Princeton Park Homes, a private rental
development.—Courtesy of Chicago Housing Authority*

High-Rise Projects

The tallest building CHA constructed prior to 1953 was the Victor A. Olander Homes. The project consists of a single fifteen-story Y-shaped building containing 150 units. It is located at 3939 South Lake Park Avenue, next to the Illinois Central Gulf Railroad tracks and Burnham Park. The architect was the firm of Shaw, Metz, and Dolio. In 1956 the Olander Homes Extension was constructed just south of the original building. The site for the first building had been vacant, but eight residential buildings had to be demolished for the extension. It is an identical concrete tower, except the veneer on the original is common brick, whereas the extension is red finished brick. Other than having a good view of the lake, which is about a quarter of a mile to the east, the project is without distinction.

The Victor A. Olander Homes consists of a single fifteen-story Y-shaped building that was the tallest Chicago Housing Authority building prior to 1953.—Courtesy of Chicago Housing Authority

In 1955 three large high-rise projects opened. One of them was the 797-unit Harold L. Ickes Homes on the west side of State Street from 22nd to 25th streets. It is reminiscent of some of the relocation projects, but on a larger and more inhumane scale. Even though part of the twenty-one-acre site was obtained when the old Wesley Hospital buildings were demolished, about forty residential buildings, with 308 units housing 449 families, were demolished for the project. Eight buildings were constructed; three of them are nine stories tall and extremely long; the other five are seven stories tall. The buildings, designed by Skidmore, Owings, and Merrill, have exposed concrete frames and small wings projecting to the west. The site

One of three high-rise projects to open in 1955 was the 797-unit Harold L. Ickes Homes. Eight buildings were constructed, three of nine stories and extremely long, and five of seven stories.—Courtesy of Chicago Housing Authority

also contains CHA's central maintenance shops and a three-story brick building which formerly housed its main office. It is located at 55 West Cermak Road, was constructed in 1961 at a cost of $750,000, and contains 30,000 square feet of office space. In recent years the CHA main office has been in the Loop, and the building on the edge of the Ickes site has been used by the Illinois Department of Public Aid. The next high-rise development, the Ida B. Wells Exten-

Row houses, formerly portion of barracks of Camp Douglas, the Civil War prison camp. This building was located at 37th Street between Ellis and Lake Park avenues on the site of the Ida B. Wells Extension.—Courtesy of Chicago Historical Society

sion, is located just north of the original Wells project. It is composed of ten buildings, each seven stories tall, with a total of 641 units. The buildings, which were designed by Friedman, Alschuler, and Sincere, and Ernest Grunsfeld, Jr., have an exposed concrete frame and brick infill, like the Ickes Homes.

Grace Abbott Homes

The final product of the period was the Grace Abbott Homes, which opened in 1955. Covering ten square blocks, with no streets running through it, the project demonstrates the "bold" planning Elizabeth Wood advocated. The massive size of the project, 1,200 units, made it the precursor of the giant high-rise projects of the late

The Ida B. Wells Extension, opened in 1955, is located just north of the original Wells project and is composed of ten buildings, each seven stories tall.—Courtesy of Chicago Housing Authority

1950s and early 1960s. Located south of Roosevelt Road at Loomis Street, it is an extension of the Jane Addams and Robert Brooks projects. The three of them together, with the adjacent Loomis Courts, make one complex of twenty-six city blocks, 3,000 housing units, and the largest slum-clearance site at that time.

The Abbott project is composed of forty buildings, seven of which are fifteen-story, Y-shaped towers, similar to the Olander Homes, and designed by the same architects. The rest of the buildings are two-story row houses on the edges of the site. More than any project built in Chicago to that date, the overall feeling is forbidding, and the human scale is completely lost. A recent study, *Defensible Space: Crime Prevention Through Urban Design*,[14] by Oscar New-

Grace Abbott Homes site before redevelopment.—Courtesy of Chicago Housing Authority

man, has found that from the standpoint of crime, the absolute
worst combination for public housing is the superblock of high-rise
buildings like Abbott Homes. His research, which dealt with public
housing in New York City, found a positive correlation between
both project size and crime rate, and building height and crime rate.

*Grace Abbott Homes, which opened in 1955, covers ten square blocks with
no streets running through it. The massive size of the project, 1,200 units,
made it the precursor of the giant high-rise projects of the late 1950s and
early 1960s.—Courtesy of Chicago Housing Authority*

Street-wise residents of public housing, and perceptive observers like Jane Jacobs in her book *The Death and Life of Great American Cities*,[15] have known this all along.

As Newman points out, streets provide security because they form prominent paths for people and cars. Low-rise housing with windows and doors facing the street extend what he calls the "zone of residents' territorial commitments," to the thoroughfare; the residents have some feeling for what is going on there. Streets permit surveillance by police in passing cars. To get to a high-rise building in a superblock, such as at the Abbott Homes, a resident must leave the street and go through the unprotected grounds. It is striking how little the open areas in this type of project are used. The high-rise buildings promote anonymous living. People don't know their neighbors, and thus are not likely to watch out for them. The Abbott Homes project is an unfortunate legacy of the Elizabeth Wood years at CHA.

With its high-rise buildings and enormous open spaces, the Grace Abbott Homes exemplified the "bold" planning popular at the time.—Courtesy of Chicago Housing Authority

6 Chicago Dwellings Association

The Chicago Dwellings Association (CDA) was chartered in 1948 as a not-for-profit corporation. It was set up at the suggestion of the Mayor's Committee for Housing Action to develop moderate-income housing for those families with incomes too high to meet public-housing eligibility standards, but too low to obtain adequate housing in the private market. Its board of directors is appointed by the mayor of Chicago. From the first, CDA was closely connected with CHA; in fact its initial working capital came from the $2.5 million 1945 state allocation to the Chicago Housing Authority, earmarked for housing to be developed by nonprofit corporations.

The initial plan for CDA was that CHA would use state grant funds in its possession not only to provide equity financing for CDA, but also to acquire the land for its projects. CDA would then get money actually to construct the buildings from FHA or conventional mortgages. CHA would take back a second mortgage for the equity financing and land-acquisition cost, to be repaid after the first mortgage was paid off. In this way very long term financing could be achieved. Although CHA and CDA are legally separate organizations, from the first CHA kept accounts for CDA and provided it with technical support. In 1955 CDA was reorganized and CHA commissioners were appointed to replace all but two of the original CDA board members. The change, together with an even closer administrative connection between the two agencies, made CDA the de facto middle-income housing arm of CHA.

Midway Gardens

The first project developed by CDA is called Midway Gardens. Completed in 1953, it is located at 60th Street, between Langley and Cottage Grove avenues, on the south side of the Midway Plaisance. The name was taken from Frank Lloyd Wright's famous Midway Gardens beer garden, which stood (from 1913 until it was demolished in 1929) on the site adjacent to the building. CHA purchased the land for the project for just under $220,000, and conveyed it to CDA. The total development cost of the building was about $4 million, of which about $2.2 million was raised by a forty-year

FHA-insured mortgage, and the rest came from CHA in the form of land and equity grants.

The project consists of one building, seventeen stories tall, with 318 apartments. About one-fifth of them are efficiencies, three-fifths have one bedroom and one-fifth are two-bedroom apartments. The

Midway Gardens, the first project developed by the Chicago Dwellings Association, was completed in 1953. It consists of one building, seventeen stories tall, with 318 apartments, that is not readily identifiable as subsidized housing.—Courtesy of Chicago Housing Authority

building is long and narrow, reflecting its block-long site, and overlooks Lorado Taft's *Fountain of Time* in Washington Park. The
lobby and elevator bank are not centrally located, but near the east
end of the building. Constructed of reinforced concrete, the building
has a red-brick veneer, and a restained use of glass brick on both
ends, which are otherwise windowless. The design, by Holabird and
Root and Burgee, is comparable to, if not better than, the average
private high-rise apartment building of the period. Unlike CHA
buildings, it is not identifiable to the passerby as subsidized housing.

Preference in renting the apartments at Midway Gardens was originally given to families of veterans or servicemen. The initial rents
ranged from $68 for an efficiency to $122 for a four-and-one-half-
room apartment on an upper floor. By 1966 the top rent had increased to only $153 a month. Income limits on admission that year
were $6,000 for one person, $7,200 for two persons, $8,400 for three
or more persons, and for continued occupancy 10 percent additional
annual income was allowed. The contract and deed between CDA
and CHA provided that neither CDA nor any future owners could
discriminate on racial grounds in the selection or eviction of tenants, and that CDA rent schedules, tenant selection policies, and
occupancy standards be subject to approval by CHA and the State
Housing Board.

West Kenwood Gardens and Manor

All endeavors that CDA entered into after Midway Gardens were
effected by the Number Two Chicago Dwellings Association. Although this was technically a new corporation, in fact it was merely
an extension of the original CDA. The second project developed by
CDA was completely different from the first. West Kenwood Gardens, completed in 1956, involved the construction and sale of
fifty-two two- and three-bedroom row houses. The site covers an
irregular area of about two square blocks, along both sides of the
4600 block of South Princeton Avenue, adjacent to Fuller Park and
just west of the Dan Ryan Expressway.

CHA cleared the former slum buildings on the site at a cost of
$232,000 obtained from city slum-clearance funds. The houses were
sold at prices ranging from $11,000 to $13,300, with only 10 percent
down payment required. Home Federal Savings and Loan Association provided FHA-insured mortgages, with monthly payments as
low as $70 for principal and interest, insurance, and taxes. In addi-
tion to the city contribution of land acquisition, there was a state
grant of $193,000 to absorb the excess costs of site development.[1] If
the two figures had been added to the purchase price, each house

would have cost $8,173 more than the prices charged. There was thus a considerable subsidy involved.

The houses themselves are two stories tall, of various colors of brick, in clusters of three, four, and five units each. The architecture is unspectacular, but not quite as severe as most of the CHA row houses. In 1962 an adjacent site was acquired and cleared for eighteen detached single family houses, known as West Kenwood Manor, and also constructed by CDA. State grant funds were used to get sales prices down to $16,250 to $17,450. Their design is typical of the postwar Chicago bungalow, which is itself a scaled-down version of the fine Chicago bungalows of the 1920s. The proposed third project of CDA, to build 125 row houses for middle-income families at 29th and Cottage Grove, was aborted. The land was cleared by the Chicago Land Clearance Commission, but instead of going to CDA the property was incorporated into the Michael Reese Hospital expansion and Prairie Shores development. Still another plan, to build a CDA project at 55th and Cottage Grove, similarly never materialized.

Drexel Square Apartments

CDA's next project, the Drexel Square Apartments, was completed in 1963. It is an early example of a high-rise building designed especially for elderly residents. Part of the Hyde Park–Kenwood Urban Renewal Project, it is located at Hyde Park Boulevard (51st Street) and Cottage Grove Avenue, overlooking Drexel Square. The

West Kenwood Manor. Constructed by the Chicago Dwellings Association in 1962 adjacent to the West Kenwood Gardens development, these eighteen detached single family bungalows were sold for $16,250 to $17,450 —Courtesy of Chicago Housing Authority

building, which was designed by Keck and Keck, is nine stories tall, with a social room and outdoor sun deck on the top floor. The $1.26 million cost was financed by a mortgage from the federal government under the Section 202 program. It provides direct loans from a federal agency to nonprofit sponsors of moderate-income rental projects for the elderly sixty-two years old and over, and for the handicapped. The subsidy is derived from the fact that the loans are made at below-market interest rates. Originally the rate was based on the interest rate of the outstanding national debt, but the law was amended in 1965 to be a flat 3 percent. The 103 units of

The Drexel Square Apartments, designed by Keck and Keck and completed in 1963 by the Chicago Dwellings Association, was an early example of a high-rise building built especially for elderly residents.—Courtesy of George Fred Keck–William Keck

Drexel Square, all of which are one-bedroom apartments, initially had rents of $92.50 to $107.50.

Medical Center Apartments

In 1941 the Illinois legislature created the Medical Center Commission to develop the area around Cook County Hospital. The

Medical Center Apartments. This eighteen-story building at 1926 West Harrison Street was built to house moderate-income personnel and students connected with the West Side Medical Center.—Courtesy of Pace Associates, Inc.

commission has the power of condemnation in order to assemble large parcels of land for expansion of the various hopitals, and for redevelopment by allied institutions. In 1962 the commission asked CDA to construct housing there. What resulted in 1964 was the 306-unit, eighteen-story building at 1926 West Harrison Street. It was financed by an FHA-insured Section 207 mortgage that carried a standard market interest rate. The land was purchased by CDA from the Medical Center Commission at full market value. The building, designed by Pace Associates, has an exposed concrete frame with pebbly concrete panels between the vertical concrete members of the frame and below the windows. It lacks the good proportions and overall design quality of the Midway Gardens building, and as its light colors have gotten dirty it has taken on an almost shabby appearance. Tenancy in the building, which has apartments ranging from efficiency- to three-bedroom units, is limited to moderate-income Medical Center personnel and students.

Englewood Scattered Site Houses

From the very first of CDA's existence, scattered site housing had been envisioned. In 1949 they engaged the architectural firm of Holabird and Root and Burgee to do a study of single-family houses.[2] The study was designed to furnish an analysis of the economics, construction, and planning of low-cost family dwelling units. The report concluded that significant cost savings could be achieved by purchasing materials in large quantities and by applying factory production-line methods to the construction of conventional housing types. The authors advocated setting up centralized fabricating shops and material warehouses, but pointed out that such an "industrialized" housing system would yield maximum benefits only if it were to be used in a large-scale building operation. The architects designed two prototype houses, each with exterior walls of concrete block. Scheme A was a one-story, two-bedroom house with a very small living space of 630 square feet. Its base estimated cost was $6,615. Scheme B was a two-story, two-bedroom house of 920 square feet and an estimated cost of $9,860.

Although these proposals were never implemented, CDA did build some scattered-site housing. By 1966 it had constructed and sold on contract 102 units in the Englewood neighborhood on the South Side, the first substantial new housing construction there since 1930. The houses, built from stock plans, are double or duplex row houses, and "bi-level" houses. The latter are similar to a bungalow in the front but the rear has two levels one a finished basement several feet below grade, with another floor above it containing three bedrooms. The prices of the houses, which were subsidized by a state grant, ranged from $15,450 to $17,600, and were sold only to families with incomes that did not exceed $10,900. One-third of the homes were sold to families who were under notice to move out of CHA projects, because their incomes exceeded limits. CDA continued to adhere to the dream of building moderately priced single-family houses on scattered sites. In 1969 it cosponsored a competition which resulted in a plan for a tiny three-bedroom house costing only $15,000.[3]

Hermitage Manor

The last of the large-scale, single-site developments of CDA was a row house project on a three-acre site in the Washington-Hermitage urban renewal area. The project, called Hermitage Manor, is at 1717 West Lake Street, next to the CTA Lake Street elevated line. In fact a spur of that line connecting it to the Douglas line runs right through the project. There are 108 units with from two to four bedrooms. Twelve of the houses are only one story, and are equipped with ramps and other special features for families with children attending the nearby Spaulding School for physically handicapped children.

The design architect for the project was Stanley Tigerman. The most surprising aspect of the design was the inclusion of large sliding glass patio doors on the rear wall of each house, an especially inappropriate feature in a high-crime inner-city area. Almost all of the occupants have installed burglar bars over the doors. Tigerman was not the supervising architect of the project, and his plans were modified by CDA to cut costs. The most noticeable modification was to elevate the houses above a high basement to save excavation costs; the original plans called for basements below grade level. Because the houses were raised over two feet, the doors are that far above gound level. CDA added to the plans temporary-looking wooden front porches, and wooden porches at the rear that look like massive flights of stairs the full width of each house, going up to the patio doors. The result is disastrous to the aesthetics.

The development was financed under the National Housing Act Section 221 (d) (3) program, which provides mortgages at below-market interest rates. Under the program the federal government, through its Government National Mortgage Association, holds the mortgage and charges only 3 percent interest on it. The program is intended to provide rental units for moderate-income tenants, but the projects built under its terms may be converted to condominiums or cooperatives, which is what was done here. CDA de-

veloped Hermitage Manor in conjunction with the Foundation for
Cooperative Housing (FCH), a national group interested in promot-
ing cooperative ownership of housing. Originally the houses were
scheduled to be completed in late 1967, but construction did not
even begin until November of that year, and when the project was
completed the apartments were rented to the prospective co-op purchasers for eighteen months.

In early 1971 title to the property was finally transferred from
CDA to the cooperative association, and management was provided
by the Foundation for Cooperative Housing. This was the first
cooperative housing project developed for moderate-income families that was sponsored by a quasi-governmental agency. Due to a
change in its structure and priorities, FCH turned over management
to a company from Indiana, and later the board of the cooperative
hired a local management agent. Things got off to a rocky start,
because the first year's real estate taxes, which were expected to be
$25,000, turned out to be $66,000. Also, the co-op sued CDA over a

The last of the large-scale, single-site developments of the Chicago
Dwellings Association was Hermitage Manor, a row-house project on a
three-acre site in the Washington-Hermitage urban renewal area.—
Photograph by Devereux Bowly, Jr.

dispute involving proration of certain real estate taxes assessed while CDA was still in charge. After the mortgage was modified twice, and the suit settled by a $30,000 payment from CDA, operations went smoothly. By 1976 all units were occupied, and the turnover had been only about a dozen new families in the 108 units in the previous three years. New owners have to pay about $400 on entrance, and monthly charges of only $150 to $180, depending on the size of the unit.

The cooperative is providing housing for some families that formerly lived in nearby CHA projects. Because the occupants own the project, none of their monthly payments go for profit to a developer or for an expensive governmental bureaucracy. The monthly charges have to be large enough only to cover the project's mortgage payments, real estate taxes, maintenance, and administrative costs. Since residents are all owners, it is in their self-interest to maintain the property. The Hermitage Manor Cooperative demonstrates that co-ops have potential for inner-city, moderate-income housing. It is curious that more of them have not been built in Chicago, as has been done in New York City and Detroit.

Modular Houses

Perhaps the most bizarre chapter in the modern history of housing in Chicago occurred in the summer of 1968. That spring the West Side of Chicago, and other areas around the country, had erupted in ghetto riots after the assassination of Dr. Martin Luther King, Jr. In Chicago hundreds of buildings were burned and housing units destroyed. Mayor Daley was deeply shocked by the riots, and thus susceptible to a proposal that promised a quick approach which could go a long way toward solving Chicago's housing problems. This plan called for the construction of single-family homes from modular components made in a factory.

The moving force behind the idea was realtor Charles R. Swibel, chairman of the CHA Board of Commissioners. The idea was proposed as a joint undertaking of CDA and CHA. Two manufacturers of prefabricated housing were engaged to build prototypes for Chicago: National Homes Corporation of Lafayette, Indiana, and Magnolia Homes of Vicksburg, Mississippi. Both companies produced four-bedroom row houses, out of components that resemble house trailers, but without wheels. A concrete foundation is laid, the units are trucked to the site and installed by a crane, which places the first-floor units on the foundation and then lays another layer of units on top of them. Any combination, from a pair of houses for a small vacant lot to an entire city block of row houses is possible.

Each house has a living room, kitchen, bedroom, and powder room on the first floor, and three bedrooms and a bath on the second.

The idea of modular housing was so exciting to Mayor Daley that it became the high-priority housing item for the city. Even though CHA has its own Information Division, a private public relations firm called Information Consultants was hired to insure publicity. Articles soon appeared in newspapers saying it was hoped houses could be purchased for $350 down, with monthly payments of only $125. The sale price of the planned houses was estimated at $14,500, not including land costs. It was stated that the goal was to build 2,000 modular houses a year on vacant lots in Chicago, and there was even discussion of the possibility of a factory in Chicago to

Because modular housing seemed to offer a quick solution to many of Chicago's housing problems, this type of construction received a high priority in 1968. These houses erected by National Homes Corporation at 69th and Parnell show the ravages of but a few years' time.—Photograph by Devereux Bowly, Jr.

produce them, financed by labor unions, insurance companies, and local industries. By August 7, 1968, the *Chicago Tribune* was reporting that a group of modular houses would be erected before the opening in Chicago of the Democratic National Convention on August 26, as an example of Chicago's intention to improve conditions in black ghettos, and to help avert any racial disorders during the convention week.

One of the units was even installed behind the podium in the International Amphitheatre to serve as a staging area where VIP's would get their TV makeup, and wait to be called for their speeches. The first project, at 50th and Blackstone, was erected in four hours on August 20, 1968, with accompanying national publicity. Thousands of people toured the houses as soon as they were completed, but the plan to bus the convention delegates out to see them never materialized, because of the more pressing events of the convention itself, and the events that occurred with the young antiwar demonstrators in Grant Park.

The prototype houses were financed by a $1 million grant from the Illinois Housing Development Authority to CHA and CDA. The 50th and Blackstone group is typical of the National Homes units put up in Chicago. It has eight units, in two groups of four houses each, one facing 50th Street and the other Blackstone Avenue. The framing of the houses is wooden, and they have sliding aluminum windows. The exteriors have panels with a one-and-three-quarter-inch veneer of stone glued to half-inch waterproofed plywood, and panels of baked aluminum sheet bonded to three-quarter-inch fiberboard. The roofs are sheet metal, and the interior partitions are covered with three-eighth-inch gypsum board.

The specifications provide that each house shall have a ten-by-twelve-foot asphalt patio, three trees, a parking space, and each group of houses is to have a paved asphalt play area. When looking at the houses in the mid-1970s it is difficult to imagine how they aroused such high expectations. They are so small they look like miniature houses compared to the adjacent apartment buildings. The construction is so flimsy it almost invites vandalism. The original intention was to sell the houses at 50th and Blackstone. Neighborhood residents, however, insisted at a public meeting held by the Hyde Park–Kenwood Community Conference that they instead be rented to moderate-income families by CHA. By 1976, eight years after construction, the lampposts of the project were broken, siding on some of the houses torn, the playground a shambles, and the garden wall all but destroyed. The houses are just one step above slums.

Several other groups of the prefab houses were built and some
sold. Many have had their mortgages foreclosed, and are burned out,
or empty and stripped. Others are still in surprisingly good condition. On the South Side there are several National Homes groups. At
64th and Dorchester there are ten units, some of which are still
occupied, but all of the landscaping has been destroyed. At 69th and
Parnell there are also ten houses, on two sites on opposite corners,
seven of which are boarded up, and only three of which are still
being lived in. On the West Side there is a total of six houses, at 406
North Avers and 405 North Springfield, sites that back up to one
another, one of which is boarded up. Both units at a site at 446 North
Harding are abandoned.

The two groups of houses built by Magnolia Homes have fared
much better. The first consists of four houses at 3310–12 West
Douglas Boulevard. These have a real brick wall at the first floor
level and wooden shake shingles on the second, which give them
less the look of trailers than the units built by National Homes. The

*Modular houses erected by Magnolia Homes at 3310–12 West Douglas
Boulevard. These have a real brick wall at the first floor level and wooden
shake shingles at the second, which gives them a more substantial appearance than the National Homes units.—Photograph by Devereux Bowly, Jr.*

other group is at 1707–15 North Larrabee, in the Lincoln Park Urban Renewal Area. Both groups are fully occupied, in good condition, and surrounded by well-maintained yards. The final group of ten houses, also in good condition, is on two sites at the junction of the Dan Ryan and Stevenson expressways. The land for them was left over when the expressways were built and purchased from the city. The houses are National Homes units but they differ from the other ones in that they have basements, as well as real brick walls at the first-floor level. The modular housing program in Chicago never got beyond the prototype stage, because the houses turned out to be more expensive and less satisfactory than expected, and failed to satisfy the requirements for FHA-insured mortgages.[4]

Receivership Program

One of the most ambitious programs in which CDA was involved started in 1965 at the urging of Mayor Daley. CDA agreed to make itself available to the judges of the Building Court for appointment as receiver of buildings with serious Building Code violations, where the owner was unwilling or unable to bring it up to code standards. CDA planned to carry out this mission in three ways.[5] These were: first, by obtaining court approval for demolition of structures where rehabilitation was unfeasible; second, by obtaining compliance through rehabilitation by the owner under CDA supervision; and finally, by meeting code standards through rehabilitation by CDA itself. Theoretically this was to be financed through the issuance of "receiver's certificates," which under Illinois law take precedence over all liens except taxes. It turned out, however, that the risk was so great that there was no market for the receiver's certificates. The program thus had to be funded from other sources, which included about $1 million in City of Chicago bond issue money.

Under the receivership program management, maintenance and rent collections were taken over by CDA, and the owner did not reacquire control of the building until it was brought up to compliance with the Building Code, and CDA's expenses had been reimbursed. The scheme had a fatal flaw from the beginning, however. It was based on the false premise that the buildings involved were potentially solvent, and simply suffered from greedy or inefficient landlords. The fact was that almost all of the buildings were in very poor condition, often partially burned out; they had high real estate tax assessments and tax arrearages, and faced enormous rehabilitation costs. They were occupied by tenants who were mostly public-aid recipients and unable to pay rents that would justify the rehab costs, and located in neighborhoods where it was impossible to get middle-income tenants even for rehabilitated buildings. Also, neither CDA nor the support services from the CHA bureaucracy were organized for, or efficient at, this type of endeavor, and bringing them into the picture merely added high administrative and legal costs.

By the end of 1966 CDA had 280 buildings, with 2,980 units under receivership. They claimed that 98 structures, with 1,140 units had achieved code compliance either by the owners under CDA supervision, or by CDA, and in addition 42 buildings with 508 units had been demolished.[6] During 1967 the receivership program included 3,035 units in 321 buildings.[7] Many of the receiverships involved specific matters such as repairing a furnace, or providing a building that had no heat with fuel. Some involved extensive rehabilitation. For example, the showcase building at 4430 North Magnolia, which was featured in CDA's 1966 Annual Report. CDA relocated the tenants, deconverted the building from 19 to 12 units, and corrected 188 violations, at a cost of about $40,000. By 1976 the building had returned to its slum status, however, with an overall shabby appearance and one apartment burned out and boarded up.

On December 31, 1972, the receivership load of CDA stood at 2,969 units, in 502 buildings.[8] The bubble was about to burst. The receivership program was suspended in February 1973 because of lack of funds. State money that had been used to fund the program was exhausted, and CDA was having severe financial problems generally. In January 1973 President Nixon had suspended the federally subsidized programs nationally. This cut off funds to CDA, and caused the cancellation of an agreement between the City of Chicago and HUD, whereby CDA was to develop 500 new single family units.

Rehabilitation Program

As early as 1965 CDA had been surveying, appraising, and planning rehabilitation of residential structures in Lawndale, Uptown, South Shore, and Lake View. The federal Department of Housing and Urban Development on May 26, 1966, announced that FHA had agreed to earmark $3 million for CDA to carry out a rehabilitation program of 500 units, under the Section 221 (d) (3) program, with forty-year mortgages covering 100 percent of the acquisition and rehabilitation costs, at only 3 percent interest. By the early 1970s CDA had seven Section 221 (d) (3) mortgages, totaling $7.5 million, covering thirty-seven buildings with 539 units. Except for a 50-unit building in South Shore, and a 24-unit building in Woodlawn, all of the properties were located in the Lawndale area of the West Side, and virtually all of them were three-story walk-ups.

The most highly publicized of the rehabilitation projects involved two groups of buildings in Lawndale renovated by United States Gypsum in 1967, as a demonstration project. The company had previously experimented with new rehabilitation techniques by renovating 120 apartments in six buildings in the Harlem section of New York City. In the Chicago program United States Gypsum entered into an agreement with CDA under which the company purchased the buildings, renewed them, and then sold them to CDA, which financed the purchases by 221 (d) (3) mortgages. United States Gypsum hoped to apply the lessons and techniques it had learned in Harlem, demonstrate its products (such as a new super-tough wallboard), and make a profit. The original estimate put the total cost at $12,000 per unit. The first package involved four buildings with 137 units, and the final mortgage figure was $1,886,500, or $13,770 per unit. The second group involved five buildings with 105 units, and a mortgage of $1,522,907, or $14,500 per unit. Even with these cost overruns, United States Gypsum did not break even on the project, much less make a profit.

The rehabilitation program as a whole did not go any better than this United States Gypsum demonstration project. Due to financial and management problems as early as June 1, 1970, CDA had turned over management of some of the buildings to CHA, and CHA ultimately managed all of them. None were financially self-supporting, and CHA had to plow in over $1.5 million in state funds to offset operating deficits before such funds were exhausted in the summer of 1973. All of the mortgages were ultimately defaulted, and the properties taken over by HUD. In a surprisingly frank report issued February 8, 1974,[9] CHA outlined the reasons for the complete failure of the rehabilitation program. It begins with the startling admission that even if there had been no mortgage payments whatsoever on the properties, they still would not have been self-supporting, that is, their income was not even equal to their real estate taxes, maintenance, and administrative expenses. The report went on to say that even if the properties had also had complete real estate tax abatement, only two of them would have become solvent.

According to the report the factors that doomed the projects were: 1) heavy maintenance costs, 2) limited rental income, and 3) high real estate taxes. The high maintenance costs were attributed to improper building rehabilitation and continuous vandalism and theft by tenants and outsiders. The rehabilitated buildings, because

they were located in a deteriorating neighborhood, were said by the
report to be the object of anger and envy on the part of the neighbors,
especially children who broke windows and did other damage. The
buildings had mostly large apartments that attracted families with
many children, and there were no play areas.

Because Lawndale has a high crime rate, a lack of city and community services, poor schools, and lack of shopping, it was almost
impossible to get middle-class families to live there. CDA rents
were only $120 to $193 a month, unrealistically low for units cost-
ing $15,000 to purchase and rehabilitate, even taking into account
the below-market interest rate on the mortgages. The report ac-
knowledges that limited management staff made it difficult to
supervise the scattered site properties. The management problems
went much deeper than that. The project from its inception was
based upon complete misjudgment and incompetence on the part of
HUD, CDA and CHA, and the city.

By mid-1973 CDA had lost its executive director, reduced its
office to a skeleton staff, and put most of its records into storage. It
did complete, by the end of 1974, the rehabilitation and sale of
sixty-six units of mostly two-flat, mortgage-foreclosed buildings,
acquired from the Federal Savings and Loan Insurance Corporation.
By 1976 CDA was still a legal entity, but for all intents and purposes
had merged into CHA, which runs the three large buildings which
CDA developed, and several other miscellaneous properties it still
owns. CDA's only going operation was a tiny office maintained to
manage a 566-unit Model-Cities-funded rent-supplement leasing
program, under which private apartments are leased by CDA, and
then subleased to poor families at a reduced rent. That program,
which involved about 1,100 units at its peak in 1974, was in the
process of being phased out.

7 Chicago Housing Authority: The High-Rise Years

The overall housing supply in Chicago improved during the 1950s. The seven-year period from the beginning of 1950 to the end of 1956, for example, saw a 5.3 percent increase in the total number of housing units in the city, from about 1,106,000 to 1,165,000. The increase of 59,000 units was accounted for by the addition of 145,000 units, and the loss of only 86,000 units. During the same period the number of families in Chicago increased by only 4.2 percent, or 45,000. The easing of the housing shortage is shown by the fact that housing-unit vacancies increased from 0.8 percent in 1950, to 1.7 percent, or about 20,000 units in 1956. Of these, 17,000 were rental units, and 3,000 were for sale. The period also saw an improvement in the quality of available units. It is estimated that the number of substandard occupied units decreased from somewhere between 246,000 and 284,000 in 1950, to between 63,000 and 107,000 in 1956.[1]

From the inception of public housing in Chicago in 1935, to 1956, the total investment in it was almost $164 million, of which about $116 million was raised by the sale of bonds and notes, and $48 million by government payments. CHA in 1956 had twenty-seven projects, with 14,205 units. They planned to increase the total in the following four years to 27,026 units, at a total cost of $317 million.[2] This tremendous growth was planned even though the housing shortage caused by World War II had eased, and a significant reduction could be seen in the demand for public housing. From 1954 to mid-1956 the CHA waiting list fell from 45,000 families to only 15,000.[3] In light of these facts the unprecedented construction of public housing in Chicago after 1956 may be viewed as a response to the increased availability of federal funding, and an attempt to improve the city and the housing stock for poor people, rather than increasing the stock of housing per se.

The failure of public housing built in Chicago after 1956 was due in large part to the type of housing built, mostly large units in high-rise, inner-city buildings. Three quarters of the apartments

CHA constructed during the period 1957 through 1968 had three, four, or five bedrooms. The sociological impact of putting large families in high-rise buildings leaves a significant question as to whether the new housing was in fact better than the housing it replaced, and the answers provided by the families for whom it was built are by no means clear. Less than twenty years after the major high-rise projects were started, they contained hundreds of empty apartments, despite the fact that CHA apartments rented in 1976 at an average of about $50 per month, a fraction of the cost of comparably sized housing on the private market.

In addition to the negative impact the high-rise projects often have on their residents, especially children, their most severe effect on the city has been to promote racial and economic segregation. As early as 1955, when about two-thirds of all CHA residents were black, CHA was heading for a virtually all black family unit occupancy. In that year 73 percent of the new families moving into CHA projects were black.[4] By June 30, 1959, the percentage of all CHA units occupied by blacks had risen to 85.[5] CHA insured that its family housing would be virtually all black, by building its major projects only in inner-city ghetto areas. The conclusion is inescapable that the locations for new projects were selected by CHA, and by the political leadership of Chicago, to contain and segregate the poor, black population.

During the period from 1957 through 1968 CHA completed 15,591 family units, of which all but 696 were in high-rise buildings. This was the great era of construction of public housing in Chicago, and the source of the current popular image of public housing as being long rows of sterile tall buildings. As early as 1951, just a year after the completion of Dearborn Homes, the first CHA elevator building project, CHA was stating in its monthly bulletin that almost all of its future units would be in elevator buildings.[6] The rationale given was the standard one dealing with keeping construction costs low, and leaving a large proportion of each site open for recreation space. The article went on to point out that the construction of CHA housing falls into a neat chronological pattern. The walk-up apartments were built basically before 1941; 90 percent of the row houses were constructed between 1941 and 1946; after 1948 CHA construction was almost completely high-rise.

Horner Homes

The first project built during the period was the Governor Henry Horner Homes on the Near West Side, adjacent to the Chicago Stadium, in the area bounded by Hermitage Avenue, Lake Street,

Damen Avenue, and Washington Boulevard. It was completed in 1957, and consists of 920 apartments in seven buildings seven stories each, and two of fifteen stories. The buildings resemble the Ickes Homes, designed two years earlier by the same architects, Skidmore, Owings, and Merrill. They have exposed concrete frames, with infill of common brick in some of the buildings, and finished brick in the others. The total development cost of $13,182 per unit makes this the least expensive CHA development built during the period.

A more interesting project architecturally is the 736-unit Horner Homes Extension which continues the site west from Damen to Oakley Boulevard. Constructed in 1961, it has seven buildings, four of which are fourteen stories tall and placed diagonally to Lake Street, and three of which are eight stories tall. The buildings are composed of duplex apartments, with living rooms, dining and kitchen areas on the lower levels, and bedrooms and bath upstairs. The alternate floors comprising the lower levels of the apartments have open galleries within the framing of the buildings, not cantilevered out from them. The alternating floor pattern gives some relief from the monotony of most public housing, as does the fact

The Governor Henry Horner Homes, completed in 1957, consist of 920 apartments in seven buildings of seven stories each, and two of fifteen stories. With exposed concrete frames and infill of common and finished brick, this project resembles the Ickes Homes designed two years earlier by the same architects.—Courtesy of Chicago Housing Authority

that the buildings are divided vertically by the elevator shafts, with
the galleries on one side of the shaft facing one direction, and those
on the other side facing the opposite direction. The architects were
Quinn and Christiansen. Even though the design of the project is
above average for CHA, its size when taken together with Horner
Homes, and its location in a semi-industrial area along the Lake
Street CTA Elevated tracks, leaves a great deal to be desired.

*The Horner Homes Extension comprises seven buildings, four of which are
fourteen stories tall and three of which are of eight stories. Constructed in
1961, the apartments are duplexes with living rooms, dining and kitchen
areas on the lower levels, and bedrooms and baths upstairs.—Photograph
by Devereux Bowly, Jr.*

Stateway Gardens

A major step in the ominous march of CHA buildings south along
State Street took place in 1958 with the construction of Stateway
Gardens, between 35th Street and Pershing Road. It has 1,684 units
in two buildings ten stories tall adjacent to State Street, and six
buildings of seventeen stories to the west, along the Rock Island
Railroad tracks. The buildings cover only about 12 percent of the
thirty-three-acre site. Designed by Holabird and Root and Burgee,
the project is uninteresting visually, but of some significance from
an engineering standpoint. Constructed of concrete, instead of having conventional short-span column-and-girder frames, the buildings have a box frame of reinforced concrete. This is perhaps the
largest development using this type of framing, which is more eco-
nomical than the traditional method. Within the box frames there

*Houses at 3707–11 South Federal Street, 1951, on site of Stateway
Gardens.—Photograph by Mildred Mead, courtesy of Chicago Historical
Society*

are vertical as well as horizontal concrete slabs, and thus interior partitions are of concrete.[7]

Cabrini-Green

The original 581 row houses of Frances Cabrini Homes were augmented in two stages to increase the total number of units more than sixfold, thus creating a single complex of more than 3,600 units. The Cabrini Extension was completed in 1958 and added 1,925 units in fifteen buildings of seven, ten, and nineteen stories. Located at Division and Sedgwick streets, immediately east of the original project, its buildings have exposed concrete frames and red brick infill. Designed by A. Epstein and Sons, they are rectangular with one or two perpendicular wings at the rear of each building. When the Cabrini Extension opened, it was the largest public housing project ever constructed in Chicago. The cost was $27 million or about $14,000 per unit. Less than 16 percent of the land is covered with buildings, and CHA included extensive landscaping at a cost of $238,768. The specifications provided for 25,000 cubic yards of new topsoil, 10,000 shrubs, 500 trees, 23,000 feet of chain link fence, and lawns covering seventeen acres of the thirty-five acre site.

It appears that officials of CHA had a premonition of future criticism of the massive project. In 1951 CHA published a booklet

Stateway Gardens. This project has 1,684 units in two buildings ten stories tall and six buildings of seventeen stories that cover only about 12 percent of the site. Uninteresting visually, this is perhaps the largest development having box frames of reinforced concrete rather than conventional short-span column-and-girder frames.—Courtesy of Chicago Housing Authority

called *Cabrini-Extension Area: Portrait of a Chicago Slum*, which described graphically the terrible conditions on the site before redevelopment. As early as 1900 the area was crowded with frame and brick tenements and industrial buildings, often two or even three buildings on a single lot. It had a large Italian population and was often called "Little Sicily." By 1940 the Negro population in the area had grown to 20 percent, and by 1950 to 79 percent, although at that time the Cabrini Homes themselves were still 75 percent white.

During the period 1940 to 1950, with virtually no new residential construction, the population of the area increased 47 percent, and by 1950 there were 3,596 families living in only 2,325 units, that is, more than 1,200 units were being shared by two families. The Cabrini Extension later caused a net reduction of 400 units on the site. Out of the 554 residential buildings before redevelopment, 242 had no baths whatsoever, and 349 had less than one bath for every two

The Cabrini Extension, completed in 1958, added 1,925 units in fifteen buildings of seven, ten, and nineteen stories to the original Frances Cabrini Homes project. When opened, the extension was the largest public housing project ever constructed in Chicago.—Photograph by Betty Hulett, courtesy of Chicago Historical Society

apartments. Only 7 percent of the units had central heating; most had to rely on coal stoves. The report further describes the area as being subjected to a constant flow of trailer trucks, having refuse-laden alleys, and presenting danger to pedestrians of falling into coal sheds located underneath the sidewalks.

The final component of the Cabrini-Green complex is the William Green Homes, situated north of Division Street, north and west of the Cabrini Extension. Designed by Pace Associates, it was completed in 1962, and consists of 1,096 units in eight buildings, fifteen and sixteen stories tall. The buildings have concrete frames, ends of almost solid concrete, except for one row of windows down the middle, and precast concrete panels below the windows on the front and rear walls. The result is an even more monolithic appearance than the other CHA high-rises. Like the other projects of the period, emphasis in Green Homes is given to many large apartments, which at least are concentrated on the lower floors of the buildings. All of the five-bedroom apartments are located in duplex units on the first and second floors. The three- and four-bedroom apartments

William Green Homes dedication, November 12, 1961. Located north and west of the Cabrini Extension, the Green Homes consist of 1,096 units in eight buildings, fifteen and sixteen stories tall.—Courtesy of Chicago Housing Authority

occupy the third through the sixth floors, with the smaller units on the upper floors.

Rockwell Gardens

A project in many ways unique in the history of CHA is Rockwell Gardens, located on an irregular fifteen-acre site bounded by Western Avenue, Van Buren, Monroe, and Rockwell streets. The development, which is adjacent to the Eisenhower Expressway and

William Green Homes. With concrete frames, ends of almost solid concrete, and precast concrete panels below the windows on the front and rear walls, the result is an even more monolithic appearance than other Chicago Housing Authority high-rises.—Courtesy of Chicago Housing Authority

just east of Maplewood Courts, is unique because an attempt was made in it to preserve many of the existing buildings on the site, rather than clearing it completely and starting from scratch. It was the first site in the nation where both federal and state funds were used to provide new public housing construction within a larger program for upgrading structurally sound buildings.[8]

In 1950 CHA conducted a survey that showed two-thirds of the buildings on the proposed site of Rockwell Gardens were either in standard condition, or at least suitable for rehabilitation, and CHA was therefore reluctant to engage in wholesale demolition of the area. The initial plan developed was for CHA to: 1) clear out the worst buildings and replace them with new housing, 2) acquire and rehabilitate neglected structures, and 3) encourage owners of buildings in good repair to retain and improve them. The State Housing

Unique for the Chicago Housing Authority is that an attempt was made to preserve many of the existing buildings on the site, Rockwell Gardens involved the demolition of buildings containing 716 units, the construction of eight new buildings of ten and thirteen stories containing 1,126 units, and the preservation of 108 buildings with about 250 units.
—Courtesy of Chicago Housing Authority

Board financed the missionary work CHA did with the private owners. State funds were also used to purchase and demolish three dilapidated buildings on a portion of the site location where new
buildings were not planned.

Beginning in 1954 buildings containing 716 units were demolished, and eight new buildings of ten and thirteen stories were
constructed in 1961. They contain 1,126 units, and were designed by
Nicol and Nicol. The buildings have red brick front and rear walls,
and exposed concrete ends. Some are rectangular and some
L-shaped. A total of 108 buildings, with about 250 units were left
standing. At first CHA planned to purchase about 50 percent of
those buildings, but as the project progressed an increasing number
of owners requested permission to retain and rehabilitate their
buildings. By mid-1956 CHA had purchased seven buildings, with
23 units, to be used as a pilot project to assess rehabilitation costs.
The work never took place, because CHA later changed its plans and
demolished the buildings. The idea of Rockwell Gardens was one of
the most enlightened CHA tried. It was a mistake, however, to
construct the new units in high-rises, and to leave 85 percent of the
cleared land vacant. The new buildings are so out of scale with the
older two- and three-story ones, and so isolated from them, that they
stick out and look awkward. The project could have been outstanding if the new units had been in well-designed walk-up apartment buildings and row houses, with a greater intensity of land use.

Prairie Avenue Courts Extension, Brooks Homes Extension, and Clarence Darrow Homes

Two additional projects were built with structures very similar to
the L-shaped buildings of Rockwell Gardens. The Prairie Avenue
Courts Extension was designed by the same architects as Rockwell
Gardens and built in 1958. It consists of a single thirteen-story
building with 203 units located just south of the Prairie Avenue
Courts at 2822 Calumet Avenue. The building is massive and lacks
the grace of its neighbors at the Prairie Avenue Courts. The Brooks
Homes Extension, completed in 1961 from plans by Mielke and
Smith, is located on a triangular eight-acre site at Roosevelt Road
and Blue Island Avenue, just east of the Brooks Homes and directly
across Roosevelt Road from Holy Family Church and St. Ignatius
High School. It is composed of three buildings of sixteen stories each
with a total of 449 units.

During the period from 1958 through 1960 CHA submitted several plans to the federal Public Housing Authority for projects of
low-rise buildings. All of them failed, however, to come within the

$17,000 per unit cost ceiling established by PHA. One of the better of the proposed developments that was never built was a 132 unit complex planned for a site at 63rd Street and Calumet Avenue. The plan, prepared by Samuel Lichtmann and Mark Kalischer, called for five buildings, four stories tall, each containing two tiers of duplex apartments. There was also to be an eight-story building, with two-story apartments on the first and second floors, and smaller apartments on the upper floors. Because the site was on fill ground, extensive foundations would have been required, even for four-story buildings. The cost estimates were thus pushed beyond PHA limits.

Lichtmann and Kalischer actually did plans for housing on about fifty South Side sites, with two-story, four-story, "row-on-row," and eight-story buildings, but they were never approved by PHA. The cost of these units would have been $20,580 each. PHA was very concerned about the fact that CHA costs averaged 22 percent more than public housing in New York City. This was despite the fact that construction wages were higher in New York than in Chicago, and that the Boeckh Index for February 1959 evaluated normal high-rise construction costs for New York at 17.8 percent higher than Chicago. At the same time Cleveland was constructing public

The Brooks Homes Extension, completed in 1961, is located just east of the Brooks Homes and is composed of three sixteen-story buildings, with a total of 449 units.—Courtesy of Chicago Housing Authority

row houses and walk-up apartment buildings for $15,348 a unit, well within the PHA limit.[9]

After looking into the situation PHA found that land costs in Cleveland averaged only about $700 a unit as opposed to $2,020 in Chicago. CHA probably could have matched Cleveland's cost, if it had built low-rise housing on outlying vacant sites, rather than on inner-city slum-clearance sites. PHA also found that in New York the housing authority let all of its building contracts, such as structural, electrical, and plumbing, separately, rather than using a general contractor as CHA did. The end result was that CHA did not change its practices, and PHA did not make exceptions to its cost limits. Therefore relatively good housing was passed up in favor of more high-rise projects. One of these was the Clarence Darrow

The Clarence Darrow Homes, built in 1961 adjacent to the Ida B. Wells Homes, continued the Chicago Housing Authority practice of building high-rise projects.—Courtesy of Chicago Housing Authority

Homes at 39th and Langley adjacent to the Ida B. Wells Homes. Built in 1961 on a site formerly occupied by substandard structures, vacant lots, and an old CTA car barn, it consists of four buildings, fourteen stories tall, with 479 apartments. The red-brick buildings were designed by Solomon and Cordwell, with open galleries facing opposite directions, on either side of the elevator cores.

Robert Taylor Homes

Probably the most famous public housing project in Chicago is the Robert Taylor Homes, whose very name has become synonymous with the stereotypes of high-rise public housing. It is not only the largest public housing project in Chicago, but the largest in the world. A moving description of life in Robert Taylor Homes, by an anonymous resident, was quoted by M. W. Newman in his excellent seven-part series on the Taylor Homes, which appeared in the *Chicago Daily News* during April 1965. The resident said: "We live stacked on top of one another with no elbow room. Danger is all around. There's little privacy or peace and no quiet. And the world looks on all of us as project rats, living on a reservation like untouchables."[10]

Construction of the development was started in 1960, which was the biggest construction year in CHA history, with a total of 8,000 units begun at Robert Taylor Homes and other projects. Taylor Homes originally contained 4,415 units, although the figure has been reduced to 4,312 through the conversion of some apartments to school and other nonresidential uses. The site, which covers ninety-five acres, is only a quarter of a mile wide, but two miles long. It runs from State Street west to the Rock Island Railroad tracks, which in turn are adjacent to the Dan Ryan Expressway, and from Pershing Road south to 54th Street. It is a straight line geographical extension of Stateway Gardens. The housing is contained in twenty-eight identical sixteen-story buildings, mostly located in U-shaped groups of three. The buildings are completely undistinguished, with red or yellow brick veneers, central elevator shafts, and fenced galleries.

Because of the magnitude of the project, it was built in four stages. The first covered the area from 47th to 51st streets, and included eight apartment buildings, a management-maintenance building, a community center leased to the Chicago Park District, and the heating plant for the entire project. The second stage covered the area from 43rd to 47th streets, the third 40th to 43rd, and the last 51st to 54th streets. Both the architects, Shaw, Metz and Associates, and the contractor Gust K. Newberg, had just completed work on the

original McCormick Place. Newberg moved their big equipment
from the one job directly to the other. They had 2,000 construction
workers pouring concrete frames at the weekly rate of seventeen
floors, and laying one-half-million bricks per week. Taylor Homes
was completed in November 1962, eleven months ahead of
schedule. In the final stages of construction CHA had more apartments than they had properly screened tenants for and thus admitted a large number of virtually unscreened tenants in the buildings
between 51st and 54th streets. It was in these buildings that the
greatest tenant difficulties developed.[11]

Robert Taylor Homes is the largest public housing project in the world.
Construction started in 1960 on a site of ninety-five acres, a quarter of a
mile wide and two miles long. The 4,312 units are contained in twenty-
eight identical sixteen-story buildings, mostly located in U-shaped groups
of three.—Courtesy of Chicago Housing Authority

The land cost $7.3 million and was a slum-clearance site of mixed uses. It had had 800 residential units and many small businesses including a number of junkyards, and in fact still contains one such yard. The area between Root (4134 South) and 43rd Streets, which formerly contained the J. W. Petersen Coal Company yards, was excluded from the project. In recent years with a decline in the use of coal as a fuel in Chicago, the site has been converted to an auto graveyard. The site is also broken by two small shopping centers, one at 51st Street and one at Pershing Road. CHA's original proposal for the site was a mixture of high-rise and low-rise buildings, but was rejected by the Public Housing Administration because of its $22,000 per unit cost. PHA financed the project in the usual public housing manner by guaranteeing the forty-year bonds CHA issued. The total development cost was $75 million, or $16,988 per unit. A possibility for the site evidently not considered by CHA would have been to make the entire project up of low-rise buildings. The buildings of Robert Taylor Homes cover a mere 7 percent of the site. All of the residential buildings are sixteen stories tall. If the same size apartments had been put in three-story buildings, there would have been 5.3 times more ground area covered with buildings, or 37.3

Interior of a Robert Taylor Homes apartment.—Courtesy of Chicago Housing Authority

percent of the total. This would still have left over 60 percent of the site for parking, landscaping, and play areas.

The justifications given for high-rise public housing on vast open sites are mostly myths. Low-rise construction would have eliminated elevator construction and maintenance costs, and the expensive foundations required for tall buildings. Each building at Robert Taylor Homes has sixty-nine caissons sunk to an average depth of thirty-four feet. More importantly, low-rise buildings would not have the problems that elevators present, such as misuse by children who play on them. Children also often use the stairways in high-rise public housing buildings as toilets, because they are too impatient to wait several minutes for the elevator to take them up to their apartments.

In 1964 the Planning Committee of the Chicago chapter of the American Institute of Architects studied the architectural problems of CHA housing. Stanley Tigerman, chairman of the committee, presented its conclusions to a meeting of the CHA Board of Commissioners. He strongly criticized the use of high-rise buildings for families with children, and showed that as many units of housing could be provided on a given site by low, row-on-row housing as in high-rises. He pointed out that this could be achieved with considerable economies, including: 1) reduction of the 20 percent of high-rise buildings devoted to elevators, stairs, and public corridors at a saving of $2,200 per unit, 2) elimination of caisson, substructure, and elevator costs of $965 a unit, and 3) low-rise units could be built in 25 percent less time than high-rise apartments.[12] The AIA Committee report has been substantiated by CHA's experience with elevators. They are a constant source of frustration to tenants, because they break down often, especially in the winter when their exposed mechanisms freeze, and are a center for crime and vandalism. They are also a major source of expense to CHA. During the four-year period 1972 to 1976, CHA spent $11.7 million to maintain its 322 elevators, in 168 high-rise buildings.[13] This averages out to more than $9,000 per elevator per year.

Some understanding of the decision of CHA to build almost exclusively high-rises can be gotten from the public letter the authority's board chairman wrote in response to M. W. Newman's series. In it he stated: "Virtually all new construction in the city is high-rise. Families who either must or want to live in an urban area will have to learn to live with the high-rise building for all large centers of population must plan for accommodating an ever increasing number of people within a prescribed land area."[14] The statement demonstrates an almost complete ignorance of conditions in Chicago. The

fact is that most of the new residential construction in metropolitan
Chicago at that time was in the form of single-family houses and
walk-up apartments in suburban areas, not in high-rise buildings.
Vast undeveloped areas remained available to CHA in the city, and
are increasing due to large-scale abandonment and demolition of old
housing in various neighborhoods. In regard to CHA's statement
about "an ever increasing number of people," the fact is that
Chicago's population has been falling since at least 1960.

An insight into the infatuation with high-rises for public housing
was offered years earlier by Catherine Bauer, a perceptive writer and
lecturer on housing. She said:

The public housing project therefore continues to be laid out as a "community unit," as large as possible and entirely divorced from its neighborhood
surroundings, even though this only dramatizes the segregation of charity-
case families. Standardization is emphasized rather than alleviated in project design, as a glorification of efficient production methods and an expression of the goal of "decent, safe and sanitary" housing for all. But the bleak
symbols of productive efficiency and "minimum standards" are hardly an
adequate or satisfactory expression of the values associated with American
home life. And all this is, in addition, often embodied in the skyscraper,
whose refined technology gladdens the hearts of technocratic architectural
sculptors but pushes its occupants into a highly organized, beehive type of
community life for which most American families have no desire and little
aptitude.[15]

The social consequences of the decision to build Robert Taylor
Homes are significant. It originally contained 27,000 residents, of
which 20,000 were children. All are poor and virtually all black. The
project was specifically designed for large families. It contains about
3,500 three- and four-bedroom units, and 1,000 of them have an
oversized bedroom, capable of accommodating three or four people.
The average Robert Taylor Homes family contains about 5.8 persons, and as early as 1965 more than half of the resident families
received Public Aid. The project even contains its own sub-district
office of the Illinois Department of Public Aid. CHA statistics
gathered shortly after construction of the project showed that there
were only 2,600 households in Taylor Homes with a mother and
father present. Because the project has few childless couples, this
essentially means there were only slightly more than 2,600 men in
the entire project. It is thus the equivalent of a good-sized town of
more than 25,000 people, composed of almost 90 percent women
and children.

As with all its projects CHA is autocratic in the management of
Robert Taylor Homes. For example, tenants have no control over

their own heat; adjustments can only be made by a CHA employee. Such rigid rules are efficient from CHA's standpoint in the short run, but very destructive to the tenants in the long run. Treating them as if they have no common sense may well produce resentment or apathy, both of which are undesirable. The inclusion of resident advisory "Building Councils" in Taylor Homes, and Firman House, a settlement sponsored by the Presbyterian Church, are positive factors, but of so little consequence in the overall situation as to be insignificant.

Washington Park and Lake Michigan Homes

During 1962 and 1963 two projects were completed on the Near South Side. The first was the Washington Park Homes. It is made up of sixty-seven buildings, on twenty-seven scattered sites in the area bounded by 39th and 63rd streets, and from Lake Michigan west to Stewart Avenue. Seven of the buildings are sixteen-story high-rises of the same design as Robert Taylor Homes. These buildings contain

Washington Park Homes is made up of high-rise buildings and row houses on twenty-seven scattered sites. Seven of the buildings are of the same design as the Taylor Homes, while the remaining are sixty groups of well-designed two-story row houses that are not much different from some of the inexpensive tract housing in the suburbs.—Courtesy of Chicago Housing Authority

a total of 1,065 units. One of them is located at 4040 S. Oakenwald
Avenue, on the site of an oddity called the "Sphinx Kiosk," which
CHA demolished in 1957. It was built by Washington Porter II, to
house an art collection said to be worth $2 million. He helped to
design the building, which he described as "Egyptian with a touch of
Italian Renaissance." A 150-foot tower was also built to observe the
Century of Progress fair which took place in 1933 and 1934 on the
lakefront just east of the property. At the time of demolition sixteen
families occupied the adjacent Porter family mansion; the walls of
the Kiosk and Tower were crumbling, and the real estate taxes delinquent.[16] The remaining 378 units of the Washington Park Homes
are located in sixty groups of two-story row houses. These houses,
designed by Lichtman and Kalischer, are red brick with flat over-
hanging roofs and aluminum sliding windows. They are well designed, and not very much different from some of the inexpensive
tract housing in the suburbs. The other project, Lake Michigan
Homes, consists of 457 units in a cluster of three of the sixteen-story
Robert Taylor Homes design buildings, on Lake Park Avenue between 41st Street and 42nd Place.

Hilliard Center

The Raymond Hilliard Center is perhaps architecturally the most
well known of all CHA projects. Located at Cermak Road and State
Street, it forms the northern end of the State Street public housing
row, which consists of five large projects. In addition to Hilliard they
are, going south, Ickes Homes, Dearborn Homes, Stateway Gardens, and Robert Taylor Homes. The projects stretch for thirty-four
blocks, with the only major break being the campus of the Illinois
Institute of Technology from 30th to 35th streets. The projects
comprise more than 20 percent of all CHA units, and house almost
30 percent of all CHA residents. It is surprising that CHA selected
the State Street site for the showcase Hilliard project. During the
late nineteenth and early twentieth centuries the site had been part
of Chicago's infamous Levee, a district of gambling houses, saloons,
and numerous brothels, the most famous of which was the Ever-
leigh Club. In later years the area became a center for used-auto-part
dealers, and the Hilliard Center today is near several auto junkyards.
Selection of the site was fought by the Metropolitan Housing and
Planning Council which was opposed to adding "more monolithic,
high-rise buildings," to the "four mile wall" of public housing already existing along State Street.[17] Their objections went unheeded,
however.

The Hilliard Center was designed by Bertrand Goldberg Associates, and was constructed in 1966 just as their famous private housing development, Marina City, was being completed downtown. Hilliard Center consists of 346 family units in two arc-shaped twenty-two-story buildings, and two sixteen-story circular buildings for elderly residents, all of reinforced concrete. The site plan, which includes an outdoor amphitheatre, is good. The arc-shaped buildings, however, which are occupied mostly by children and have outdoor galleries, magnify sound and make for a high noise level throughout the project. It was hoped when the Hilliard Center was built that it would be racially integrated, and initially it was. By 1974, however, it had no whites in the family units, and only 40 of the 364 units in the elderly buildings were occupied by whites.[18] If

The Raymond Hilliard Center is perhaps the most well known architecturally of all Chicago Housing Authority projects. It was designed by Bertrand Goldberg Associates and constructed in 1966 just after completion of their famous private housing development, Marina City.—Courtesy of Chicago Housing Authority

the project had been built for exclusively elderly occupancy, or the family units put in low-rise buildings, and if it had been located on a less desolate site, it could have been one of the best public housing projects in the city.

Criticism of its high-rise projects was not the only problem CHA had to contend with during the 1960s. A controversy simmered since 1963 when Mayor Daley appointed Charles R. Swibel chairman of the CHA Board of Commissioners. Swibel had been on the board since 1956 and had often been the subject of attention by the press because of his background. On the one hand he had been one of the developers of Marina City, but at the same time he was president of Marks Company, which managed West Madison Street skid-row hotels and held mortgages on other slum properties.[19] The criticism was continued through the years but had no apparent effect on Swibel. In 1975 he was fined $700 in Housing Court for failing to clean up the McCoy Hotel, located at 945 West Madison Street, which he and his wife acquired in 1959.[20] He was also accused by the Better Government Association and reporters for the *Chicago Sun-Times* of having some CHA funds deposited in interest-free accounts at a bank that assisted him in the financing of Marina City, and further of having a $6,500 burglar alarm system installed in his Winnetka home by a company which got large CHA contracts shortly afterward but did not bill Swibel for his system for six years.[21]

Scattered Sites and Hyde Park Homes

The last projects built by CHA during the period were completely different from the others but involved only a small number of units. The first, built in 1967, is simply called Scattered Sites, and is composed of 300 apartments, in nineteen buildings on twelve sites in the area bounded by 35th Street, Lake Park Avenue, 63rd Street, and State Street. The units are in three-story buildings with semi-enclosed stairways. While all of the buildings are similar in design, they range from twelve to thirty-six units in size. The designs, by Schiller and Frank are not extraordinary, but the idea of scattering small buildings is a good one. The unfortunate thing about the Scattered Sites project is that the buildings are located exclusively in low-income South Side black neighborhoods, not distributed throughout the city.

A completely atypical project, because it is located in the highly desirable integrated area near the University of Chicago, is Hyde Park Homes. It is composed of two groups of six row houses each, one at 5120–24 South Blackstone Avenue, and the other at 5604–12

South Dorchester Avenue. Originally there was to have been a third group on the east side of Blackstone at 50th Street, but that site was absorbed by the construction of Kenwood High School.[22] The two rows of houses are identical, although at one site they are placed parallel to the street and at the other perpendicular to it. Except for the simplicity of construction, and the somewhat smaller scale of the buildings when compared to those surrounding them, they are unidentifiable as public housing. The houses have full basements, living room and kitchen on the first floor, and two or three bedrooms on the second floor. The architects were Y. C. Wong–R. Ogden Hannaford Associates.

The houses were built only after considerable controversy. As early as 1958 opposition was mounted to the Hyde Park–Kenwood Urban Renewal Project by Monsignor John J. Egan and the Cardinal's Committee on Conservation and Urban Renewal, because the plan made no provision for the poor people who were to be displaced.[23] The plan originally had only one public housing site at 4949 South Cottage Grove Avenue, on the extreme western edge of the community. This land was later developed as the Washington Park Apartments, a 92-unit CHA building for elderly tenants. After

Hyde Park Homes is composed of two groups of six row houses each. The houses have full basements, living room and kitchen on the first floor, and two or three bedrooms on the second floor.—Courtesy of Chicago Housing Authority

much effort independent Alderman Leon M. Despres was able, with the help of the Hyde Park–Kenwood Community Conference and liberal supporters, to get the plan amended in the City Council to provide 120 units of scattered-site public housing. Nowhere near that number were ever built, however. There was continuing opposition by some residents of the community to public housing, and the Department of Urban Renewal claimed that sufficient sites could not be obtained. In addition to the 12 family units, CHA did construct 22 units for the elderly in single-story buildings on two additional sites.

Sale of Racine Courts

In an unprecedented action, in 1968 the Chicago Housing Authority sold the 122 row houses of Racine Courts. This was the first time urban public housing in the United States was sold to its occupants. A cooperative was formed under the guidance of the Foundation for Cooperative Housing to hold the property. It in turn is owned by the occupants of the units. The terms of the sale were very advantageous to the tenants. The price was only $1.7 million, the cost of the project in 1950, and CHA took back a forty-year mortgage for the full purchase price at only 3 percent interest. Down payments were $200, with another $250 payable at $10 a month over twenty-five months. Monthly payments range from $87 to $112 for a three bedroom unit, up to $149 for a five-bedroom one. A unique feature of the transaction is that interest rates paid by the individual buyers vary from zero to 6 percent, depending on their income, so as to keep payments at a level of 21.8 percent of each buyer's income.[24] Approximately 85 of the purchasers were current residents of Racine Courts, 20 were over-income residents of other CHA projects, and the remainder came from the general public.

With the sale of Racine Courts, families in the $5,700 to $7,500 income range were able to buy homes, and some of the former "excess income" tenants actually pay less per month as owners than they did as tenants. Families unable to purchase their units were transferred to other projects at CHA expense. The contract between CHA and the cooperative contains provisions to insure that the development will continue to serve moderate-income families. Resale is limited to families whose incomes are below $11,000. Management is by an eleven-member board of directors, six of whom are owners, and five CHA appointees. The first few years of cooperative ownership of the project were not without difficulties, however. Mortgage payments to CHA were not always on time, and were not always for the full amount due. Deadlines had to be extended, and

CHA more than once considered foreclosing the mortgage and taking back the property. The situation slowly improved, and payments became current. The sale of Racine Courts was relatively successful because it is a virtually unique project among those developed by CHA. It is a small development, well designed, has large units, and is integrated into a middle-class neighborhood. The idea of selling other CHA projects to their occupants may be possible for a few developments but is very questionable for the great bulk of CHA projects.

By 1968 CHA had been operating public housing in Chicago for thirty years, and had assets of more than $500 million. In that year it revised its income limits for new tenants, and also the limits for continued occupancy. Under the new rules hundreds of families, who had been under notice to move because their incomes had risen above the continuation limits, won a reprieve. The new regulations provided, for example, that a family of four could have an income of $6,000 for admission, or $6,900 for continued occupancy: a family of eight could have $8,400 and $9,600 respectively: a family of twelve $10,000 and $11,500.[25] Even with these liberalized income limits, because of the sites selected and the kind of housing it constructed, CHA was never able to regain the racial and social mix it had had in some of the early projects.

At the end of 1968 the CHA population was just under 150,000 people, of which more than 97,000 were minors. If the units occupied by the elderly were not considered, there was an average of approximately 4 children per unit. One half of the families had 5 or more children, and more than 2,500 of the families had 9 or more members. In 1963 51 percent of all CHA units were occupied by families with both a husband and wife present, 16 percent by elderly persons or childless couples, and 33 percent by one-parent families.[26] By 1968 the proportion of CHA families with a mother and father present had fallen to 38 percent. Of the over 36,000 CHA units, less than 40 percent were occupied by self-supporting families; the other 60 percent received Public Aid, Social Security, VA benefits or Unemployment Compensation. Public Housing in Chicago had essentially been transformed from what was hoped would be a temporary way-station for families moving up the economic ladder, to a permanent repository for a whole underclass of basically large, poor, black families.

8 The Community Renewal Foundation and the Kate Maremont Foundation

There was little activity in the field of subsidized moderate-income housing in Chicago during the 1940s and 1950s other than that of the Chicago Dwellings Association. There were two interesting low-budget projects built on the South Side by private developers, but they were not subsidized. Both of them, however, anticipated in many respects the design of later housing in the city, both subsidized and nonsubsidized. They are both composed of two-story row houses on compact sites.

The earlier development, built at the end of World War II in 1944, is called the George Washington Carver Garden Homes, and is located on a split site on either side of Michigan Avenue at 37th Street. It was built by the late Newton Farr and his large Loop real estate firm of Farr, Chinnock, and Sampson. Farr constructed the project, originally on a part-rental and part-sale basis, as an experiment to see if a private developer could build moderate-income housing in the inner city for a profit. His company was familiar with the Near South Side because it had dealt with industrial property there, and had done extensive land assembly for the expansion of the campus of the Illinois Institute of Technology. The land chosen for the Carver project was occupied by marginal residential buildings which were purchased and cleared. The instructions to the architects, Skidmore, Owings, and Merrill, were to build solid but not fancy houses. Each of the fifty-four houses has two bedrooms and a full basement. The cost of the project was about $290,000, with the original rents set at $56 per month and the sales price at $6,250 per unit.[1] As time went on more and more of the residents asked to purchase their homes and eventually all were sold at a profit.

The other project, called Drexel Gardens, is located at 48th Street and Drexel Boulevard. It was built in 1954 by Jack Witkowski, a real estate appraiser, and Bertrand Goldberg. Their hope was that racially integrated housing could be privately developed without subsidy, at a cost equal to or less than that being spent for public housing. Early in the development Arthur Rubloff and Company was brought into the endeavor, and two of their officials, the late Stanley Goodfriend, and Abel Berland, became co-developers. Each of the men put up about $5,000 equity money, with Goldberg in charge of design and construction, and Witkowski taking care of the financial and technical real estate matters.

The fifty-two units, each of which has three bedrooms, are grouped in seven rows of houses. They sold for $13,950, with a $2,500 down payment. It turned out that the hoped-for integration

Built in 1944, the George Washington Carver Garden Homes were designed as an experiment to see if a private developer could build moderate-income housing in the inner city for a profit. They were planned on a part-rental and part-sale basis, with initial rents set at $56 a month and sale prices at $6,250 per unit. Eventually all were sold at a profit.—Photograph by Mildred Mead, courtesy of Chicago Historical Society

did not materialize, since none of the units were purchased by white families. The savings and loan association that provided the mortgages did not encourage purchases by whites, because it felt that white families who would purchase housing in an integrated development would be so "radical" as to not be good mortgage risks. The market for the houses turned out to be not as strong as expected, and not all of them were sold. Some were rented by Rubloff, and later sold off in a package. Although all of the contractors were paid in full, the four investors lost about half of their equity money.[2] Goldberg won an award in 1959 from the Chicago chapter of the American Institute of Architects and one from *Progressive Architecture* magazine for the project.

Both Drexel Gardens and the Carver Homes have extensively landscaped courtyards for their houses. Carver is constructed of red brick, Drexel Gardens of concrete block painted pastel colors. Both groups of houses have a large expanse of glass in the front and rear

The Drexel Gardens were built in 1954 by Jack Witkowski, a real estate appraiser, and Bertrand Goldberg with the hope that racially integrated housing could be privately developed without subsidy at a cost equal to or less than that being spent for public housing.—Courtesy of Bertrand Goldberg Associates

walls. Both are well designed and integrate the houses in pleasant surroundings. Unfortunately, since they were built on limited budgets, they are no longer in ideal condition. Some of the owners of the units have not maintained them, and the projects have become generally run down.

By the early 1960s the strong social action movements in the United States had manifested themselves in the Chicago housing picture through the work of two philanthropic organizations, the Community Renewal Foundation and the Kate Maremont Foundation. The impetus for housing action by groups such as these came from Section 221 (d) (3) of the federal Housing Act of 1961, under which nonprofit sponsors could secure 100 percent, forty-year mortgages for moderate-income housing at below-market interest rates.

In November 1967, the Chicago City Missionary Society, which later changed its name to the Community Renewal Society, set up a special Middle Income Housing Committee which engaged architects, lawyers, and college professors as consultants to explore the possibility of becoming active in the housing field. The organization, which was chartered in 1882, is related to the United Church of Christ, and is engaged in various activities aimed at improving urban conditions. Less than two years after the special committee was appointed, the Community Renewal Foundation (CRF) was incorporated as a not-for-profit organization to develop housing by itself and also in conjunction with other organizations. The parent Community Renewal Society gave it $100,000 to use as seed money, and in 1965 the foundation embarked on an ambitious program of housing construction, rehabilitation, and receivership.

Hyde Park West

For each of the projects built by the CRF a separate corporation was set up, to limit the liability of the foundation in case the project failed. In the case of the development called Hyde Park West, the special corporation's title was the Chicago City Missionary Society Dwellings Corporation No. 2. The land for the project, over one half a square block at 53rd Street and Cottage Grove Avenue across from Washington Park was acquired from the Chicago Department of Urban Renewal, and was part of the Hyde Park–Kenwood Urban Renewal Project. What resulted was the best development of the CRF, and in many ways one of the best of its type in the city.

The 1968 project, designed by Ezra Gordon–Jack M. Levin and Associates, consists of a total of 160 units in a single twelve-story apartment building and twenty-eight row houses. All are sheathed in dark brick like the older buildings in the area. The project is laid out well, with the high-rise having an open view to the park, but surrounded on the other three sides by the town houses, so it does not look isolated. Some of the houses face Maryland Avenue, the next street to the east of Cottage Grove, and help to weave the project into the fabric of the area, as does its manageable size. The total cost was $2,479,000 or $15,500 per unit,[3] an impressive figure in light of the quality of the construction.

Kedvale Square and Dauphin Apartments

The next CRF project, built in 1969 and developed under the corporate name of Federated Lawndale Buildings Corporation No. 2, is called Kedvale Square and located at 19th Street and Karlov Avenue on the West Side. It consists of 116 units in eight walk-up buildings of three stories each designed by Louis Rocah. The loca-

Hyde Park West. Built by the Community Renewal Foundation in 1968, this well-planned development consists of a total of 160 units in a single twelve-story apartment building and twenty-eight row houses, all sheathed in dark brick.—Courtesy of Ezra Gordon–Jack M. Levin & Associates

tion was a difficult one insofar as attracting moderate-income tenants because it is in the middle of an area of extreme poverty. The project has suffered from vandalism, and it is the only CRF project where there was, from the beginning, a major problem of unpaid rent by tenants. Physical problems also developed shortly after construction including roof leaks, standing water in the courtyards, and deterioration of the exterior doors, all of which had to be replaced. By 1976 the development was a near slum, and the subject of a building court suit involving numerous building code violations. The Dauphin Apartments were also built in 1969, at 9200 South Dauphin Avenue, under the name Essex Development Corporation. Here 37 units are located in a single five-story building of yellow and orange brick. The location is in a low-density residential area across from a railroad embankment. Designed by Erick Anderson, the building lacks any architectural distinction and was constructed at a low cost of $14,684 per unit.[4]

Kedvale Square, built in 1969 and the second Community Renewal Foundation project, was poorly constructed and placed in an area of extreme poverty with the result that it has suffered from the beginning from vandalism, and has become a near slum.—Photograph by Devereux Bowly, Jr.

Southeast Englewood

In many ways the most interesting of the CRF projects is a group of five buildings, with a total of eighty-one units, on scattered sites in the Englewood community. The sites are at 69th and Parnell Avenue, 70th and Parnell, 73rd and Vincennes, 70th and Wentworth, and 73rd and Yale. The technical sponsor was the Southeast Englewood Building Corporation. The apartments were the first privately developed, scattered site, moderate income, subsidized housing in Chicago. The two and one-half acres comprising the sites were purchased from the Chicago Department of Urban Renewal as part of the Englewood Urban Renewal Project. The buildings, which were completed in 1969, are all three-story walk-ups of brown brick, a simplified version of the type of housing that was so prevalent in Chicago through the 1920s. They vary from three flats to over twenty units, depending on the lot sizes. About a quarter of them are one-bedroom units, half have two bedrooms, and the remainder three bedrooms. The buildings were of what is called "ordinary con-

The Dauphin apartments, thirty-seven units in a single five-story building of yellow and orange brick, was built in 1969 at the low cost of $14,684 per unit.—Photograph by Devereux Bowly, Jr.

struction," which means they have interior wooden structural framing, and exterior brick supporting walls. The architect was John
Moutoussamy, of Dubin, Dubin, Black, and Moutoussamy.

Rehabilitation Projects

In addition to the four new construction projects, the Community
Renewal Foundation rehabilitated three large apartment buildings.
The architects for all of these projects were Swann and Weiskopf.
The first, rehabilitated in 1966 under the name Chicago City Missionary Society Dwellings Corporation No. 1, is at 5350 South
Maryland Avenue. It is an old twenty-two-unit, three-story building
adjacent to Hyde Park West. The mortgage was for $192,219,[5] or
only $8,737 per unit, showing how much more economical well-
executed rehabilitation can be than new construction. The other
two CRF rehab projects were on the West Side. In both instances the
original contractors did not finish the jobs, so the CRF itself had to
act as the general contractor to get the work completed. One of them

*The Southeast Englewood apartment building at 69th Street and Parnell
Avenue was abandoned because of youth gang pressure. This is one of a
group of five Community Renewal Foundation buildings, with a total of
eighty-one units on scattered sites in the Englewood community. The
buildings, completed in 1969, are all three-story walk-ups with brick exterior supporting walls and interior wooden structural framing.
—Photograph by Devereux Bowly, Jr.*

was a forty-five unit court building at 3410 West Douglas Boulevard, rehabilitated under the name Federated Lawndale Buildings Corporation No. 1. The other was a twenty-three-unit building at 4650 West West End Avenue, sponsored by the Federated Lawndale Buildings Corporation No. 3. The mortgages on these two buildings were much larger than on the Maryland Avenue property, in part because of the switch in contractors. The cost of the Douglas Boulevard building was $13,684 per unit, and the one on West End Avenue ran to $12,757 per unit.[6]

Serious problems developed almost from the beginning with the various projects of the Community Renewal Foundation. Less than a year after the Englewood scattered sites buildings were occupied, youth gangs in the area demanded protection money from the tenants and management agents at two of them. The late 1960s represented the height of gang activity on the South Side, and they literally frightened away the residents of the two buildings at 69th and 70th and Parnell. Both of them were vandalized and gutted, and have stood for years as empty hulks, without plumbing or kitchen fixtures, windows or doors, with their interior plasterboard walls kicked in—a sad commentary to the problems that plague the inner cities.

By 1971 the CRF decided it could not maintain the Englewood project. Because the buildings were spread out and relatively small, they did not have resident custodians, and it was not economically feasible to hire guards for each of them to control the vandalism. The CRF therefore deeded the buildings to the federal Department of Housing and Urban Development in lieu of foreclosure. The other properties did not fare much better for a variety of reasons, the most serious of which were cost overruns and confiscatory real estate taxes. The experience of the CRF was that the so-called 100 percent mortgages for nonprofit sponsors under the 221 (d) (3) program did not pay all the costs of the projects. They calculated that the mortgages covered in fact only 95.7 percent of the costs.[7] The major omission of the federal program was its failure to make adequate provision for interim or construction financing, and the "discount" the sponsor had to pay the mortgage company to get the financing. Also, delays in construction and cost overruns pushed costs beyond original FHA commitments. The net result was that during the seven-year period of 1964 to 1971, the CRF had to secure $350,000 in additional loans and loan guarantees from the Community Renewal Society, as well as an additional $200,000 from the society for contributions to general operating expenses.[8]

All the normal landlord costs, such as janitor service, repairs and decorating, were above estimates, but the worst problem, and one shared by virtually all the private sponsors of federally subsidized housing in Cook County, was real estate taxes. In 1970, for example, they varied on the CRF new-construction projects from a low of 35 percent of gross rentals for the Dauphin Apartments, to a high of 41 percent for Hyde Park West, a figure that averages out to $525 per unit per year. The following year taxes at Hyde Park West went up to 44 percent of the rentals. The Cook County Assessor's Office was assessing the properties on about the same basis as privately built housing, without taking into account the fact that rents paid in the 221 (d) (3) buildings, due to federal regulations and the income of the residents, are considerably less than those for comparable apartments on the open market.

Apartment building at 4650 West End rehabilitated by the Community Renewal Foundation at a cost of $12,757 per unit.—Photograph by Devereux Bowly, Jr.

When mortgage payments, management, and maintenance expenses are considered, virtually no low-rental property can survive at the tax assessments that existed on the CRF new-construction properties. The tax levels on the rehabilitation properties were not much better, varying from 21 to 31 percent of gross rental income in 1970.[9] Negotiations were held with the Cook County Assessor's Office, although HUD failed to intercede on behalf of the CRF, and reductions were promised, but they failed to materialize until the CRF hired lawyers to represent it in the matter. By that time the projects were financially beyond the point of being salvaged.

As early as 1969 the CRF had decided to complete its projects under construction, and then reduce the scope of its housing activities. It had concluded that the problems were such that it should not develop any more housing. Because of its good location and design, the foundation tried to convert Hyde Park West into a cooperative. The tenants, however, organized against the idea and blocked it. By 1972 all seven of the projects were completed, but all seven of the mortgages were in default, and Southeast Englewood was in the process of being deeded to HUD. Four years later the mortgages on four more of the properties had been foreclosed in court proceedings. All that remained in CRF ownership were Hyde Park West, about $300,000 behind in its mortgage payments, and the Dauphin Apartments. The mortgages on both of these projects had been assigned to HUD, and the properties were subject to what HUD calls Provisional Workout Arrangements, which means the mortgages could be either caught up (which is unlikely), renegotiated, or foreclosed at a later date. The situation remained clouded, however, because of confusion and lack of coordination between the main HUD office in Washington and the local Chicago office.

Receivership Program

The other major housing program of the Community Renewal Foundation involved court-ordered receiverships of deteriorated buildings. In 1964 CRF received a $209,000 grant from HUD for a two-year demonstration of the validity of receivership as a device to rehabilitate substandard housing. Research from the 1960 Census by the CRF spotlighted the overwhelming building code enforcement problems in Chicago. They found that 105,400 Chicago families with incomes of $5,000 or less were living in substandard housing. Of the 532,000 residential structures in Chicago, 122,000 or 23 percent had significant code violations or deficiencies.[10]

During the two-year period the CRF was appointed receiver of fifteen buildings, only three of which were actually rehabilitated, the largest of these was a twelve-flat at 5338–44 South Greenwood where $75,000 was spent. In litigation concerning the receivership, attorneys for CRF got the Illinois Supreme Court in 1970 to establish not only the validity of court-appointed receiverships, but the fact that the receiver could issue certificates to raise money for rehabilitation which became prime liens on the property, even superior to mortgages. It was hoped that this fact would provide a strong deterrent to the owners of the buildings, and the banks holding the mortgages, not to let their properties run down so far that a receiver would be appointed. By 1970, however, the cost of rehabilitation had gone to an extremely high level, and rents had not kept

Receivership Program apartment building at 5338–44 South Greenwood Avenue. The Community Renewal Foundation, as court-appointed receiver, spent $75,000 restoring this twelve-flat structure.—Photograph by Devereux Bowly, Jr.

pace because of the greater availability of housing for poor people in
Chicago. Thus the economic facts of life effectively killed the idea of
large-scale receivership programs. Of the remaining buildings dealt
with by the CRF, seven were repaired by their owners or mortgage
holders because of the threat of receivership, three were demolished,
and two dropped from the program.

Kate Maremont Foundation

The other major experiment in privately sponsored subsidized
housing in Chicago during the 1960s was conducted by the Kate
Maremont Foundation (KMF). It was established in 1948 by Arnold
Maremont in memory of his mother, and in its early years had
operated in the fields of the arts, education, and social reform. Mr.
Maremont, an industrialist and civic leader, was appointed in 1962
as chairman of the Illinois Public Aid Commission. His suggestion
of establishing a publicly supported family-planning program for the
indigent caused an enormous controversy, and he left his post only
nine months after his appointment. During that time, however, he
became acutely aware of the housing problems of public-aid recipients and poor people generally. Upon leaving the commission in
April 1963, he changed the thrust of his foundation to the field of
low- and moderate-income housing, and channeled virtually all of
its resources to that end.

To head up the new program Maremont hired Victor de Grazia,
who had been active in independent politics and executive director
of the Illinois Board of Economic Development. He had had no experience in the field of housing, except for a year's employment a
decade earlier as a field representative for the City of Chicago Housing and Redevelopment Coordinator's Office. In less than ten years
the KMF participated or advised in the development or rehabilitation of 2,890 units of housing, with mortgages and investments
totaling almost $40 million.[11] The basic program of the Maremont
Foundation involved the purchase and rehabilitation of substandard
buildings. After meeting with Robert Weaver, head of the federal
Housing and Home Finance Agency, which in 1965 became the
Department of Housing and Urban Development (HUD), Arnold
Maremont initially put up about $500,000 in seed money to get his
program started.[12] The work of KMF was considered a pilot project
of national significance, because it was the first really large-scale
attempt at renovation of slum housing under Section 221 (d) (3).

The initial rehabilitation work of the KMF, which took place between 1963 and 1968, involved thirteen buildings containing 597
apartments. They varied from 18 units up to 92 units and were

located on the North, West, and South sides of the city. Most were three-story courtyard buildings, constructed between 1910 and 1930, that had been neglected and allowed to become run down. The acquisition costs totaled $2.4 million or about $4,000 per unit, and another $5,000 per unit or almost $3 million was spent on rehabilitation and indirect costs. The mortgages totaled $5.3 million or $8,914 per unit.[13] Rents were set at $65 to $95 per month for the two- and four-room apartments in the first building finished, at 3024–38 North Halsted Street. A subsidiary, called the Chicago Rehabilitation Management Foundation, headed by de Grazia, was set up to manage the Chicago properties, and to conduct a national program of housing rehabilitation and construction for KMF.

One of the theories on which KMF operated was that the more successful buildings would generate excess income that could be used to carry the less successful ones, and also be used as seed money for expansion of the program. This turned out not only to be overly optimistic, but completely unrealistic. In fact federal regulations provide that separate books have to be kept on each property, and the funds segregated; pooling is not permitted. This difference in philosophy was later to become one of many sources of dispute between federal officials and the foundation.

Michigan Boulevard Garden Apartments

In 1963 the KMF purchased the Michigan Boulevard Garden Apartments, Julius Rosenwald's early experiment in model housing, to be the flagship of its program. The Rosenwald Foundation had sold the property in 1957 to a private party, who in turn sold it to the Maremont Foundation. The original intent of KMF was to rehabilitate it with Section 221 (d) (3) funds, but several attempts failed. FHA would not allocate enough money for the project, and the residents objected because they felt they would be displaced in the process. In March 1967 it was announced that the foundation would spend $2 million to rehabilitate the buildings and convert the property to condominium ownership. A model apartment was opened and sale prices were set ranging from $6,265 for a one-bedroom unit, to $9,215 for a three-bedroom one. Down payments were to be as low as $845, and monthly payments from $123.75 to $152.27, with fifteen year mortgages.

Within a month tenants in the complex organized against the condominium conversion. They were concerned about a number of things, including the low-income tenants who would be forced out, especially the 44 percent who were more than sixty years old, almost all of whom lived on fixed incomes.[14] Most of the tenants refused to show their apartments to prospective buyers. Because of the tenant objections, and less interest by outside purchasers than expected, the condominium plan fell through. In 1973 the Chicago Department of Urban Renewal purchased the property for $1.8 million by condemnation, and has since operated it. During the decade KMF owned it, Arnold Maremont personally obligated himself on notes to finance the purchase of the property, and it is estimated that the foundation had a total investment in it of $2.6 million.[15]

Another large South Side project, considered by the KMF in 1965, was the acquisition and rehabilitation of all the buildings of the so-called "Canyon," on the edge of the Hyde Park–Kenwood Urban Renewal Area. The Canyon is the 4700 block of South Ingleside Avenue, which is made up of a solid wall of three-story buildings on both sides of the street, all of which are in poor repair, and many of which have been cut up into smaller units than when the buildings were constructed. The block contains 650 units, and was not cleared as part of the urban-renewal project because of the tremendous number of people who would have had to be relocated. The KMF's idea was to demolish two buildings on each side of the street to let in light and provide recreation space, and rehabilitate the rest. The proposal never went ahead, in part because the various owners held out for high prices for their properties.[16] Also in 1965, in another ambitious plan, the KMF obtained an option to purchase the Marshall Field Garden Apartments for a Section 221 (d) (3) rehabilitation. It did not pan out, however, and the option was never exercised.

In 1964 KMF began assisting The Woodlawn Organization (TWO) in building Woodlawn Gardens as a major housing development at 61st Street and Cottage Grove Avenue. (Since the primary sponsor of the project was TWO, it will be considered in chapter 9.) The KMF assisted in two other projects sponsored by Chicago community organizations. The Apostolic Church of God, located in the Woodlawn area, asked the KMF to act as general contractor and managing agent for an eighteen-unit rehab it sponsored under the name Kimbark Development Association. The Fifth City Citizens Redevelopment Corporation used KMF as a consultant on a grant it received from the Illinois Housing Development Authority, to plan renewal of their neighborhood, on the West Side.

The Kate Maremont Foundation was also involved in major housing endeavors in other parts of the country. These included the Metro North East Harlem Project, under which 135 housing units and ten stores in five old-law tenement buildings on East 100th

Street in New York City were rehabilitated by a neighborhood organization. In connection with a group called FIGHT in Rochester, New York, 149 new units were developed. The KMF itself built two large 221 (d) (3) projects in the San Francisco Bay area. One is called Crescent Park, located in Richmond, California, and has 378 units. The other, called Glenridge, has 275 units, and is located in Diamond Heights, California.

Lawndale Freedom Movement–KMF Development Association

Dr. Martin Luther King, Jr., and his Southern Christian Leadership Conference (SCLC), was the catalyst for the formation of the Lawndale Union to End Slums. It was part of his Chicago Campaign of 1966 and 1967. The Lawndale Union to End Slums entered into an agreement on April 17, 1967, with Mrs. Eva Atlas, owner of eleven apartment buildings in Lawndale, which had 264 apartments and about 1,000 residents. Under the agreement, which ended a nine-month rent strike against the buildings, Victor de Grazia was named as arbitrator of disputes between the landlord and tenants, with the power to bind both groups. It was planned that extensive repairs would be made by Atlas to bring the buildings up to code standards. An option to purchase the buildings was also granted to KMF. The foundation did in fact obtain them, in trade for a $700,000 building it owned on West Sheridan Road,[17] and the Lawndale Freedom Movement–KMF Development Association was formed. A 221 (d) (3) loan was obtained to rehabilitate six of the buildings, with 71 units, at a total cost of $1,089,500 or $15,345 per unit. It was originally hoped the other buildings could be converted to condominiums, but that expectation was completely unrealistic considering their location and condition. It turned out that the Lawndale project was the beginning of the end of the KMF housing program in Chicago.

In June 1967 the Maremont Foundation, together with the Community Renewal Foundation, financed a two-day conference on the future of Lawndale, addressed by a variety of experts including Jane Jacobs; Claude Brown; M. Justin Herman, executive Director of the San Francisco Redevelopment Agency; Charles Abrams, chairman of the Department of Urban Planning at Columbia University; and Daniel Watts, Harlem architect and editor of *Liberator Magazine*. They proposed that new low-rise apartments be constructed on vacant lots, and residents of existing buildings be moved to them while their buildings were being rehabilitated. The visionary dreams of transforming Lawndale to a viable community were pretty much

scuttled less than a year later, in April 1968, when the riots following the assassination of Dr. King destroyed the commercial base of
the area, along with hundreds of units of housing.

Almost from the time of obtaining the Lawndale buildings the
KMF had difficulties. The minority contractor who was engaged to
rehabilitate them went out of business, and the foundation had to
step in and become its own general contractor. Vandalism was
constant, maintenance costs were high, and one of the buildings
burned down. Disputes arose between the foundation and the Lawndale Freedom Movement (LFM) over, among other things, who was
to collect the rents, and a rent strike occurred. A suit was filed by
the LFM against the KMF although it was later dismissed. Mechan-
ics' liens were put against the properties, and suits were filed by
unpaid subcontractors. In all, KMF lost between $900,000 and $1
million on the Lawndale Project.[18]

Lawndale was not the only problem of KMF. A fifty-six-unit building it rehabilitated at 5 South Central Park Boulevard was hit by a
rent strike in February 1968. The strike was called by the East
Garfield Tenants Union because of a $12-per-month rent increase,
which raised the rents to an average of $102 and a maximum of $130
for a five-room apartment. The foundation contended it had lost
$15,000 per year on the building for the previous two years, in part
because of a high rent-delinquency rate.[19]

By 1971 it was becoming known in the housing field that the KMF
was in trouble. Transfers of funds from the properties holding their
own to the others could not save the sinking ship. The causes of the
situation, in addition to the Lawndale problems, were very similar
to those of the Community Renewal Foundation, and in fact many
other nonprofit housing sponsors across the country. The KMF also
had special problems with HUD. Although Secretary Weaver and
the Washington office viewed the KMF as a prototype for the entire
country, the foundation felt that the local office of HUD was inefficient if not outright uncooperative. The local office, for its part, had
no great love for the foundation. In 1963 John M. Ducey, a retired
Loyola University professor who had worked with Arnold Maremont in setting up the Maremont Foundation housing program, got
Weaver to establish a special task force out of the Washington office
to get the projects through the bureaucracy and effectively skirt the
local office.[20]

Although de Grazia and the other people at the KMF were in-
telligent and aggressive, they lacked housing and real estate experience, and more importantly, were completely naïve about the depth
of the problems of inner-city Chicago neighborhoods. They paid too

much for some of the properties purchased, suffered from constant vandalism and cost overruns, and for some buildings set rehabilitation budgets insufficient to really put them in proper condition. They were overly ambitious and tried to build a housing empire practically overnight, rather than operating slowly based upon experience learned along the way.

In late 1970 Michael Maremont, son of Arnold Maremont, had become active in KMF and its Chicago Rehabilitation Management Foundation. A real estate developer by profession, he quickly came to realize that the housing program was in serious trouble, and he recommended the buildings be refinanced or deeded to HUD. In April 1971 it was agreed that in fact the foundation would deed them in lieu of foreclosure. At that point payments on the mortgages had not been made in some months. When it became publicly known that the KMF was going out of the housing business it caused quite a stir, because the foundation up to that time had enjoyed frequent and favorable press coverage, in part because it was represented by the energetic Mort Kaplan Public Relations firm.

On Sunday, December 5, 1971, the *Chicago Tribune* carried a front-page, three-column article entitled "Fear Huge Loss of FHA Funds on Three Housing Projects Here: Blame Mismanagement." The story cited the allegations of unnamed FHA officials that more than $6 million in federal funds could be lost because the KMF projects "were burdened by exorbitant administrative fees, irregular accounting procedures, the refusal by the Foundation to turn over its financial records without long delays and excuses, and serious violations of standard FHA rules and regulations." The basic specific allegation was that management and administrative fees averaged 17 percent, and ran as high as 24 percent of the rents of one of the KMF buildings, when FHA regulations permit only a 5 percent administrative fee. The article quoted, but did not name, local FHA officials and former officials, who were bitter because the Maremont projects were approved directly from Washington, not through the local office.

The next day the *Tribune* ran another front-page story,[21] saying that John Waner, who had then been federal housing director for the Chicago office for two months, was going to ask the FBI to investigate the Maremont situation. The following day the third *Tribune* article appeared, saying Waner had ordered records concerning the KMF properties put under tight security, and that a "top level" FHA employee who worked on the Maremont projects was being investigated.[22] The *Tribune* exposé had all the signs of being politically motivated. Not only did the paper itself have a long-standing opposition to public and subsidized housing, but Waner was a prominent local Republican leader who had run against Mayor Daley in 1967. FHA had been under Democratic control during the period of 1965–68 when the projects had been approved in Washington. Arnold Maremont was influential in Democratic politics in Illinois, at one time aspiring to be governor. Most importantly, at the time the articles appeared de Grazia had left the KMF to be the campaign manager for Daniel Walker, who was then seeking the Democratic nomination for governor.

On December 6, after the first two articles appeared, Michael Maremont issued a statement stating that the Maremont Foundation had itself lost more than a million dollars on the housing program. On December 7, de Grazia gave an interview to the *Sun-Times*, which was published the following day, in which he defended his actions. In regard to the management fees, he pointed out that if income drops for a building, which happened because of various problems in the Maremont properties, the administrative costs remain the same, but become a larger percentage of the reduced income. He also pointed out that other sponsors of private rehabilitation projects, including the Community Renewal Foundation and United States Gypsum Corporation, had had about the same experience as the Maremont Foundation.[23] The *Tribune* ran still another article, on December 20,[24] complaining, among other things, that KMF administrative costs included more than $6,000 for taxi, parking, and auto expenses, $4,500 for meals, first-class air flights, and $40-a-day hotel rooms.

The end result of all the allegations was that no evidence of wrongdoing by KMF or FHA officials was found. The unfortunate aspect of all this controversy was that no attempt was made to evaluate the real problems and mistakes of the Maremont Foundation. Their program was the most ambitious private attempt at housing rehabilitation, and it resulted in complete failure, as well as the loss of $1.5 to $2 million by Arnold Maremont.[25] After 1972 the two projects in California were all that remained solvent of the Maremont-sponsored projects. The fact remains, however, that even if the Community Renewal Foundation and the Kate Maremont Foundation had moved more slowly, picked their buildings and sites more carefully, and engaged more competent and experienced employees, there is no guarantee they would have succeeded in light of the problems of excessive real estate taxes, delays and difficulties in dealing with the federal bureaucracy, high rehabilitation costs, and vandalism.

9 Federally Subsidized, Privately Sponsored, Housing

The Housing sponsored by the Community Renewal Foundation and the Kate Maremont Foundation constituted only a small fraction of federally subsidized, but privately owned, multi-family housing in Chicago. Such housing was developed basically during the decade from 1963 to 1973, under the Section 221 (d) (3) and Section 236 programs. The developers were of three types: nonprofit organizations, cooperatives, and limited-dividend entities. The latter are profit-making businesses, limited to a 6 percent return on their investment. The basic theory of both the 221 (d) (3) and 236 programs was that federal funds could be used to stimulate the private sector of the economy to produce housing for moderate-income families. This represented a major departure from public housing, which was financed by the federal government, and built and managed by local governmental bodies. Under the 221 (d) (3) and 236 programs, a total of 143 projects were built or rehabilitated in Chicago containing 19,927 units.[1]

Section 221 (d) (3) of the National Housing Act was enacted in 1961. It provided 3 percent mortgages for housing developments which met its cost and tenancy requirements. The cost saving of the below-market interest rate allowed the developer to charge lower rents for the units than would be possible if the project were financed by a market-rate mortgage. The Section 221 (d) (3) mortgages are held by the Government National Mortgage Association, a federal agency under the Department of Housing and Urban Development. The units covered by the mortgage can be either new construction or rehabilitated existing housing. Each project must consist of five or more units, which may be detached houses, row houses, or apartment buildings. Nonprofit sponsors are eligible for mortgages covering 100 percent of the cost of the land, construction, professional fees, and organization expenses. Limited-dividend entities can get 90 percent mortgages. The mortgages run up to forty years in length.

Under the Section 221 (d) (3) program, income limits are set for the tenants by HUD, based on a formula which takes into account the size of the family, the cost of living in the local community, and the public-housing income limits there. Tenants generally pay about 20 percent of family income for rent. The rents are set by HUD, based on the expenses and debt service of the project. The tenants' income must be recertified annually, and if it goes above the income limits established for initial occupancy in the apartment, the rent is raised to an established "adjusted market rent." Although 221 (d) (3) is basically a rental program, projects constructed under it can be converted to ownership by the occupants through cooperatives or condominiums.

The Section 236 program was enacted as part of the 1968 Housing and Urban Development Act to replace and expand Section 221 (d) (3). It is similar in its general design to the earlier program, but the objective is carried out by slightly different mechanisms. Under the Section 236 program the mortgages are held by private mortgage companies and financial institutions, although they are insured by the federal government. The holder of the mortgage charges market-interest rates, but FHA subsidizes the mortgages by "interest reduction payments" to the lender on behalf of the tenants in the project. These payments can lower the interest rate the developer has to pay down to 1 percent per annum. The amount the government pays towards the interest varies with the income of the tenants, and thus with the rents paid by the tenants. The lower the tenants' incomes and rents, the higher is the subsidy for the project.

Under the Section 236 programs each tenant pays the basic subsidized rent set for his unit, or such greater amount as represents 25 percent of his income, up to the market rent. The upper income limit, for families to be eligible to have assistance payments made on their behalf, is 135 percent of the local public housing initial occupancy limit. In Chicago in 1974, for example, the limit for a family of four was about $9,750. The 236 program allows for a greater mix of income levels than the 221 (d) (3) program. Under Section 236 20 percent of the units can be used for very low income tenants requiring an additional rent supplement subsidy, and 20 percent can be occupied by "exception limit" tenants with incomes above the regular 236 limits.

At first blush the Section 221 (d) (3) and 236 programs would seem to be quite attractive to developers, because of the low mortgage rates. It must be remembered, however, that although the mortgage rates are below market levels, the rents are also below market, and are controlled by HUD. There are other advantages to the programs, however. Nonprofit developers could build housing with 100 percent financing and thus almost no investment on their part. Limited-dividend developers could build with an investment of only 10 percent of the cost of the project. Even though their profit is limited to 6 percent, the developers are building equity, and most importantly, can achieve significant tax benefits with a small investment. Many of the entities set up to develop 221 (d) (3) and 236 housing are limited partnerships made up of wealthy persons wishing to "shelter" some of their income from federal income taxes. Because the investors are limited partners they are not personally liable if the project goes bankrupt, but only lose the actual investment they made. The tax advantages of such investments are derived from the device of accelerated depreciation, and the ability to deduct on the investor's tax return the interest paid on construction loans, and real estate taxes paid during the period of construction. Also, some of the developers set up their own management companies to run their developments and derived additional profit through them.

The Section 221 (d) (3) and 236 projects that were developed in Chicago range from 6 to 803 units, and are located in three major sections of the city, the South Side, the West Side, and the north lakefront from about Division Street to Bryn Mawr Avenue. Many of them are twenty- to twenty-five-story concrete buildings, containing perhaps 200 units, and often located near the Lake. Most of these buildings lack any distinction, architectural or otherwise, and were built merely to comply with minimum HUD standards. About a dozen of the projects are notable, however, for one reason or another.

South Commons

In many ways the best private housing development in Chicago containing 221 (d) (3) or 236 housing is South Commons. It is located in the area bounded by 26th Street, Michigan Avenue, 31st Street, and Indiana and Prairie avenues. The thirty-acre tract was purchased from the Chicago Department of Urban Renewal in 1964, for $34,875 an acre. Before redevelopment it had 181 structures housing 306 families and 224 single persons.[2] The completed development has 1,619 units, subsidized and nonsubsidized, and represents an investment of about $25 million. The developer, McHugh-Levin Associates, submitted one of four bids for the site. Their proposal was selected not only because of the variety and quality of housing types it envisioned, but because its social plan called for racial integration and a wide variety of income levels among residents.

The site is in the middle of the Near South Side, almost completely rebuilt by urban renewal. It is adjacent to CHA's Prairie Avenue
Courts, Mercy Hospital, and the Illinois Institute of Technology,
and is near Michael Reese Hospital, Prairie Shores, and Lake Meadows.[3] The architects, Ezra Gordon–Jack M. Levin and Associates,
who won several awards for the design of South Commons, con-
sciously created a setting like a small village. it has a shopping area
and community building in the center, surrounded by a variety of
types of residential buildings, gardens, play areas, low brick walls,
and sculpture. Most importantly, the development has a fairly high
intensity of land use. This is in stark contrast to earlier developments like Lake Meadows that were influenced by Le Corbusier and
contain merely isolated high-rise towers in a park setting. By the
late 1960s those projects, with vast open spaces that rarely contain a
person walking or a child playing, were disfavored by many architects and developers.

South Commons was basically constructed in four stages. The
first, which had Solomon, Cordwell, Buenz as associate architects
and was constructed in 1967, is composed of three apartment buildings in a cluster at 29th and Michigan. It is called Windsor Mall, and
is made up of a 200-unit, twenty-four-story concrete high-rise, and
two 68-unit, five-story red brick buildings. The lower buildings are
really five and six stories tall, because each has four duplex apartments on its top floor, alternating with conventional apartments,
creating a variegated roof line. None of this group of buildings is
subsidized; their tenants pay full market rents.

The second stage included the shopping center and community
building, and three apartment buildings near 28th Street and Prairie
Avenue, called York Terrace. The buildings, all of which were
financed under Section 221 (d) (3), are a twenty-one story 240-unit
building, and two- and five-story maisonettes, with a total of 91
units. Each maisonette building is made up of two structures, one
four story and one five story, served by a single elevator and connected by an overhead bridge. The first-floor apartments in the five-
story sections are conventional apartments entered directly from
ground level. The rest of the units are duplex apartments entered
from interior hallways at the second and fourth floors of the five-
story sections, and the first and third floors of the four-story ones.

The third stage of construction, at the south end of the development, is called Oxford Mall. It is adjacent to, and virtually a twin of
the first three buildings constructed, except that the high-rise is
three stories taller. Next to it is a low concrete garage, one of several
located at various points along the perimeter of the site, and con-

cealing much of the automobile parking. At the time these buildings
were constructed, forty-two two- and three-story row houses were
built at 28th and Michigan called Stuart Townhouses. Later, thirty
additional row houses were added to the north, and to the northeast
an eighteen-unit cluster called St. James Townhouses. All of them
are built of brown brick and handsomely designed, and sold for
$29,000 to $49,000 with conventional financing. The final phase of
construction occurred at the northeast corner of the site, and was
composed of two high-rise buildings. One is called Cambridge
Manor and was financed under Section 236; it has 312 units for
elderly tenants. The other, Stratford Mall, is a 207 unit nonsubsidized family building. One of the most significant things about the
planning and architecture of South Commons is that when walking
through it one cannot tell which are the subsidized buildings and
which are not.

Of equal importance to the physical plan of the development was
the social ideal, which sought economic and racial integration. In

*In many ways one of the best private housing developments in Chicago
containing some subsidized housing is South Commons. The award-
winning project was designed to resemble a small village with a variety of
structures and facilities and intense land usage. York Terrace, one part of
South Commons, is depicted here.—Photograph by Devereux Bowly, Jr.*

order to attract middle-class families it was decided that a special
school would have to be created for the youngsters of South Commons, instead of the local public school whose students were almost
entirely from the nearby public housing projects. The Chicago Board
of Education was persuaded to hold classes in the South Commons

*Cambridge Manor (right, foreground) and Stratford Mall (left, background),
the final phases of construction of South Commons. The former is a subsidized building for the elderly while the latter is a nonsubsidized family
building.—Courtesy of Ezra Gordon–Jack M. Levin & Associates*

Community building. The South Commons branch of the Drake School opened in 1968 for kindergarten and the first three grades. Grades four and five were added in 1972 and 1973 respectively, and by the fall of 1976 the school had classes through the seventh grade.

The high quality of the design of the development, and its amenities, were initially enough to attract the desired economic and racial mix. In 1970, when South Commons was about one-half completed, it had families with annual incomes ranging from $6,900 to over $60,000, and a racial balance of 60 percent white and 40 percent black.[4] Although the economic diversity remained over the coming years, the racial integration did not. South Commons was not immune from racial tension, and some of the white children were intimidated by children from Prairie Avenue Courts. The children from the public housing project, for their part, as well as those from the Section 221 (d) (3) York Terrace buildings, resented the fact they could not swim at any of the three pools at South Commons. In June 1973 a change was made in the procedures allowing them use of one of the pools from 2:00 to 4:30 P.M. on weekdays. By 1973 the racial balance at South Commons was already beginning to shift. It was not so much that the white families fled the development, but that when they moved in the normal course of events, they were usually not replaced by new white tenants. In 1973, out of 650 children living in South Commons, only 151 attended school in the public South Commons-Drake School, and the South Commons Preschool. The rest, black as well as white, went to private schools.[5]

By 1976 the population of South Commons was approximately 90 percent black, and the school about 95 percent black. The townhouses, with about half white owners, remained the only well-integrated segment of the development.[6] A decade and more earlier, when planning for the development was first undertaken, there was no way to have foreseen the black militancy that followed the riots of the mid-1960s, and the assassination of Dr. Martin Luther King, Jr., in 1968, or the white backlash that followed. South Commons by most criteria has to be considered a success. It remains physically attractive, and economically diverse. It would have been a greater success if it had remained well integrated racially.

Lawless Gardens Apartments

A second large 221 (d) (3) project, also on the Near South Side, is the Lawless Gardens Apartments. It is located just east of King Drive, along Rhodes Avenue, from 35th to 37th streets. The thirteen-acre site, between Lake Meadows and Ida B. Wells Homes, was purchased from the city's Department of Urban Renewal for $391,000. The developers were the late Dr. Theodore K. Lawless, and other prominent black business and professional men.

The project designed by John Moutoussamy, of Dubin, Dubin, Black, and Moutoussamy, was built in two stages. The first was started in 1967, and involved the construction of two twenty-four-story towers, each with 240 units. In the second stage, constructed in 1969, a third matching tower was built together with 54 two-

Lawless Gardens Apartments were developed by the late Dr. Theodore K. Lawless and other prominent black business and professional men. —Photograph by Hedrich-Blessing, courtesy of Dubin, Dubin, Black, and Moutoussamy

story, buff colored, rental row houses. The initial rent schedule for the development ran from $115 per month for a one-bedroom apartment to $155 for a three-bedroom one, with income limits of $7,250 for a family of two, to $9,850 for a family of five or six.

Woodlawn Gardens

The most ambitious Section 221 (d) (3) project undertaken by a community organization was Woodlawn Gardens, developed in 1969 by The Woodlawn Organization, and the Kate Maremont Foundation, under the name of TWO-KMF Development Association. As early as 1959 some of the ministers in the Woodlawn area had consulted Saul Alinsky about organizing the community, and by 1960 he and his chief organizer, Nicholas von Hoffman, later to become a well-known newspaperman, were organizing Woodlawn. In that same year the University of Chicago announced a plan to expand its South Campus, located on the edge of Woodlawn, by an urban renewal project. TWO was formed in large part in response to the expansion plans. In its early years TWO experienced very favorable media attention, especially by Georgie Anne Geyer in the *Chicago Daily News*. Charles E. Silberman, in his best-selling book, *Crisis in Black and White*, published in 1964, devoted thirty pages to TWO, and asserted: "TWO is the most important and most impressive experiment affecting Negroes anywhere in the United States."[7]

A compromise was reached under which it was agreed TWO would not oppose the South Campus plan, and it in return would be the developer of moderate-income housing along both sides of Cottage Grove Avenue, from 60th to 63rd streets. The site is adjacent to CDA's Midway Gardens, and generally only one-half block deep on either side of the street. It had been a dilapidated strip of forty-four commercial buildings, including the once-famous Trianon Ballroom, but had few residential units. It was cleared by the Department of Urban Renewal with the intention that the project would be built before clearance for the South Campus, so at least some of the persons to be displaced could move to the new building. The 504 units that were ultimately built, however, represented less than half as many as were eliminated for the South Campus area.

The 9.1 acres of land for Woodlawn Gardens was sold to TWO-KMF in 1967, for $562,800. The original scheme for the development, for which planning began in 1964, called for 762 units, some of which would be rented, and some owned by the occupants on a cooperative basis.[8] It was scaled down, however, and plans for cooperative ownership abandoned. The architect was Stanley Tigerman who was careful to keep the entire project low-rise. It has twenty-four three-story buildings, which have conventional apartments on the first floor, and duplex apartments on the upper floors. There are a pair of four-story buildings, each of which contains sixty-three efficiency and one-bedroom apartments. There is also a community building, and at 63rd Street a small shopping center.

All of the buildings are of dark brown brick with severe lines and no ornamentation. Structurally, the buildings have timber joists, with masonry bearing walls and concrete block partitions. The human scale and good proportions of the design are admirable, but the arterial street bisecting the project, its preponderance of parking lots, and the monotony of the architecture make it a pretty drab place. The initial rents at Woodlawn Gardens ranged from $93 to $100 for an efficiency apartment, up to $160 for the three-bedroom, one-and-one-half-bath duplex units. Income limits started at $6,400 for a single person, and went to $10,500 for a family of six. The low-income tenants who had federal rent supplements paid rents of

Woodlawn Gardens, built by The Woodlawn Organization and the Kate Maremont Foundation, includes twenty-four three-story buildings with conventional apartments on the first floor and duplex apartments on the upper floors.—Courtesy of Stanley Tigerman and Associates, Ltd.

only $50 to $80 a month. The total cost of the project was $9.3 million, or about $18,450 per unit.

When the *Chicago Tribune* did its exposé of the Maremont Foundation in December 1971, Woodlawn Gardens was already experiencing severe financial difficulties. Its real estate taxes had been projected at $152,000, but were in fact $334,000, and its operating expenses, estimated to be $109,000, actually amounted to $227,000 a year.[9] In the original budget there was no provision for security expenses, but they ran to $90,000 in 1971. On December 8 the *Tribune* reported that TWO had in June 1971 fired the Chicago Rehabilitation Management Foundation, a subsidiary of the Maremont Foundation, as the manager of Woodlawn Gardens, because it was not keeping proper books and records.[10] The following day it was reported that the current manager of the project alleged that more than $45,000 in security deposits collected by KMF could not be accounted for.[11]

From a financial standpoint TWO had only slightly better success managing Woodlawn Gardens than had the Maremont Foundation. The project deficit of $120,000 in 1970 went up to $274,000 in 1971, dropped to $236,000 in 1972 and $204,000 in 1973.[12] According to HUD records the mortgage went into default in March 1971.[13] TWO continued to pay the interest, but by early 1975 only $30,000 of the principal had been paid.[14] In 1973 after vigorous protest, and the assistance of a special consultant hired for TWO by the Ford Foundation, a $255,000 real estate tax rebate was received by TWO. The money was used to rehabilitate the then four-year-old project, which had suffered some vandalism and damage due to defects in the original construction. As of late 1976 HUD had not instituted a foreclosure action against the project, although no payments were being made on principal, only interest. Since HUD was not anxious to take over the property, it appeared that the only long-range solution to the default would be to renegotiate the mortgage from $9 million down to perhaps $6 million.

Campus Green

Campus Green is a major Section 236 development, located on a 9.5 acre site at Ashland Boulevard and Polk Street. It was developed in 1972 by a group headed by John Baird on land obtained from the Near West Side Urban Renewal Project. The Department of Urban Renewal selected the plan from three proposals submitted. It was designed by Robert C. Friedman and Associates, and consists of two buildings of twelve stories each, with a total of 410 units, and forty-six three-story row houses, which were not subsidized, and were

sold to individual families. The original plan also called for two
apartment buildings of four or five stories, but they were eliminated
in favor of more town houses which are closer in scale to the old,
predominately Italian neighborhood to the east. The high-rise buildings are located on the western edge of the site, and form a visual
transition to the heavily built up West Side Medical Center immediately across Ashland Boulevard. Personnel from the medical
center make up a large segment of the tenants of the development.

The apartment buildings are concrete, with brick veneer and bal-
conies on the sides, and exposed ribbed concrete on the ends. They
were the first buildings in Chicago to use the Van den Heuval concrete system. Developed in Holland, and used widely elsewhere in
Europe, it is based upon poured concrete bearing walls, instead of
traditional column and beam construction. In this respect it is like
the construction of Stateway Gardens, built fifteen years earlier.
Under the Dutch system, special steel forms are used, which are

*The Campus Green Apartments buildings were the first buildings in
Chicago to use the Van den Heuval concrete system, which employs
poured concrete bearing walls instead of column and beam construction.—Photograph by Devereux Bowly, Jr.*

nine feet high and thirty feet long. They produce not only the floors, but eight-inch-thick concrete walls between apartments. The interior surfaces of the forms are polished, and create such a smooth surface that it is painted directly, without a coating of plaster.

Barbara Jean Wright Courts

The other major Section 236 project on the Near West Side is the Barbara Jean Wright Courts, at 14th and Morgan streets. It was built in 1973 by a nonprofit community group called the Residents' Development Corporation, and the architects were Environment Seven. The development consists of 272 units, in fifteen groups of two-story row houses, and twelve buildings of four stories each. The latter have conventional apartments on the lower two floors, and two-story maisonettes on the upper floors. The entrance to each apartment is no higher than the third floor, so elevators were not necessary. Also, a simple timber structural system could be used.

Barbara Jean Wright Courts, two-story row houses. The hoped for integration of this project never materialized because of location, construction, and landscaping problems.—Photograph by Devereux Bowly, Jr.

The exteriors of the buildings are well designed, and employ over-sized brick and sloping roofs.

The original intent was to have a three-stage development of almost 1,000 units. It was hoped that because the development is near the University of Illinois at Chicago Circle, and the West Side Medical Center, it would have a racial and economic mix. Problems developed early, however. The contractor went bankrupt during construction, and the firm's bonding company had to be sued. Because of the trouble with the contractor the landscaping was not done, giving the grounds an utterly naked appearance. By late 1976 the suit had been settled, and the landscaping work substantially completed. The project had received a real estate tax reduction, and was economically still afloat. In fact, a final stage of 195 additional units was being planned. The desired integration never materialized, however. All of the tenants were black, and heavily concentrated at the lower end of the Section 236 income spectrum. There have been some problems with broken windows and other vandalism. One of the reasons it has been difficult to attract middle-income residents is that the site is next to the South Water Street Wholesale Market with its heavy truck traffic, the CHA Brooks Extension proj-

Barbara Jean Wright Courts, four-story building. These buildings have conventional apartments on the lower floors and two-story maisonettes on the upper floors. —*Photograph by Devereux Bowly, Jr.*

ect, and vast parcels of vacant land owned by the Department of
Urban Renewal. In a better location, without the construction and
landscaping problems, the Barbara Jean Wright Courts might have
been one of the better subsidized housing developments in Chicago.

Lake Village

Architecturally the best subsidized housing in Chicago, since
Frank Lloyd Wright's Francisco Terrace, is found at Lake Village.
It was designed by Harry Weese and Associates, and Ezra Gordon–
Jack M. Levin and Associates, and is located along the south side of
47th Street, between Lake Park and Ellis avenues, at the northern
edge of the Hyde Park–Kenwood Urban Renewal Project. The developer was a partnership headed by Jared Shlaes. The first phase of the
project, with Ezra Gordon in charge of design, is called Greenwood
Park, and was built in 1971. It occupies the two block fronts at the
western edge of the site, and consists of 122 units in ten apartment
buildings of two and three stories each, financed by a Section 221 (d)
(3) mortgage. The site is a long narrow one, and the buildings are
basically in two rows, facing an interior, heavily landscaped, mall.
The manageable scale, excellent proportions, and general quality of

*Architecturally the best subsidized housing in Chicago, since Frank Lloyd
Wright's Francisco Terrace, is found at Lake Village. The first phase of the
project, with Ezra Gordon in charge of design, is called Greenwood Park,
built in 1971.—Courtesy of Ezra Gordon–Jack M. Levin & Associates*

design come together to make an inviting space. Greenwood Park was one of twenty-one projects cited in the 1971 Distinguished Buildings Awards Program of the Chicago chapter, American Institute of Architecture.

Moving east, the second part of the development was to have been a group of 100 two- and three-story non-subsidized town houses, designed by Benjamin Weese. Fifteen of them were built, at 48th Street and Kenwood Avenue, and sold at prices of $40,000 to

Lake Village East high-rise. Designed by Benjamin Weese, this unusual twenty-six-story building has thirty-eight exterior sides and an irregular shape.—Photograph by Philip Turner, courtesy of Harry Weese & Associates

$54,000. The rest were never developed, however, because of high interest rates and construction costs, and a softer market than expected. The land on which the additional houses were to have been built has reverted to the city, and thus the project is now divided by an enormous vacant lot, two and one-half blocks long.

The most dramatic element of the development is the Lake Village East buildings, at 47th Street and Lake Park. Designed by Benjamin Weese, its main feature is a twenty-six-story building, with thirty-eight exterior sides, and an irregular shape, closer to a circle than a rectangle. It was the first building of what Weese calls

Floor plan of Lake Village East high-rise. This design, called Minimum Perimeter Architecture, offers several advantages, among which are construction cost savings, compactness, no long corridors, and cross-ventilation of virtually all apartments.—Courtesy of Harry Weese & Associates

Minimum Perimeter Architecture. He discovered that such a building has less exterior wall area than a traditional rectangular building enclosing the same amount of space. In the case of this building, 3,500 square feet less, which saved $45,000 in construction costs. The building cost $3,091,000 or only $15,455 per unit in 1973. Other advantages of the building are that it is compact and does not disrupt its surroundings by its size and shadows the way a larger building would, and it has no long corridors. From some apartments you can see out in three directions, and virtually every apartment has a lake view and cross ventilation.

There is almost no limit to the flexibility of floor plans that can be incorporated into such a building, because it is literally designed from the inside out. At Lake Village East there are eight different apartment plans. Each floor contains two efficiency units, three one-bedroom, and three two-bedroom apartments. Because Weese recognized that high-rise buildings are not good places for children to live, the eighteen three-bedroom apartments are located in a pair of three-story walk-up buildings adjacent to the tower. The tower's exterior attractiveness is due not only to the large number of facets, but to the fact that the vertical spaces between the windows are covered with dark brown brick, which matches the low-rise buildings of the development and surrounding community. Lake Village East won the 1974 Honor Award of the Chicago chapter, American Institute of Architects, as the best new building in Chicago that year.

Cooperative Housing

The Foundation for Cooperative Housing (FCH) was instrumental in the development of three major 221 (d) (3) projects in Chicago: Noble Square, London Towne Houses, and Eden Green. Noble Square is located on the Near Northwest Side, on Division Street just west of the Kennedy Expressway and adjacent to Holy Trinity Church and Schools, on land obtained from the Department of Urban Renewal. It was developed under what is called an "investor sponsor program." The FCH entered into an agreement with the builder, McHugh-Levin Associates, to develop the project as a rental property under Section 221 (d) (3). The contract between them provided that when the FCH sold memberships in the cooperative for 90 percent of the units, the property was then to be sold to the cooperative, which would assume the mortgage. The tenants thus became the owners. Noble Square was built in 1970, and became cooperatively owned in August 1971. The system used to develop the project was the same as CDA used when it built Hermitage Manor.

Noble Square was designed by Perkins and Will, and has two components, a high-rise tower and row houses. The tower is twenty-eight stories tall, constructed of concrete and glass, and contains 213 one- and two-bedroom units. The 168 houses are two and three stories, have simple brick walls and a few accent walls of stucco. From an architectural standpoint the scale of the buildings leaves much to be desired. The high-rise, because of its height and severe lines, tends to dominate the existing church and school buildings which are the focus of the site. The houses, on the other hand, are overpowered by the church, and from the expressway are reminiscent of piles of children's building blocks in Holy Trinity's front yard. From an economic standpoint Noble Square represented a considerable housing bargain. Initial down payments were only $450 for a three-bedroom house with a basement, monthly payments $137, and the purchase price $17,000.[15]

Noble Square, one of three major Foundation for Cooperative Housing projects, was built in 1970 and became cooperatively owned in August 1971. It consists of two components, a high-rise tower of twenty-eight stories and row houses, some of which latter are depicted here.—Courtesy of Perkins & Will

The London Towne Houses and Eden Green were both developed in 1967 under a different method, called "presold management programs." Here the FCH enters into a contract with a builder under which the builder constructs and owns model houses. The FCH then sells, on the basis of the model units, cooperative memberships for 90 percent of the units in the proposed project, and on the basis of that advance sale, gets a loan for the development. Under Section 221 (d) (3) cooperative sponsors, like nonprofit ones, qualify for mortgages of 100 percent of the cost of the project. The builder then constructs the houses, and sells off the models as co-ops, or continues to own them and rents them out.

Both developments are located on large tracts of land on the Far South Side, and both are built in the mode of the monolithic suburban subdivision. The larger of the two, the London Towne Houses,

London Towne Houses, another Foundation for Cooperative Housing project, was developed in 1967. With 803 units it is the largest privately owned subsidized housing development in Chicago. All of the buildings are two-story red brick row houses located on curving streets.—Photograph by Devereux Bowly, Jr.

is located at 101st Street and Cottage Grove Avenue, and has 803 units, making it the largest privately owned subsidized housing development in Chicago. All the units are in two-story red brick row houses, located on curving streets. Eden Green is centered at 133rd and Indiana Avenue, about one-half mile west of CHA's Altgeld Gardens, of which both developments are reminiscent. Eden Green has 439 units, again two-story row houses but of less substantial construction than the London Towne Houses. The units at Eden Green have from one to four bedrooms, with membership down payments of $415, and monthly charges of $135 to $195. Financially Eden Green has not been a success; its mortgage has been in default since June 1971.[16] It is adjacent to Eden Green North, a 348-apartment, Section 221 (d) (3) rental project, developed by the Antioch Missionary Baptist Church.

Eden Green, also developed by the Foundation for Cooperative Housing in 1967, has 439 units, again in two-story houses.—Photograph by Devereux Bowly, Jr.

Rehabilitation Projects

A large number of the 221 (d) (3) and 236 mortgages in Chicago were obtained for the purchase and rehabilitation of existing housing. A major rehabilitation project, financed by a Section 221 (d) (3) mortgage and completed in 1970, involved the Town and Garden Apartments, originally the Marshall Field Garden Apartments. By the mid-1960s the property had deteriorated significantly, and racial change had occurred so that 62 percent of the tenants were black by 1966. A rent strike started in September of that year, and in March 1967 a subsidiary of the Community Renewal Foundation announced it had purchased the property and planned to rehabilitate it. The plan fell through, however, and after being placed in receivership, the development was purchased by McHugh-Levin Associates. An extensive rehabilitation occurred in 1969 and 1970, under the direction of Dubin, Dubin, Black, and Moutoussamy. The interiors of the apartments were completely rebuilt, including new kitchens and baths. By 1976 the project showed some signs of wear and tear, but was basically in good condition. A two-bedroom apartment rented for $163 to $184.

Parkway Gardens

The largest rehab project in Chicago involved Parkway Gardens, a 694-unit apartment complex located on a fifteen-acre tract on the west side of King Drive from 63rd to 66th streets. The site had originally been part of White City, one of the major American amusement parks.[17] It had been built between 1904 and 1906, much of it in the Venetian architectural style, complete with two dance halls, roller coasters, Ferris wheel, and a scenic tunnel railroad art gallery, built of cast concrete panels. Although it took its name from the World's Columbian Exposition of 1893, which took place less than a mile from the site, it had no connection with that world's fair. A massive fire occurred at White City in 1927, and it never recovered. It went into receivership in 1933, and the remaining buildings were razed as a hazard in 1939.[18]

The apartment buildings were designed by the firm of Holsman, Holsman, Klekamp, and Taylor, who were also involved in the development work, under the name the Community Development Trust. The project was built in 1950, and consists of thirty-five buildings, all three- or eight-stories tall, with exclusively two-and three-bedroom apartments. The exterior of the buildings is common brick, and some have undulating walls to break the monotony of the rectangles. They also have concrete trim, including relief sculpture.

The layout makes intensive use of the site, but is skillful enough to avoid a feeling of congestion.

The project was not built as a cooperative, but it was mutually owned by the residents, who held certificates of beneficial interest in the Parkway Gardens Trust, which held legal title. Each of the residents, all of whom were black, owned twenty-five shares, with a par value of $100 each, for an investment of $2,500. Before construction was completed the developer got into serious financial difficulty, and had to sell off the northwest corner of the property, where a supermarket was later constructed. The original plan had called for a hotel on that site. Initially about three-quarters of the units were occupied by owners of shares in the trust; the remaining units were rented out.

Parkway Gardens, built in 1950, consists of thirty-five buildings, all three or eight stories tall, with exclusively two- and three-bedroom apartments. The layout makes intensive use of the site but is skillful enough to avoid a feeling of congestion.—Photograph by Devereux Bowly, Jr.

Because there was not enough money to pay fully the contractors, they were issued Class B shares in the trust, and became part owners of the development. Since the purpose of the trust was to provide housing at a reasonable cost, and no dividends were paid, the shares were of virtually no value to the contractors. They brought suit against the trust, and got judgment for about twenty cents on the dollar owed them. The payment of several hundred thousand dollars to the contractors, and for legal fees, was so great a burden on the trust that it was not able to keep up the mortgage payments. By the early 1960s some of the original owners, who had larger incomes and a somewhat more open housing market, moved out of the development to single-family homes. A greater proportion of the units were occupied by renters, and by 1971 the trust was on the verge of losing the property. The trustees sought funds to refinance the mortgage, rehabilitate the property, and pay off the owners, all of whom by that time had increased their investment to $3,250.

An interim loan of $12.15 million was secured from the Illinois Housing Development Authority, and HUD approved a Section 236 mortgage. The mutual owners got their investment back, about $1.5 million. More than $3 million was spent to renovate the property and the rest to pay off the existing mortgages. The rehab included new heating plants, new roofs, tuckpointing, and some interior work. When the Section 236 mortgage was obtained, the property was converted to a strictly rental basis, owned by a specially created not-for-profit corporation, King-Parkway Development, Inc. In 1971 the rent scale was set by HUD. The market rents were at a level sufficient to sustain the property, and a basic rent was set at a lower level for low-income families, to be subsidized by the federal inter-est assistance payments. Because of increasing expenses the figures were raised in 1973, to $158 basic rent and $224 market rent for a two-bedroom apartment, and $188 and $267 respectively for a three-bedroom unit. When the Parkway Gardens development was originally built it had middle-class occupants, such as post office employees, civil servants, and even a few lawyers. By 1976 only about 150 families in the project were paying the market rent. The rest were paying the basic rent, except for about 100 elderly tenants and 20 families who were not paying even the basic rent, but were receiving rent supplements.[19]

Douglas-Lawndale

Another major Section 236 rehabilitation mortgage was issued for the Douglas-Lawndale project. The stimulus came from the Douglas-Lawndale Urban Renewal Plan produced by the city. The site is Douglas Boulevard, on the West Side, part of the boulevard system connecting major parks in Chicago. The boulevard is almost a mile long and runs east and west at 1400 South; it connects Independence Square, which is 3800 West, to Douglas Park. It was laid out in 1869 and transferred from the Chicago Park District to the City of Chicago in 1959. It includes a wide landscaped park area in the center, with traffic lanes on either side.

The urban renewal project, started in 1968, involved several hundred housing units on the 145 parcels of real estate facing Douglas Boulevard. The boundaries of the project go only to the alleys behind the buildings on both sides of the boulevard, about one-third of a block away.[20] Most of the structures in the project area are three-story apartment buildings, but the site also includes several schools and churches. The hope was that, by focusing great attention on a relatively small site, the once luxurious apartments there could be

*Douglas Boulevard, laid out in 1869, is almost a mile long with a wide landscaped park area in the center, and traffic lanes on either side. An extensive urban renewal effort, started in 1968, involved several hundred housing units on the 145 parcels of real estate facing the boulevard.
—Photograph by Devereux Bowly, Jr.*

transformed from slums to a model moderate-income area. Virtually all the residential buildings were purchased and rehabilitated by the city and a group of public and private agencies including CHA, CDA, Community Renewal Foundation, Beacon Development Corporation, and a community group established for the project, the Douglas-Lawndale Corporation.

The project was a complete fiasco, and because of the number of agencies involved, it probably will never be known how many millions of dollars it consumed. Almost all of the agencies had problems during rehabilitation of higher costs than expected, vandalism, thefts of building materials, faulty work, and underestimation of taxes and expenses. It was never possible to attract any significant number of moderate-income tenants to the area, and thus the population was almost exclusively very low income. The Douglas-Lawndale Corporation by December 1972 had completed the rehabilitation of 126 units in seventeen buildings. The corporation and the buildings went through a series of management companies, but the project was a financial disaster regardless of who was running it. On December 2, 1975, HUD announced foreclosure proceedings against the properties, and alleged the corporation was $1.6 million behind in its mortgage payments. Other mortgages in the Douglas-Lawndale project, involving 344 additional rehab units, were also foreclosed. By 1976 HUD had hired its own manager for the properties, but their future remained uncertain.

Except for some sprucing up of the median strip, one passing along Douglas Boulevard in 1976 would not guess that it was the site for a major experiment in upgrading of housing. Although hundreds of units were rehabilitated, tenants complain some of the work was defective from the start, and most of the buildings have been inadequately maintained. The agencies involved complain about poor housekeeping and vandalism by tenants and neighbors. The project demonstrates the complexity of the problem of providing adequate housing for poor people, and that it cannot necessarily be improved simply by massive funding, particularly if the administration is by inept governmental agencies and well meaning, but totally inexperienced community groups.

Real Estate Taxes and Subsidized Housing

The most prevalent single complaint by the developers of Section 221 (d) (3) and 236 housing in Chicago, was that real estate taxes were set at an unreasonably high level. The Cook County Assessor's Office originally assessed those projects in roughly the same way it assessed comparable privately funded real estate, in disregard of the lower rents charged by the subsidized project. It appears such practice was the result of habit, ignorance, and possibly the belief that no matter what happened, the federal government would bail out the projects.

Complaints about many aspects of the operation of the Assessor's Office caused the appointment of Richard A. Michael, a law school professor, to conduct hearings during the summer of 1972, and prepare recommendations concerning assessment classifications and practices. He recommended, in regard to Section 221 (d) (3) and 236 housing, that the practice of assessing such properties on the basis of their replacement cost be abandoned, and that they be assessed rather on the basis of income-producing experience, taking into account the low rent charged. Such charges had in fact been made earlier in 1972, affecting subsequent years.[21]

A comprehensive inquiry into the matter of real estate taxes and subsidized housing was completed for the Assessor's Office in 1974. It involved a two-part study financed by the Ford Foundation. The first report, by Appraisal Research Counselors, Ltd., like the Michael report, recommended that assessment of subsidized housing be based not on a cost approach, but rather on market value determined by the technique of capitalization of net income, arrived at by taking gross income and subtracting vacancy collection allowances, and fixed and operating expenses of the property.[22] The other report, written by a man who had been chief of real estate in the Cook County Assessor's Office from 1972 to 1973, played down the importance of real estate taxes in the problems of subsidized housing. It concluded that the investors in such projects have little interest in the welfare of the tenants, but rather are attracted by the tax shelter opportunities, and that even if there were a total elimination of real estate taxes on such properties, most of them would still have a negative cash flow after all expenses.[23]

Rent Supplements

Section 23 of the United States Housing Act was enacted in 1965, and although it involved a relatively nominal number of housing units, it heralded a change in policy away from developments specially built for the poor and toward getting the poor into the private housing market. Under the program the local housing agency, in Chicago CHA, leases privately owned apartments, and in turn subleases them to families with incomes low enough to qualify for public housing, at rents set at only 25 percent of the adjusted annual income of the family. The federal government pays the difference to CHA.

CHA began its participation in the Section 23 Leasing Program in 1966. By March 31, 1968, it had 785 apartments under leases, 722 for elderly tenants, and 63 for families. By 1975 there were 3,000 apartments under lease, 2,160 for the elderly, and 840 for families, housing a total of 5,600 people. The apartments were in 615 buildings, with 385 separate owners. The average income of the families in the leased units was $3,435, and for elderly households, $2,535. The average rent paid by CHA was $131 a month, and that paid by the tenants was $46.[24] Also part of the Housing Act of 1965 was the Rent Supplement Program which applies to the low-income tenants in 221 (d) (3) and 236 projects. They receive a greater subsidy than the other tenants and only have to pay one-quarter of their adjusted income for rent.

The Housing and Community Development Act of 1974 replaced the Section 23 program with a new Section 8 system of Housing Assistance Payments. This legislation represented a significant departure from the Housing Act of 1949, which had laid out the basic federal program of slum clearance and urban renewal. Under the 1974 act the categorical grant programs were eliminated in favor of a revenue-sharing type of block grants to the states and local governments. The basic thrust of the housing portions of the act work toward an economic mix in subsidized housing, and thus avoidance of geographical concentration of poor families, with their often present social problems. Although the statute provides that up to 100 percent of the units in any one development can be subsidized, HUD is instructed by the act to give preference to applications where only 20 percent or less of the units require Housing Assistance Payments.

The eligibility requirements for families to qualify for Housing Assistance Payments are considerably higher than under Section 23. Under Section 8 a family can qualify if its income is equal to up to 80 percent of the median income for the area. For example in 1976 in Chicago, a single person could have an income up to $7,950 and still qualify; a couple up to $10,200; and a six-person family up to $14,300. The top limit on rents to be paid the owner of the apartment vary from $165 for an efficiency apartment in a walk-up building, to $315 a month for a four-bedroom unit in an elevator building, including utilities. As with the earlier programs, most tenants pay 25 percent of their adjusted income, and the rest of the rent is made up by the federal government. The Section 8 program applies to existing housing and to new or rehabilitated housing. Although the subsidy is actually paid to the landlord and not to the tenants, the families who are selected to participate in the program are issued a

Certificate of Family Participation, and are free to go out and find their own housing. For new construction HUD will guarantee the subsidy on a specified number of units for twenty years, but as of the end of 1976 the program had not stimulated a significant number of units to be built nationally, and almost none in Chicago.

Because of the tremendous amount of paper work involved, many landlords are reluctant to participate in the Section 8 program. Also, an order in the *Gautreaux* case, which deals with CHA racial segregation policies, mandates that 60 percent of the nonelderly families in the program in Chicago must live in the basically white North and Southwest sections of the city, where blacks have trouble getting housing. The most important restraint of the Section 8 program is that it is implemented at such a low level that there are only a token number of slots available. Although there are an estimated 600,000 families eligible for the program in the Chicago area, as of the end of 1975 only 1,373 slots had been allocated.[25] CHA, which administers the program as to existing housing in the city, received only 571 slots, 343 for families, and 228 for elderly households. Under the *Gautreaux* decision, half of the slots are available to the public, a quarter to present CHA tenants, and a quarter to those on the CHA waiting list.

Although CHA began to implement the Section 8 program on March 1, 1976, actual leasing did not begin until July 1. CHA as of that date still had almost 3,000 apartments under the Section 23 program, all of which are expected to be eventually transferred to Section 8. There is speculation about an 800-unit net increase in the Section 8 program in Chicago in 1977.

Preliminary discussions took place in 1976 among CHA officials as to the possibility of some day using Section 8 to solve one of CHA's own problems. CHA by the mid-1970s was suffering a financial drain resulting from its 1,400 unit city-state projects. Although more humanely designed than the federally funded projects, the city-state developments are not eligible for annual federal subsidies or modernization funds, and their rents are not enough to cover operating expenses and proper maintenance. Some of them are in poor condition, showing the results of deferred maintenance. The strategy of CHA would be to issue a Section 8 certificate for each unit in those projects, so they could receive a full market rent. That level of rent would support a mortgage which CHA could obtain to raise the funds needed to renovate the projects. It remains to be seen whether federal officials will approve such a scheme.

10 Chicago Housing Authority: The Fourth Decade

During the period of 1967 through 1976 the Chicago Housing Authority constructed only a fraction of the number of family units as in the previous decade, in part because of disillusionment and challenge by many of those formerly supporting public housing. One notable exception to the otherwise gloomy picture from the standpoint of CHA was the housing for the elderly program, which met with considerable success. From the earliest years of its existence CHA had had a few elderly tenants in its various projects. By the late 1940s, with the increase in the elderly proportion of the population, CHA began to receive complaints from private and public welfare agencies about the problems the elderly had in securing adequate housing. In 1948 65 percent of the over-sixty-five-year-old population of Chicago had incomes of less than $1,000 per year, and almost half of those reported no income at all.

As of 1951 CHA had fewer than 1,200 tenants over sixty-five and they occupied only 5 percent of the total CHA units. There were 312 couples, 150 widows and widowers, and 400 elderly persons living in their children's apartments.[1] An early action was taken that year, with an eye toward helping the elderly, when the one-bedroom units at Archer Courts were designed in such a way that each could be converted into two units, with a shared bath and kitchen. This was never actually done, however. Also, an "Oldsters Club" was set up at the Ida B. Wells Homes, and a "Golden Agers" club at the Jane Addams Houses.

Lathrop Apartments

The first CHA building designed for elderly occupancy was the Lathrop Apartments at 2717 North Leavitt Street. It is on the western edge of the grounds of the Julia Lathrop Homes, overlooking the Chicago River. Designed by Loewenberg and Loewenberg, it is eight stories tall and contains ninety-two efficiency and one-bedroom apartments. Special features of the building include waist-high ovens, grab bars in the bathrooms, nonslip floor surfaces, bathtubs with low sides, doorways wide enough to accommodate wheel chairs, and a social room. The building was constructed in 1959 as a prototype project, before the federal legislation for senior citizen housing had been implemented. The $1,125,000 cost of the Lathrop Apartments was paid for out of CHA corporate funds left unspent from the city-state housing program.

Federally Financed Housing for the Elderly

The first of the federally financed elderly projects in Chicago was the Washington Park Apartments, at 4949 South Cottage Grove Avenue. Completed in 1961, it is typical of most of the CHA elderly projects that followed. It is a single building, on a business street, not part of a larger CHA development. The elderly program expanded quickly after 1961, when the federal Public Housing Administration approved CHA plans for eight buildings for the elderly, containing 1,009 apartments, at a cost of $15.6 million. All but two

Lathrop Apartments, the first Chicago Housing Authority building designed for occupancy by the elderly. It is located on the western edge of the grounds of the Julia C. Lathrop Homes and overlooks the Chicago River.—Courtesy of Chicago Housing Authority

of those projects are high-rise buildings, containing an average of about 160 units each. The financing is by the same technique as CHA's family housing; CHA issues forty-year bonds, the principal and interest of which are paid by the federal government.

Architecturally the most famous of the elderly projects are the two sixteen-story circular buildings of the Hilliard Center, at Cermak Road and State Street constructed in 1966. A year earlier CHA had completed renovation of the Surf Hotel, on the southwest corner of Surf Street and Pine Grove Avenue, into 173 apartments. Renamed the Britton I. Budd Apartments, it was the first CHA experiment in acquiring and rehabilitating an existing building for elderly housing. In 1964 CHA had purchased the Hayes Hotel, at 64th and University, for just under $200,000. The plan was to demolish the original section, built in 1893 for the Columbian Exposition, and the section built in 1915, but to rehabilitate the fireproof section constructed in 1922 into 100 apartments for elderly tenants. The projected rehabilitation cost was $400,000, which would have meant a total cost for acquisition and rehabilitation of only $6,000 per unit. The plan did not work out, however, when the cost figures came in considerably above the initial estimates. CHA decided to demolish the entire hotel building and replaced it with a 165-unit building for the elderly, called the Kenneth Campbell Apartments.

Two additional rehabilitation buildings for the elderly did work out, however, both completed in 1966. One involved the seven-story apartment hotel at 5040 North Kenmore Avenue, which was purchased and rehabilitated into 136 apartments for $1.1 million, or just over $8,000 per unit. This was not only much less than the cost of new construction but saved the time-lag of new construction. The other rehabilitation project was the 1039 West Hollywood Avenue Apartments, comprising 117 units at a total development cost of $1.4 million.

Unlike CHA family housing, CHA buildings for the elderly were constructed in all parts of the city, much of it on the North Side. Three projects were located on Sheridan Road alone, at 4645, 4945, and 6400 North Sheridan. Because of the locations and designs of the projects, and the fact that poverty is most prevalent in the older population, the elderly projects have not suffered the stigma attached to the family projects, and have always had a substantial white occupancy. At the end of 1965, for example, there were 1,273 white elderly tenants, and 1,139 nonwhite ones.[2] This does not mean that each elderly project was well integrated. In fact, most of them were predominantly white, or black, depending on the loca-

tion. In 1965 CHA set the limit of total assets elderly tenants could
have and still qualify for housing at $15,000, but that rule was re-
scinded in 1975. Income limits for elderly tenants remained in force,
however, and stood in 1976 at $3,600 for one person and $4,200 and
$5,500 respectively for continued occupancy.

The year the greatest number of CHA elderly units were built was
1967, when six projects opened containing over 1,100 units. The
most interesting of them, and by far the smallest, was the 22-unit
Hyde Park Apartments. They comprise two groups of one-story row
houses, fourteen along 55th Street from Kimbark to Woodlawn
avenues, and eight on the southwest corner of 53rd and Woodlawn.
The land for the houses was obtained from the Hyde Park–Kenwood
Urban Renewal Project, as part of the settlement of the controversy
concerning inclusion of public housing in the overall plan. Each unit
has a living room, kitchen, bedroom, and bath, and is independent of
the others, even with its own tiny garden. Architecturally the buildings, designed by Wong and Hannaford, leave much to be desired.
The scale is so low that they are sometimes mistaken for garages. Of
greater concern, all of the windows face the rear gardens with none
whatsoever in the front. They are in this respect similar to the
well-known Atrium Houses that Y. C. Wong designed six years earlier a few blocks away in Madison Park. It is one thing for middle-

*Hyde Park Apartments. Built in 1967, this twenty-two-unit project for
the elderly consists of two groups of one-story row houses with all of the
windows facing the rear.—Courtesy of Chicago Housing Authority*

class families to build houses facing interior courtyards, but quite another for a public agency to build them for elderly residents, and thus cut them off from any chance of vicarious participation in the street life adjacent to their homes, and thereby reinforce the isolation so often associated with old age.

In late 1976 construction was underway on a 168-unit building at Lake and Parkside, on the Far West Side. It was the last planned CHA building for senior citizens because of the phase-out in federal financing for such projects. The seventeen-year CHA program for the construction of elderly housing, which totaled forty-six developments with 9,607 units, was thus brought to an end. Chicago's was the largest senior citizen housing program in the country on a per capita basis. There are twice as many elderly units per 100,000 population in Chicago as in New York City, which although it has a population more than twice that of Chicago, has only 2,000 more federally funded public housing elderly units.[3] There is a possibility of a revival of federal financing for the elderly program, because the housing bill signed by President Ford on August 4, 1976, makes provision for it. It remains to be seen, however, how it may be implemented by HUD.

The Summit Agreement

By 1966 opposition was mounting to the massive high-rise CHA projects. That year Dr. Martin Luther King, Jr., and his Southern Christian Leadership Conference (SCLC) set up an organization in Chicago called the Chicago Freedom Movement, which was aimed primarily at fighting racial discrimination in housing. During the summer of the "Chicago Campaign," Dr. King led massive marches through various parts of the city, including the Marquette Park area of the Southwest Side. In an effort to stop the marches Mayor Daley agreed to meet with Dr. King, together with various other civic and governmental officials. The sessions were convened by the Chicago Conference on Religion and Race, and soon were being called the "Summit Meeting."

After a week of sessions a "Summit Agreement" was entered into on August 26, 1966, under which the Chicago Freedom Movement agreed to a cessation of neighborhood housing demonstrations, and the governmental and civic groups agreed to take certain steps to promote open housing. One such step was the creation of the Leadership Council for Metropolitan Open Communities, a nonprofit organization which seeks to enforce open housing legislation and promote racial integration in the city and suburbs. The Summit

Agreement also contained a provision under which the Chicago Housing Authority agreed to promote fair housing and recognized "that heavy concentrations of public housing should not again be built in the City of Chicago." CHA agreed further, in regard to its family projects, that: "In the future, it will seek scattered sites for public housing and will limit the height of new public housing structures in high density areas to eight stories, with housing for families with children limited to the first two stories. Whenever possible, smaller units will be built."[4]

The United States Housing Act of 1968 mandated that no new family public housing located above the third floor was to be approved. Although the Summit Agreement and the 1968 act stopped construction of new high-rise projects not then approved, they did nothing specific to promote construction of new public housing outside the black ghettos. In 1968 housing discrimination was outlawed by Title VIII of the Civil Rights Act of 1968, and by the United States Supreme Court in the case of *Jones v. Alfred M. Mayer Co.*, where it was held that an 1866 Reconstruction era civil rights act prohibited racial discrimination in the sale or rental of housing. The task of restraining CHA's discriminatory practices had, in 1968, already been in progress for more than two years.

Gautreaux v. Chicago Housing Authority

In the fall of 1965 the Illinois Division of the American Civil Liberties Union set up a Civil Rights Committee, and it was decided by that committee that public housing site selection in Chicago was a problem that warranted attention. Alexander Polikoff, then a partner in a large law firm and later the executive director of Business and Professional People for the Public Interest (BPI), agreed to head up a team of lawyers to pursue litigation seeking to change CHA practices. On August 9, 1966, a class action suit was filed in federal court against CHA and its then executive director, Alvin E. Rose, on behalf of Dorothy Gautreaux, three other black CHA tenants, and two black CHA applicants. The complaint in the case alleged that since 1950 substantially all of the sites selected for CHA family housing projects were "in Negro neighborhoods and within the areas known as the Negro Ghetto because the Authority has deliberately chosen sites for such projects which would avoid the placement of Negro families in white neighborhoods."[5]

The complaint alleged further that the effect of the CHA policies was governmental action to deprive the plaintiffs and other black CHA tenants and applicants of the right to reside in public housing outside the black ghetto, in violation of the due process and equal protection guarantees of the Fourteenth Amendment to the United States Constitution, and Section 601 of Title VI of the Civil Rights Act of 1964. Title VI provides that programs receiving federal financial assistance may not discriminate on the basis of race, color, or national origin. The lawsuit and the Summit Agreement, both of which materialized in August of 1966, symbolized an interesting turn of events. In the early years of public housing its strongest advocates had been social reformers. They were in the forefront of those urging the construction of massive projects to house the poor. By 1966, however, the defenders of large-scale public housing projects were the old-line conservative political forces, and the social reformers had become the most severe critics of such housing.

A bombshell in the *Gautreaux* case occurred during a deposition of C. E. Humphrey, a longtime CHA employee, and later its executive director from 1968 to 1973. He admitted the so-called Kean-Murphy deal that was made in 1955 between Gen. William Kean, then CHA's executive director, and Alderman Murphy, chairman of the City Council's Housing and Planning Committee. The secret agreement provided for an aldermanic veto system under which CHA would not submit a proposed site to the City Council until it had informally been approved by the alderman in whose ward the site was located.[6] Although it was obvious to any observer that CHA was constructing virtually no family housing in white communities, the Humphrey deposition was the first public admission of the actual mechanism used by CHA in the site-selection process.

On February 10, 1969, Judge Richard B. Austin entered his initial Memorandum Opinion in the case, in which he denied CHA's motion for a summary judgment, and found that CHA had practiced both racially discriminatory tenant assignment and site selection. The judge found that CHA imposed a racial quota in four predominantly white projects, Trumball Park, Lathrop, Lawndale Gardens, and Bridgeport. He found further that CHA family housing was 99 percent occupied by blacks, and that 99.5 percent of its units were in black or racially changing neighborhoods. The court directed that the parties formulate a comprehensive plan to remedy the situation.

The parties were not able to agree on such a plan, so on July 1, 1969, Judge Austin handed down his Judgment Order, which essentially followed the pattern suggested by the plaintiffs. It remained the basic order in the case. The order designates what is called the "Limited Public Housing Area," as those census tracts with 30 percent or more nonwhite population, including a one mile buffer from the perimeter of such census tracts. The "General Public Housing Area" is the remainder of the city, basically the North, Northwest, and the Southwest sides. It was ordered that CHA not build any family housing in the Limited Public Housing Area until it had constructed 700 units in the General Public Housing Area, and thereafter only on a quota basis, with three units in the General Public Housing Area for each unit in the Limited Public Housing Area. No single housing project may, under the order, contain units designed for more than 120 persons, except in special cases when the limit can go to 240. No new public housing can be built that would aggregate more than 15 percent of the total housing units in its census tract. Finally, no new units for families with children can be located above the third floor.

The order covered the CHA leasing program, except for a small number of units then being leased in the Limited Public Housing Area. It specifically exempted, however, 1,458 units in several proposed CHA projects in the Limited Public Housing Area, the sites for which had already been selected, and federal approval granted. It was further ordered that CHA eliminate its discriminatory tenant assignment practices, except that the order specified that 50 percent of all residential units be made available to neighborhood residents, the intent being that the new housing in white areas would be at least half-white, which would not be the case if it were filled exclusively from the CHA waiting list, which was predominantly black.

The judge also ordered CHA to come up with a special plan to insure that the four white projects would not eventually become all-black, as the other CHA family housing had done. Pursuant to that order CHA set up a Tenant Assignment Plan for those projects which limited black occupancy to 15 percent, and total minority occupancy to 25 percent. It is ironic that a suit by black CHA tenants and applicants, because it stopped construction of new CHA family housing in black areas and set up neighborhood resident quotas for the housing that was later to be built, actually had the effect of making family public housing in Chicago more attractive to whites, and thus providing less public housing to black families than would have otherwise been the case. It is doubly ironic that the original complaint in the case was based, in part, on the de facto CHA quotas in the four so-called white projects, but the litigation resulted in the court-approved imposition by law of just such quotas in those projects.

On September 15, 1969, Judge Austin exempted 601 CHA Rent Supplement Program units in the Limited Public Housing Area, that were located in developments with Section 221 (d) (3) and 236 mortgages. The rationale of the exemption was to permit CHA to carry out commitments made to the developers and city agencies prior to the July 1, 1969, order. During the year after that order CHA did little toward the construction of scattered-site low-rise housing in white neighborhoods, except that in December 1969 it hired Community Programs, Incorporated, to work toward community acceptance of public housing, and to recruit whites to the CHA waiting list.

Because of CHA's foot-dragging, Judge Austin on July 20, 1970, entered his second major order in the case. It provided that within a month CHA was to refer sites for 1,500 family units to the Chicago Plan Commission for their approval, and that within two months the sites be referred to the City Council. CHA appealed the July 20 order, and the United States Court of Appeals for the Seventh Circuit affirmed it. The United States Supreme Court denied CHA's Petition for Certiorari, and thus declined to hear the case. On March 5, 1971, CHA finally submitted the proposed sites for the 1,500 units to the City Council, and made them public. The sites were for single-family units, two- and three-flat walk-up buildings.

In 1971 the plaintiffs sought to have $26 million in Model Cities funds withheld from Chicago, because the City Council was not proceeding to approve the sites that had been submitted to it, and Judge Austin did in fact enjoin payment of the money. The Court of Appeals for the Seventh Circuit, however, in an opinion handed down March 8, 1972, reversed the action, holding that there had been no finding by the trial court that the Model Cities programs, which involved much more than just housing programs, had been administered discriminatorily. In February 1972, the plaintiffs filed a supplemental complaint, naming the City of Chicago, all fifty of its aldermen, and Mayor Daley as defendants in the case. This was done to force the City Council to approve the sites. As of June 1971 the council had approved sites sufficient to accommodate fewer than 200 units. Judge Austin on April 10, 1972, in an effort to get around the City Council, ordered that the provision of the Illinois Revised Statutes that requires CHA to get City Council approval of the sites it purchases "shall not be applicable to CHA's Actions." On May 18, 1973, the Court of Appeals affirmed that order, saying that the District Court had the power to suspend the operation of state statutes that hinder federal constitutional guarantees.

When the original suit was filed against CHA, a companion case was filed against the federal Department of Housing and Urban

Development. Judge Austin initially stayed proceedings in that case pending resolution of the CHA suit. On September 1, 1970, however, he dismissed the complaint against HUD. In an opinion handed down a year later the Court of Appeals reversed his decision, and held that the secretary of HUD, in funding CHA projects, had violated the Due Process Clause of the Fifth Amendment, and Section 601 of the Civil Rights Act. On December 23, 1971, pursuant to the opinion of the Court of Appeals, Judge Austin issued an order that the plaintiffs and HUD formulate a comprehensive plan to remedy the past effects of the unconstitutional public housing site selection in Chicago.

The two cases were then consolidated, but an order was entered on September 11, 1973, under which Judge Austin denied plaintiff's motion for a metropolitan plan of relief, that would include the suburbs as well as the city. The Court of Appeals for the Seventh Circuit reversed his decision in August 1974, saying that relief restricted to the City of Chicago was "not only too little but also much too late in the proceedings." The court went on to say "anyone reading the various opinions of the District Court and of this Court quickly discovers a callousness on the part of the appellees [CHA and HUD] towards the rights of the black, underprivileged citizens of Chicago that is beyond comprehension."

On April 20, 1976, the United States Supreme Court, in what is considered a landmark decision, affirmed 8 justices to 0, the decision of the Court of Appeals.[7] It was held that metropolitan relief is proper in the case, although the matter of how the housing would be built or leased was left to the District Court. The decision was given considerable space in the Chicago newspapers, complete with speculation concerning the possibility of large-scale construction of public housing in the suburbs. Such an eventuality seems unlikely, however, not only because of the lack of federal funds for such projects, but because of the ability of suburbs to zone out such projects with minimum lot sizes and other devices.

One step has been taken, pursuant to the *Gautreaux* litigation, toward a metropolitan solution to the problem raised in the case. On July 7, 1976, HUD and Alexander Polikoff announced a plan to place 400 families, currently living in CHA housing or on the CHA waiting list, in existing private Chicago and suburban apartments, throughout the six-county metropolitan area. The one-year plan called for placing 100 of the families in Chicago, 100 to 150 in suburban Cook County, and 25 to 40 families in each of the other five counties, with rents subsidized by the federal government. The program, to be administered by the Leadership Council for Metropolitan Open Communities, was agreed to by the parties to the litigation to get information on how to carry out a metropolitan housing plan.

The *Gautreaux* case up to 1976 was in many ways an exercise in frustration. To many, including the leaders of some black community organizations who spoke out against it, the fact that the case stopped construction of all but a few exempted public housing projects in the inner city, accelerated the decline of those areas. It is not clear, however, how much public housing would in fact have been built in the absence of the case, in light of the federally subsidized housing moratorium imposed by President Nixon on January 5, 1973. It is clear that the *Gautreaux* case consumed a tremendous amount of effort during the ten-year period, and cost untold amounts in the time of lawyers, judges, and other governmental personnel. The major pleadings in the case fill thirteen large volumes. Mrs. Gautreaux herself never lived to see the results of the case that bears her name; she died a few years before the Supreme Court decision. The case demonstrates the inherent difficulty in fashioning relief, in a situation that involves the funding and execution of complex social programs by several levels of government, especially in an area that much of the population considers controversial, such as the promotion of racially and economically integrated housing.

Gautreaux Exempted Projects

The July 1, 1969, order of Judge Austin exempting 1,458 units of proposed CHA housing involved a dozen separate projects. The sites for them had been selected in 1965 and 1966 and were all in the inner-city Limited Public Housing Area. Without the exemption they could not have been built. The first of the projects, and the most modest, is known by its location, 75th and Eggleston. It was built in 1968 and consists of a single row of six houses, two stories tall, on high basements. They are constructed of red brick, and have quasi-mansard roofs. Because they blend in with the surrounding area they are not identifiable as public housing, and thus are similar to the "new look" housing CHA was later to construct to comply with the *Gautreaux* decision.

The other exempted developments are made up of several housing types. The most diversified is the 43rd and Princeton project, designed by Keck and Keck. Opened in 1969, on a thirteen-acre site actually centering on 42nd and Princeton, it consists of ninety-seven units, each two and three bedrooms, in twenty-three bungalows, nineteen pairs of duplex houses, and five groups of row houses. The variety of housing types, the quality of their design, and the fact that the buildings are low-rise, make it one of the best single-site developments CHA has constructed. The buildings were designed for the possibility of sale to residents at some future date. A high-rise building for the elderly is also located on the site.

Four exempted projects were completed by CHA in 1969 and 1970, all composed of a combination of three-story, and mid-rise seven- or nine-story buildings, and all in the same architectural style, by the same architect, James Economou. The first is again known by its location, Adams and Wood. It consists of 109 units in a seven-story building, and two three-story ones. The buildings are all clad in dark red or brown brick. The taller one is very simple, in fact stark in appearance. The three-story ones have outdoor galleries,

The 75th and Eggleston project, built by the Chicago Housing Authority in 1968, consists of a single row of six houses. Constructed of red brick with quasi-mansard roofs, they blend in with the surrounding structures and are not identifiable as public housing.—Courtesy of Chicago Housing Authority

facing toward the center of the project, giving them something of the appearance of a motel.

The largest of the group is the 450-unit Madden Park Homes, at Pershing Road and Ellis Avenue. It holds the dubious distinction of being the last really large family project constructed by CHA. It has three buildings of nine stories each, and seven of the three-story ones. Just two blocks south of the Madden Park Homes is the third project of the group: 41st and Cottage Grove. It consists of 151 units in one of the nine-story buildings, and three of the three-story ones. The project completes the massive CHA concentration in the area which in addition to several buildings for the elderly and scattered-site family projects, includes the Ida B. Wells Homes and Extension, Olander Homes and Extension, Lake Michigan Homes, Clarence Darrow Homes, and Madden Park Homes. They total more than 5,000 units, and have almost 20,000 residents. The final project of the four designed by Economou is on the West Side, at 12th Place and Washtenaw adjacent to Ogden Courts. It has five of the three-story buildings, with 90 units, and a nine-story one with 97 units.

The 43rd and Princeton project. This diversified development opened in 1969 and contains twenty-three bungalows, nineteen pairs of duplex houses, and five groups of row houses. The variety of housing types and the fact that they are low-rise make this one of the best single-site projects constructed by the Chicago Housing Authority.—Courtesy of Chicago Housing Authority

The next group of five exempted projects are again of similar architecture. One gets the impression that by this time CHA was tired
of individual designs for each project, and even tired of selecting
names for the projects, preferring to identify them merely by location. The first of the group, with eighteen units, is called Lincoln
Park and located on sites obtained from the Lincoln Park Urban
Renewal Project, at 420 to 430 West North Avenue, and 1911 North
Sedgwick Street. The three story buildings resemble the earlier scattered sites CHA buildings on the South Side, designed by the same
architects, Schiller and Frank. The same design was used for the
Lawndale Area Buildings, also built in 1969. They consist of 186
units on eighteen scattered sites. Three similar groups, designed by
CHA's own architectural staff, were completed in 1974. The first
has seventy-two units in three buildings at Congress Parkway and
Millard Avenue, and at Franklin Boulevard and Albany Avenue. The
second has thirty units on three nearby South Side sites at 550 East
41st Street, 4120 South St. Lawrence Avenue, and 4140 South
Langley Avenue. The third consists of sixteen units in two buildings

*Madden Park Homes, built in 1970, was the last really large family project
constructed by the Chicago Housing Authority. It has three buildings of
nine stories each, and seven of three stories.—Courtesy of Chicago Housing
Authority*

at 525 and 537 West 56th Place which differ from the rest in that they are only two stories tall.

The remaining exempted project was the Lawndale Area Rehabilitation. Carried out in 1970 and 1971 it was the only renovation CHA has done of family housing, except the work it did in connection with CDA. The project involved the rehabilitation of 118 units in three old three-story buildings, at 1400 South Albany Avenue, 1332 South Harding Avenue, and 3718–28 West Douglass Boulevard. The total development cost of the work was $2,462,000 or $20,865 per unit. CHA personnel were generally not happy with the results. They felt that the constraints of working with old buildings prevented them from creating the exact types of units they wanted, and they expected the buildings would be more costly to maintain than new ones.

Congress and Millard project, completed in 1974, has seventy-two units in three buildings.—Photograph by Devereux Bowly, Jr.

New Look Housing

The first CHA housing that complied with the requirements of the *Gautreaux* case was the six-unit building at 1052–54 West Byron Street. Built in 1970, it is indistinguishable from other contemporary small apartment buildings often found on the outskirts of Chicago and in the suburbs. The building was actually constructed by CDA, in cooperation with a Japanese-American community organization, but purchased by CHA when CDA got into its financial difficulties. The first housing specifically built to comply with the

Lawndale Area Rehabilitation building at 3718–28 West Douglas Boulevard. This was one of three old three-story buildings renovated by the Chicago Housing Authority in 1970 and 1971. The cost per unit was $20,865.—Photograph by Devereux Bowly, Jr.

Gautreaux decision is a sixty-three-unit group of twenty-one
three-flat apartment buildings, on eleven scattered sites in the Uptown, Lake View, and West Town communities of the North Side.
Construction began on the buildings, which are identical to one
another, in September 1974. Like the Byron Street building they are
of a standard design and not identifiable as public housing. In ac-
cordance with the court edict, half of the tenants are from the surrounding neighborhood. In addition, all of them were given special
screening to find "model tenants."[8]

On December 10, 1975, CHA submitted a list of 420 possible sites
for additional housing to the federal district court. It was basically a
list of vacant lots north of North Avenue and in the Southwest and
Far South areas of the city. There was no guarantee that many of the
sites might not turn out to be too expensive, or would fail to meet
HUD environmental standards. In some areas mere publication of
the list started neighborhood groups working to get the sites privately developed, so that they would not be available to CHA. The
second major group of CHA housing to comply with the *Gautreaux*
decision was again located in the Uptown and Lake View neighborhoods. CHA avoided in its site selections the Southwest and

*New Look Chicago Housing Authority housing at 5325 North Paulina
Street.—Photograph by Devereux Bowly, Jr.*

Northwest sides of the city, where opposition to public housing was the strongest. This housing consists of six six-flat buildings, two three-flats, two two-flats, and five single-family houses. The total is thus fifty-one units, in fifteen buildings, on twelve sites. A $1.4 million contract for construction of the buildings was awarded in June 1976.

The final phase of the post-*Gautreaux* housing, in the planning stage in 1976, calls for 153 units. It will round out 267 units approved before the Nixon moratorium of January 1973. As of August 1, 1976, options had been obtained on land for one-quarter of the phase three units, but no sites actually acquired. It is clear CHA has not moved quickly to build housing in complaince with the *Gautreaux* decision, and after the initial 267 units are completed, it is not certain how much additional housing CHA will construct. Not only will the availability of federal funding be determinative, but the effect of the April 20, 1976, United States Supreme Court decision, permitting a metropolitan solution to the problem of housing low-income families, is difficult to predict.

Existing CHA Family Housing

By 1970 it was evident CHA was going to have serious problems during the coming decade, not only because of the *Gautreaux* litigation, but because of a partial breakdown in major areas of CHA activity. In that year two studies were published relating to different aspects of CHA housing. One of them involved a survey by the Welfare Council of Metropolitan Chicago of social welfare and health services to CHA residents.[9] It was commissioned by CHA, which contributed $50,000 for it out of funds obtained from HUD. CHA had long had the policy of providing space in its projects for public and private agencies engaged in health, social services, and recreation programs but not of contributing to the operating expenses of such programs.

The major conclusion of the Welfare Council study was that of the forty-four public and voluntary agencies providing services to CHA residents, such as the Chicago Board of Health or the settlement houses, most came in contact on a regular basis with only a small number of the residents. The offices of the Cook County Department of Public Aid served the largest number, 39 percent, and the Chicago Park District about 14 percent during a typical month. The other agencies averaged considerably less, many serving only 1 or 2 percent of the residents of the local project. The results of the study tend to discredit the view that providing social services in public housing projects has a major effect on the residents. The fact is the agencies fail to even come in contact with the great majority of the residents.

The other study, financed by HUD and the Chicago Model Cities program, sought to determine how public housing can be utilized to improve the quality of life for its residents.[10] Interviews were conducted with 1,200 CHA families, in twelve projects, and family characteristics, life histories, and problem variables drawn from CHA records were considered. Over half of the adults sampled were born in the rural South, and only 20 percent were born in Chicago. Nearly one-fourth had lived in CHA projects more than ten years, and 63 percent more than five years. It was found that once a family is admitted to public housing it is not likely to leave voluntarily, and there was a growing propensity, involving about 25 percent of the younger families, for the heads of new CHA families to have grown up in CHA buildings themselves.

The study also found, not surprisingly, that large CHA families have more problems than smaller ones. The most striking findings involved crime rates of CHA residents. Among those who live in buildings under five stories, only 4.1 percent of the residents had CHA records of criminal or antisocial behavior, whereas 28.4 percent of those in buildings over five stories had such records. It was concluded that some, although by no means all, of the differences can be attributed to the fact that large families are concentrated in the high-rises. It is not clear for what specific purpose CHA commissioned the two studies, or what policy decisions, if any, were later based upon their findings. These were used, presumably, as input for general long-range CHA planning, to the extent that it exists.

Modernization Program

In 1968 CHA started a massive modernization program paid for by funds obtained from the sale of bonds to be paid off by HUD. The purpose of the program was to improve physical conditions in the various projects by work ranging from the replacement of kitchen stoves, refrigerators, sinks, and cabinets, to upgrading apartment electrical service, adding closet doors and bathroom tile where the original construction omitted them. There were major heating plant renovations, and the installation of large garbage compactors for twenty-three projects, to replace incinerators. Also included was the construction of thirteen community and day care centers at a cost of $8.4 million. Through 1971 over $10 million had been expended under the modernization program. At the end of that year CHA personnel numbered 1,790, of which 523 were administrative employees and 1,267 were maintenance workers. The maintenance staff was 344 smaller than a year earlier, several hundred craft workers having been laid off due to a major budgetary cutback. By July 31, 1976, the total spent or obligated under the modernization program stood at $50.5 million, out of about $60 million that had been approved by HUD. In addition, CHA had special programs at Cabrini-Green and Robert Taylor Homes.

In the summer of 1970 two Chicago policemen assigned to a "Walk-and-Talk" patrol were murdered by a sniper at Cabrini-Green. This and other crimes caused, of course, considerable CHA and public concern, and led to the creation of a special security program there. The plan for the program was published in 1972, its goal being a prototype to demonstrate that high-rise public housing can be made significantly safer. The plan gives some indication of the magnitude of the crime problem at Cabrini-Green by citing statistics for the period of May 25, 1972, through December 6, 1972. The homicide rate at Cabrini-Green was 6 times higher than the rate for the city as a whole, 5 times greater for rape, 3.3 times greater for robbery, and 4.5 for aggravated assault.[11] These figures may be lower than the reality of the situation, if one considers the widespread speculation that a greater proportion of crime goes unreported in public housing than in the community as a whole.

The basic change called for in the plan was the remodeling of the ground floors of four of the twenty-three high-rise buildings at Cabrini-Green. The work included redesigning the lobbies and installing security stations to be staffed twenty-four hours a day. They are to be equipped with electronic monitoring devices including fourteen television cameras, as well as communication devices in the elevators, and sensors on fire exit and office doors. The plan also calls for converting 4,200 feet of space on the ground floor of two of the buildings from apartments to convenience stores for the tenants. One of the buildings involved, at 1150–60 North Sedgwick, in 1970 had a closed-circuit television system installed with a camera in each of the four elevators, monitored by CHA guards. The telephone communication system in the building permits security personnel to communicate with each apartment and get permission from residents before visitors are admitted.

The budget for work on the four buildings, nearing completion in late 1976, was set at $2.6 million, including increased personnel costs for the first year. The ultimate budget, for such facilities in all the high-rise buildings was set in the report a $6.7 million, including $1.56 million for one-year extra staffing costs. Later estimates, however, have set the cost of enclosing lobbies in the other nineteen Cabrini-Green buildings at $10 million, and all the modernization and security work proposed for Cabrini-Green would add up to $21 million.[12]

In early 1976 CHA submitted to HUD a proposal for a special $1.2 million Target Projects Program (TPP) for the Robert Taylor Homes. Under it management offices, staffed by resident employees, would be set up in each of the twenty-eight Taylor buildings. One of the main goals of the special programs at Cabrini-Green and Taylor Homes was to stem the tide toward large-scale vacancies in those projects. At the end of 1974 Taylor had 732 vacant apartments and Cabrini-Green 516. Taylor reached its all-time-high vacancy rate, for the week ending October 24, 1975, when 1,026 units, or just under one-quarter of the total apartments in the project, were unoccupied.

In the following months a dramatic drop occurred, to 880 Taylor vacancies as of December 26, 1975, and only 478 as of August 6, 1976. Similarly, Cabrini-Green fell to 467 vacancies as of the end of 1975, when the top four floors of three nineteen-story buildings were actually closed off, and to 330 as of August 1976.[13] The vacancies were present despite the fact that at the end of 1975 CHA had about 10,000 families on its waiting list, and waits of five years or more for certain of the low-rise projects. There was no wait, of course, for apartments at Taylor or Cabrini-Green, and those projects were used by the Tenant Relocation Bureau of the city's Department of Urban Renewal to relocate families displaced by emergencies such as fires.

The improved occupancy rate at Robert Taylor Homes cannot be attributed to special programs there, because it occurred before they were implemented. It seems to be due, rather, to the shortage of housing for very poor families, caused by the abandonment and demolition of thousands of slum buildings, and the fact that CHA rents average only about $50 per month. At Cabrini-Green the figures are not quite as dramatic, but CHA officials say light can be seen at the end of the tunnel. They contend that from April 1975 to July 1976 vandalism costs were reduced 26 percent, incoming tenants outnumber those leaving by a two-to-one ratio, and that a greater proportion of the residents were employed.[14] In 1976 a $75,000 study was commissioned by CHA to examine the feasibility of converting two high-rise buildings at the Cabrini Extension from family to elderly housing. If this is carried out, relocation of families from those buildings would eliminate vacancies at the project.

With the reduction in the vacancy rates at Taylor and Cabrini-Green, CHA prevailed, at least in the short run, over the observers who predicted those projects would go the same route as the infamous Pruitt-Igoe development in St. Louis. Those two public housing projects were built in 1954 and 1955, at a cost of $36 million, on adjacent sites totalling 57.5 acres. They contained thirty-three eleven-story buildings, 2,700 units, and had 10,000 residents. Pruitt-Igoe suffered from tremendous crime, drug, and vandalism problems. In 1971 a massive rent strike occurred. The next year a study was undertaken to see if the projects could be rebuilt and saved. The housing authority dramatically demolished three of the buildings in 1972, by the use of dynamite, but the plan to retain thirteen of them, reduced to a height of three or four stories was scrapped, and the entire remainder of the project was leveled in 1976.

Although the vacancy rates for Cabrini-Green and Taylor Homes have fallen, the rate for CHA units as a whole has risen somewhat. At the end of 1965 there was virtually no CHA vacancy rate. Of the 307 unoccupied apartments, 234 were in buildings just completed but not fully occupied, and 73 units were in the process of being redecorated for new tenants.[15] By the end of 1972 CHA had an overall vacancy rate of 2.8 percent of the 41,191 apartments under its control. It had at that time a waiting list of 22,696, of which 12,119 were for senior-citizen apartments.[16] By the end of 1974 the overall vacancy rate had jumped to 4.8 percent; 6.1 percent in the family housing buildings, and 0.2 percent in the elderly housing.[17] At the end of 1975 the figures stood at 4.9 percent overall, 6.3 percent in the family housing, and 0.2 percent in the elderly units.[18]

It is not possible to predict with certainty what will happen to the existing projects of the CHA family-housing program in the late 1970s and beyond. If federal operating subsidies continue to keep the rents at an extremely low level, if modernization funds continue, and the option remains open to convert excess family units to elderly housing, it seems likely the system can be sustained in essentially its present form for the foreseeable future.

11 The Illinois Housing Development Authority

In 1965 the Illinois Legislative Commission on Low Income Housing was appointed. Under the chairmanship of State Representative Robert E. Mann, the commission issued its report in 1967 recommending legislation giving the State Housing Board the power to issue bonds for the purpose of providing mortgages and "seed money" to nonprofit and limited-dividend corporations to construct or rehabilitate housing for low- and moderate-income families.[1] The first such state housing finance agency was established in New York in 1960, with New Jersey, Massachusetts, and Michigan following in 1966. By 1975 thirty states had them.[2] The economic impetus for the establishment of such agencies lay in the provision of federal law regarding the tax exempt status of bonds issued by states and their instrumentalities. The interest paid on such bonds is exempt from federal income tax. They are thus attractive to investors, particularly those in the higher tax brackets, who will purchase the bonds even though they carry lower rates of interest than taxable securities. Mortgages financed by such bonds are typically 2 percent below the market rate of interest for conventional mortgages, and about one-half of one percent below HUD insured loan rates.[3]

Pursuant to the recommendations of the Mann Commission, legislation was enacted in 1967 establishing the Illinois Housing Development Authority (IHDA),[4] the fifth such state housing finance agency in the United States. Under the legislation the major function of the agency is to make construction loans and long-term mortgages to nonprofit and limited-profit entities for construction or rehabilitation of rental, cooperative, or condominium housing for persons of low or moderate income. Under the act limited-profit entities may distribute annually as profit, a maximum of 6 percent of their equity in a development. Equity is defined as the total development cost, less the amount of the mortgage loan. IHDA mortgages are for a period of forty years, and the notes and bonds issued to finance them are obligations of the agency itself, not a debt of the State of Illinois.

The act also empowers IHDA to finance, by grants or loans, research and demonstration projects in techniques for increasing the quality and supply of low- and moderate-income housing. The agency may also make grants to lower the rents of certain housing units. IHDA can make loans to lending institutions which in turn loan the money out in mortgages to achieve specified objectives. Finally, IHDA can provide nonprofit and limited-profit housing groups with advisory, consultative, technical, training, and educational services in the production and management of housing. In 1968 the state housing finance agencies, including IHDA, received a further boost from federal legislation. Section 236 of the 1968 Housing Act provided for subsidies to the developers of housing with state housing finance agency mortgages. Pursuant to the legislation, HUD set aside special funds for this purpose. The HUD Section 236 interest reduction subsidy can be applied to some or all of the units in a project. For the units receiving the subsidy the developer pays an interest rate of only 1 percent, and HUD pays the difference between the 1 percent and the actual interest rate. The developer is required to pass along the savings to the tenant in the form of lower rent. The developments are also eligible to receive federal rent supplement funds that directly subsidize the rents of specified units reducing them to a level where they can be rented by low-income families.

The rule of thumb is that IHDA's lower finance costs generate average rent savings of about $50 per unit, per month, as compared to similar projects financed by conventional mortgages. With Section 236 interest-reduction subsidies, rents can be up to $140 per month lower. The federal Tax Reform Act of 1969 provided still additional incentives for the development of such projects. These included: 1) continuation of the highly accelerated double declining balance method of depreciation for new housing; 2) establishment of a new five-year write-off for rehabilitation of buildings for occupancy by low-income tenants; and 3) limitations on the amount of tax on the sale of Section 236 developments.[5]

In April 1972 IHDA published a study entitled *Illinois Housing Needs 1970–1980*, which concluded that during that decade Illinois must construct or rehabilitate 1,132,000 units to house adequately the state's population. Most of the units would be created by the private market, but the report pointed out that during 1970, 27 percent of all new housing construction in Illinois was assisted by various federal and state subsidy programs. The study found that as of that year 408,000 households, or 11.4 percent of the total in Illinois, had incomes low enough to qualify for entry into public hous-

ing, and were in need of financial assistance in order to rent aver-
age-quality standard housing. It predicted the number would increase to 452,000 by 1980.[6]

Harper Square

The first project financed by IHDA in Chicago, and the largest it
has financed to date in the state, is called Harper Square. It is a major
component of the Hyde Park–Kenwood Urban Renewal Project, located on a site one and one-half blocks long at 48th Street and Lake
Park Avenue. The developer was the United Dwellings Foundation
of Metropolitan Chicago which was set up by the Amalgamated
Clothing Workers Union of America. This union had built two
dozen housing developments in New York over a period of many
years. Like the New York projects, Harper Square is a cooperative,
with down payments required of $880 to $1,700 for the one- to
three-bedroom apartments. Although that sum is refunded when the
family leaves a unit, and there are tax advantages to cooperative
ownership, Harper Square is currently structured so that the tenants
do not build up an equity in their apartments.

The project has 591 units, all but 22 of which are located in twin
twenty-five story buildings. The 22 remaining units are four-bedroom row houses adjacent to the towers. Designed by Keck and
Keck, the development has much open space, giving it an almost
suburban feeling, which seems somewhat out of place in its mid-
city location. The massive size of the buildings appear heavy-handed
when compared to the Lake Village East high-rise, which is on the
adjacent site to the north. Questionable architectural solutions
at Harper Square include the space between the towers, which
contains a circle of benches surrounding large, and noisy, air-
conditioning equipment, and the five-story parking garage, which is
located so that it cuts off the view from Lake Park Avenue of S. S.
Beman's beautiful Blackstone Public Library built in 1904.

Harper Square has been a success from a social and economic
standpoint. Constructed in 1971, the total development cost was
just under $16 million, or about $27,000 per unit. Although that
figure is not extremely low for that date, it was justified by the large
land area, the relatively large rooms of the apartments, and the high
quality of the construction. It has been found that state housing
finance agency projects are generally at least as costly as HUD ones,
even though the projects have lower financing costs. The mean cost
of IHDA projects processed through its Chicago office for 1970–73
was $22,688 per unit, as compared with only $19,564 for HUD projects.[7] The IHDA projects generally have amenities, such as central

air conditioning, often not found in the federally financed ones. The monthly payments at Harper Square initially range from $101 for the least expensive one-bedroom unit, up to $349 per month for a town house, depending on the size and location of the unit and whether it received Section 236 assistance. The development, like its neighbor Lake Village East, is well integrated racially; it is well managed, and has a day care center on the premises established and run by residents.

Park West Tower

A less ambitious development than Harper Square, built a year later by a private developer, is the Park West Tower at Clark Street and Fullerton Avenue. It consists of a single nineteen-story building

Harper Square, the first project financed by the Illinois Housing Development Authority in Chicago, was designed by Keck and Keck. This 591-unit cooperative development has been a success both from a social and economic standpoint since it was constructed in 1971.—Courtesy of George Fred Keck–William Keck

with 180 apartments. The architects were Dubin, Dubin, Black, and Moutoussamy. The building's birdcagelike exposed concrete frame, with infill of glass, is similar to several other buildings the architects have designed along the north and south lakefront in Chicago. The building includes a swimming pool and restaurant. The location is dubious for this type of building. Clark Street at that point is a gaudy overcommercialized thoroughfare of "New Town," and Fullerton contains a handsome group of late nineteenth- and early

Artist's rendering of Park West Tower, which was built in 1972 by a private developer. This single nineteen-story building of 180 units does not relate well architecturally to its commercial or residential neighbors.
—Courtesy of Dubin, Dubin, Black, and Moutoussamy

twentieth-century Victorian houses. The Park West Tower does not relate well to either street.

The mortgage for the project was $4,485,000 which represents 90 percent of the development cost. Under IHDA rules, for-profit developers can get only 90 percent mortgages, whereas nonprofit developers get 100 percent ones. When the 10 percent equity is added, the cost of each unit at Park West Tower averages about $27,500. Park West Tower has only 33 percent of its units subsidized by Section 236 payments, whereas Harper Square has 62 percent of its units so subsidized.[8]

Jackson Park Terrace

Jackson Park Terrace marked the beginning of a new era for IHDA. In April 1973 Irving Gerick became the director of IHDA, and Bruce

Jackson Park Terrace, completed in 1974, is composed of twenty-four three-story walk-ups and a fifteen-story reinforced concrete building. Although it was hoped that the project would be well integrated, as of mid-1976 the racial composition was 94 percent black and only 6 percent white.—Photograph by Devereux Bowly, Jr.

Sagan its chairman. Both residents of Hyde Park–Kenwood, they
have special concern for housing conditions on the South Side of
Chicago. IHDA already had a start there with Harper Square, and its
efforts were extended to Woodlawn, the next neighborhood to the
south with Jackson Park Terrace, and later to South Shore.

Gerick had previously worked as a project manager for CHA, as
executive director of the Hyde Park–Kenwood Community Conference, in the housing program of the Community Renewal Foundation, and as midwest director of the Nonprofit Housing Center, Incorporated. He is enough of a realist to understand that massive
social problems cannot be solved merely with brick and mortar.[9]
Rather than financing projects all over the city, without relation to
one another, Gerick tried to have a degree of concentration along the
south lakeshore, in the hope that one project will reinforce the next,
and strengthen the entire area.

Jackson Park Terrace, at 61st Street and Stony Island Avenue, is
located a mile south of Harper Square on land obtained by the University of Chicago as part of its South Campus Urban Renewal Project, and leased by it to the developer, a subsidiary of The Woodlawn
Organization. The university not only leased the land for ninety-
nine years, but gave TWO a seed-money loan of about $500,000 to
get the project started. The architects were Whitley and Whitley, a
black firm headquartered in Cleveland.

The project, which was completed in 1974, consists of 332 units
in twenty-four three-story walk-ups, and a fifteen-story reinforced
concrete building. The total building cost was $8.1 million. The
eight-acre site, although located on the edge of the troubled Woodlawn community, is a good one. It is adjacent to Jackson Park and
the lakefront, and only one-half block from the Midway Plaisance.
Although it was hoped the project would be well integrated, as of
mid-1976 the racial composition was 94 percent black, and only 6
percent white.[10] Despite the fact that sufficient Section 236 and rent
supplement funding was available to subsidize all units of the
development, over one-quarter of the tenants have incomes too high
for those programs, and thus pay market rents.[11] These rentals range
from $213 for the least expensive efficiency apartment to $390 for
the most expensive four-bedroom unit.

Grace Street Housing for the Elderly

The Grace Street Housing for the Elderly, built in 1975, is a single
eighteen-story building on Grace Street (3800 north) just west of
Lake Shore Drive. It has 36 studio apartments, and 144 one-bedroom
units, and is constructed of concrete with a brick veneer and an

irregular shape. Designed by Benjamin Weese, it is the second
example in Chicago of his Minimum Perimeter Architecture. It is
not quite as dramatic as the earlier Lake Village East building, however, because the site is tightly surrounded by other tall apartment
buildings. Developed by Marvin Myers Associates, the cost was
about $4.4 million, or $24,688 per unit. The Grace Street building
was the first IHDA-financed project for elderly tenants in Chicago.
As early as 1973 IHDA allocated $30 million of their mortgage loan
funds for 1,500 special senior citizen housing units statewide. Their
studies had found the elderly among the most poorly housed people
in the state.[12] Two-thirds of the apartments at Grace Street are Section 236 rent-reduction units, while the other third of the tenants
pay market rates. In 1975 Illinois received a $48.4 million Section 8
assistance program allocation for low-income families and the elderly. Of that amount $25.6 million was set aside for IHDA proj-
ects.[13]

New Vistas

The New Vistas development was unique when it was started in
1974, because it was the first IHDA project that involved purchase
and rehabilitation of existing housing. The 148 units included in the
project are located in five buildings, three stories each, in the 6900
block of South Crandon Avenue, and around the corner on 70th
Street, in South Shore. The developer is a for-profit organization
called RESCORP, which stands for Chicago Area Renewal Effort
Service Corporation. It was organized in 1972 by the savings and
loan industry in the Chicago metropolitan area to assist in the solution of urban problems. The various savings associations put up the
seed money for the developments and own the stock of RESCORP. It
is RESCORP's hope that by engaging in rehabilitation in areas where
deterioration is still reversible, it can serve as a catalyst in stimulat-
ing community stabilization and renewal. It purposely concentrates
its activities within a limited geographical area, so as to create
maximum effect. Similar service corporations, created by savings
institutions, have achieved success in Boston, Hartford, Pittsburgh,
and Cincinnati.

The New Vistas project was financed by an IHDA mortgage of
$3,360,000, or just over $24,970 per unit, when the 10 percent equity
is added. Although the cost may seem high for rehabilitated units, it
must be remembered the apartments have more rooms and are
superior in most respects to new construction. The rooms are large
and the ceilings high; there are separate dining rooms, almost
unheard of in new buildings. The cost on a per-square-foot basis is

still considerably lower for rehab projects than new construction. As a spin-off of the New Vistas projects, RESCORP also in 1975 initiated the rehabilitation of the nineteen-unit Paxton Arms building at 69th and Paxton Avenue one block west of the New Vistas site. Although this building was basically in good condition and did not need as much work as the others, the kitchens were repaired, the mechanical systems upgraded, and a conventional mortgage obtained to finance the undertaking. RESCORP in late 1976 was planning New Vistas II, a $4.2 million rehabilitation project of 154 units in six buildings near 69th and Paxton, also to be financed by IHDA.

A separate South Shore project of IHDA involved a $2.7 million loan for the purchase and rehabilitation of the sixteen-story, 183-unit building at 7000 South Shore Drive. Typical of the high-rises

New Vistas I rehabilitated apartment building. This is a RESCORP project located at 6909–25 South Crandon Avenue.—Courtesy of RESCORP

built in the 1920s on Lake Shore Drive and South Shore Drive, it is constructed of dark brick with limestone trim and overlooks the South Shore Country Club Park. Once a luxury building, it had grown somewhat shabby with the uncertainty caused by the large-scale racial change of the neighborhood. IHDA provided merely the interim loan, with the long-term financing coming from a conventional FHA mortgage. The rents in 1976 range from $155 to $475 per month, for efficiency to four-bedroom apartments, with thirty-seven of the units having Section 8 rent subsidies.

Near West Side Apartments Rehabilitation

Another major IHDA-financed rehab project in Chicago carried out in 1975 and 1976, involved fifty-four apartments in six buildings

One of six apartment buildings with fifty-four units, located at Laflin and Polk streets, in the Near West Side area between the University of Illinois at Chicago Circle and the West Side Medical Center, rehabilitated in 1975–76 under financing obtained from the Illinois Housing Development Authority.—Photograph by Devereux Bowly, Jr.

at Laflin and Polk streets, in the Near West Side area between the University of Illinois at Chicago Circle and the West Medical Center. The mortgage loan was for $1.1 million or just under $20,000 per unit. Twenty-two of the apartments have Section 8 subsidies. In a second rehabilitation project on the West Side, IHDA provided interim financing of $1.2 million to the Fifth City Organization. Its development includes fifty-eight units in four buildings in the East Garfield area, all subsidized under the Section 236 program.

Elm Street Plaza

The most elaborate IHDA-financed building in Chicago is the Elm Street Plaza, at Elm and Dearborn streets. Developed by McHugh-Levin Associates, it is a thirty-four-story building, with 396 studio, one- and two-bedroom units. Located in the Rush Street area of the Near North Side Gold Coast, the building has the amenities of its luxury neighbors, including a swimming pool and 240-car garage. IHDA provided a 90 percent mortgage loan of $12,940,000 for construction and permanent financing. When the building opened in the spring of 1976, rents ranged from $229 for a studio on a low floor, to $441 for a two-bedroom apartment on a high floor. Twenty percent of the apartments have Section 8 subsidies.

The architects were Ezra Gordon–Jack M. Levin and Associates, who designed the building with bay windows, and clad it in brick. Due to the location, and the high quality of design and construction, the per-unit cost of the building was $35,945, the most expensive subsidized rental housing ever constructed in Chicago. It is questionable whether the tenants, who pay for example up to $350 a month for a one-bedroom apartment, are "low and moderate income" families. The IHDA Act defines such families as those who cannot afford to pay costs at which private enterprise, without assisted mortgages, is providing a substantial supply of decent, safe, and sanitary housing. At the Elm Street Plaza for the first time a few moderate-income families, because of the Section 8 subsidies, live in luxury apartments in a high-rent area. An examination of the loans in process by IHDA in mid-1976 indicates, however, that this is not the first of many such projects IHDA will finance in the future. The trend seems to rather be toward rehabilitation projects in the middle-class sections of the city.

Loan to Lender Program

During the early 1970s a major controversy developed in Chicago over allegations by the Citizens Action Program (CAP) and various neighborhood groups that financial institutions were not issuing mortgages in the older neighborhoods of the city, but were instead lending in the suburbs and locations in other states as far away as California. In an attempt to reduce this "redlining" and make more money available for mortgages for moderate-income housing in

Elm Street Plaza, the most elaborate building in Chicago financed by the Illinois Housing Development Authority. This thirty-four-story building with 396 studio, one- and two-bedroom units has amenities including a swimming pool.—Courtesy of Illinois Housing Development Authority

Chicago, IHDA in 1974 undertook a $22.9 million Chicago Loan to Lender program. Illinois is one of the few states whose housing finance agency has the statutory power to implement such a plan.[14]

Under the program IHDA sold its own tax-exempt securities, and loaned the proceeds to banks and savings and loan associations in Chicago, who in turn loaned the money out at slightly higher rates as home mortgages. Each lending institution was restricted in its use of funds to the financing of houses and two- to four-unit apartment buildings in the financial institution's "primary Chicago service area," which is composed of those contiguous Zip Code areas where 60 percent of the institution's City of Chicago deposits originate. The IHDA funds had to be matched on a one-to-one basis by funds from the institution itself. Mortgage limits were set at $35,000 for single-family residences, and $70,000 for two or four flats. Because of the matching fund requirement, more than $45 million was initially pumped into Chicago neighborhoods. In 1975 the program was expanded to $63.5 million and extended state-wide. Of that amount $42,150,000 was earmarked for Chicago, $12,850,000 for the suburban areas around Chicago, and $8,450,000 for communities in downstate Illinois.[15]

IHDA also engages in several activities ancillary to its main function. One of them involves non-interest-bearing preconstruction loans of seed money to nonprofit housing sponsors. The loans are made from a special revolving fund established by the legislature. When a long-term mortgage is ultimately made, the short-term loan is repaid to the fund, and thus available to be lent to another group. The purpose of these loans is to help pay planning costs, including architectural and engineering fees, and even costs of land acquisition. During the fiscal year ended June 30, 1975, IHDA made such Development Advance Loans totaling $806,765, to fourteen groups. Included in these loans were funds for what is called the Bulk Sale Program, under which community organizations purchase from HUD abandoned homes whose mortgages have been foreclosed, for rehabilitation and resale. The families ultimately purchasing the houses often get their mortgages from financial institutions participating in the Loan to Lender Program. In fiscal 1974 there were two loans for this purpose, totaling $145,000, which covered eleven buildings on the Northwest Side of Chicago. In 1975 the program was expanded to eight organizations, and involved thirty-one small apartment buildings.

In addition to development loans, IHDA makes outright development planning grants. In fiscal 1975 five organizations received such grants totaling $198,000. They are to enable community groups to get full-time professional staff help, and occasionally are made directly to organizations providing technical services. For example, a grant of $30,000 went in 1975 to the Chicago Architectural Assistance Center, an organization providing free architectural services to community organizations and individuals involved in housing rehabilitation or repair, but unable to hire private architects. IHDA itself also provides technical help to groups interested in developing housing.

In its first seven years of active participation in housing financing, IHDA achieved a good record. In sharp contrast to HUD, none of its projects have gone into default, except when a temporary problem occurred with a project in downstate Illinois. This has been the general pattern of state housing finance agencies, except the New York Urban Development Corporation, which has had severe financial difficulties and has defaulted on some of its bonds. The New York situation is unique, because NYUDC, in addition to providing mortgages, is itself a housing developer. In the projects it develops it cannot pass along the risks to the developer, but carries them itself.[16] It is also subject to political pressure to develop projects that are economically questionable.

IHDA is a mortgage lender, rather than a mere insurer of mortgages, as is HUD in most of its programs, and it keeps in closer contact with the status of the properties on which it grants mortgages than does HUD. In fact HUD acts rather passively in regard to monitoring its developments, relying on its Special Risk Insurance Fund to cover defaulted mortgages. The state housing finance agencies control their risks by becoming much more involved in project operations of their developers.[17] For example, IHDA has been wise enough to grant mortgages for projects in viable neighborhoods, but not in those where there is almost no chance of success for the development. The picture of all IHDA-financed buildings is not completely rosy, however. With interest rates rising during the early 1970s, the mortgage rates established at the final closings of some IHDA projects were higher than the developers anticipated. Some have also been hit by inflation of maintenance and management costs above the rent increases permitted by IHDA or justified by market demand.

IHDA assumes an aggressive role in the management of the projects it finances. Its Marketing and Management departments have a staff of twelve professionals to instruct in and help develop programs and budgets, especially for community organizations. They assist borrowers in both renting and marketing the apartments, and visit each development at least twice a month. They check on

vacancies, rent delinquencies, and spending above budgets each
month. Finally IHDA, unlike HUD, has a small staff, and is relatively informal in its operations. It is much more efficient than the
massive federal bureaucracy, where decisions are so spread out that
there is a lack of accountability. The quality of leadership has been
high at IHDA and at most other state housing finance agencies.

Because of the January 1973 moratorium on federal subsidized
housing programs, together with the severe drop in private housing
construction in the mid-1970s, state housing finance programs became more important. In 1974 and 1975 one in every three new
rental units in Illinois was financed by IHDA. There were 18,700
such units constructed, of which IHDA financed 6,100.[18] As of April
30, 1976, IHDA had outstanding mortgages of $272 million, on a
total of fifty-nine separate developments, with 12,510 units either
completed or under construction. In addition, it had another $57
million committed to developments likely to close, as well as pre-
feasibility proposals before it for an additional $154 million,[19] and
about $63 million outstanding under the Loan to Lender program. In
mid-1976 IHDA's list of future mortgage commitments included
four projects in Chicago, and the feasibility of a dozen more proposed projects, also in Chicago, was being studied. IHDA has used
up or committed more than two-thirds of its $500 million statutory
bonding limit, and has more than enough proposals to use the remainder. It is likely the legislature will increase the limit, but initial
efforts to do so have failed due to political bickering.

12 Overview

The more than half century of experience to date with major subsidized housing projects in Chicago could have taught many lessons.
The unfortunate fact is, however, that the history of Chicago's subsidized housing is in many respects a story of decline. The first
substantial wave of activity, from 1919 to 1930, saw the construction of the Garden Homes, the Michigan Boulevard Garden Apartments, and the Marshall Field Garden Apartments. They are all still
standing, and provide better housing than the great majority of the
public housing that followed. Although the three projects have been
successful socially, and are well designed, none were viable economically. They showed that the problem of providing adequate housing
for poor people could not be solved by philanthropic endeavors.

In 1976, as the Chicago Housing Authority approached the for-
tieth anniversary of its creation, it had become the largest landlord
in the city, and the second largest local public housing agency in the
country. It owned 30,462 units of family housing, another 9,175
apartments for the elderly, and controlled 3,098 private units under
its leasing program. The units owned by CHA were in 1,273 separate
buildings, which cost $563 million, including land acquisition.[1] As
of June 30, 1976, the total CHA tenant population stood at an estimated 140,000 people, or about 4.5 percent of the population of
Chicago. This was down from 144,188 at the end of 1975,[2] and
147,842 at the end of 1974.[3] The decrease reflect a slightly higher
vacancy rate in CHA units and the overall trend toward smaller
families.

Although it has built and now maintains a massive number of
housing units, CHA has failed to fulfill the expectations of the social
reform movement from which it sprang. That movement saw public
housing as a major component in the effort to rid the city of slums,
and transform those at the bottom of the social spectrum into
healthy, upwardly mobile citizens. CHA has eliminated large slum
areas, and constructed a body of sound, safe, and sanitary housing for
poor people, a not insubstantial accomplishment. There is no evidence, however, that the housing has helped to make the residents
more self-sufficient or contented, in fact the opposite may well be
the case.

Among the residents of CHA family housing at the end of 1975,
there were 40,439 adults and 91,074 children.[4] Only 13 percent of

the families had both parents in the home, and that same percentage
(although not necessarily the same families) were self-sufficient, the
rest receiving some form of governmental income grant, mostly
AFDC.[5] Of the total CHA households, 13 percent had annual incomes under $2,000, 24 percent between $2,000 and $2,999, 25 per-
cent between $3,000 and $3,999, 10 percent between $4,000 and
$4,999, and 28 percent over $5,000.[6] Of the family housing population, 95 percent were black, 3 percent white, and 2 percent Spanish
surname. In the CHA elderly units, 50 percent of the residents were
black, 48 percent white, and 2 percent Spanish.[7]

The original intent of the federal public housing program was that
rental income would be enough to cover operating expenses of the
housing projects. Construction was paid for by the sale by the local
housing authority of forty-year bonds, the principal and interest
of which are paid by the federal government. There are thus three
major subsidies involved in such housing: 1) the direct federal payment of the construction bond principal and interest, 2) the loss to
the federal treasury due to the fact that the holders of such bonds do
not have to pay income tax on the interest received from the bonds,
and 3) the loss to local taxing authorities due to the fact the housing
authority does not have to pay real estate taxes, but only an amount
equal to 10 percent of the shelter rents, which for CHA in 1975 was
only $695,290.[8]

Through the early 1960s rents paid by CHA tenants were at least
enough to pay the operating expenses of the projects, and as late as
1965 there was a small operating budget surplus, called "residual
receipts," which was used to reduce the federal payment of construction bond principal and interest. After that date rental income
failed to keep up with greatly increasing operating and maintenance
costs. In 1967 the federal government started paying CHA an operating subsidy for each elderly apartment at the rate of ten dollars per
month. The major federal operating subsidies came with the Brooke
Amendment, however. Senator Edward Brooke inserted a provision
in the 1969 Housing Act that limited a tenant's rent in the federal
public housing program to 25 percent of the family's adjusted gross
income, with the federal government paying the local housing authority the difference between the actual operating cost and the rent
received.[9]

By 1976 the basic rent schedule on units for families at or below
CHA income admission limits was $50 for an efficiency, $60 for a
one-bedroom, $70 for a two-bedroom, $80 for a three-bedroom, $90
for a four-bedroom, and $95 for a five-bedroom apartment. Because
of the Brooke Amendment, however, the great majority of the ten-

ants paid even less than these basic rents. As of the end of 1973, the
average rent of CHA federal developments was $45.15 per unit, per
month, which represented 42 percent of the total operating cost per
apartment. Those costs averaged $106.81.[10] By the end of 1975 the
average rent had increased to $53.54 but it represented only 39 per-
cent of the operating cost of $137.64 per unit.[11] CHA's income
figures demonstrate its increasing reliance on direct federal subsidies. In 1971 CHA received a total of just over $31 million from
the federal government: about $19 million for debt service, $3.5
million for the Brooke Amendment subsidy, $6 million for the el-
derly and other special programs, and $2.7 million for the leased
housing program.[12] By 1975 the total from Washington had more
than doubled to $67 million, broken down approximately as follows:
$25 million for debt service, $37 million for the deficit subsidy, $3.6
million for the leased housing program, and $1.6 million for the
Target Projects program.[13] In 1975 CHA tenants paid only $23.8
million in rents for the federal projects.[14]

The 42,735 units controlled by CHA in 1976 constituted less than
4 percent of the total residential housing units in Chicago. Although
the absolute number of CHA units is large, as a proportion of the
total number of units in the city, it is statistically almost insignificant, and even the majority of the poor families in Chicago live
in private housing. In light of these facts, the public housing program might have achieved more if it were conceived and carried
out as a demonstration of high-quality housing design and innovative construction techniques, instead of being scaled down to the
bare minimums. It is difficult to ascertain the exact design consideration of early public housing projects in Chicago, because they were
not articulated by the administrators or architects. Economic considerations played a part in the design of the housing, of course, but
they were by no means the entire picture.

Although the reasons for the decisions that were made are now
somewhat a matter of conjecture, it is possible to isolate certain
factors that were present. They included: 1) in the understandable
concern for quickly replacing some of the terrible slums that
existed, too little attention was given to the aesthetic and social
implications of the new type of housing, 2) the federal and CHA
officials responsible for the projects knew little about architecture,
3) a conscious effort was made to make the buildings modest, to
blunt public criticism that poor people were getting something for
nothing from the government, and also so that public housing would
not compete with the private housing market, and 4) the overly
detailed specifications formulated by the governmental bureau-

cracies inhibited creativity. Also of importance was the fact that there was not much public pressure on CHA to produce well-planned and designed housing. What resulted were dreary rows of barracks-like dwellings, physically better than the slums they replaced, but not very attractive compared to the majority of the housing in the city.

One of the ultimate ironies of the history of public housing is that the social reformers who were its most dedicated early supporters neglected the social dimensions of what they were creating. The very people who should have been most sensitive to the consequences of building massive projects inhabited solely by poor families, and containing no facilities for broad social interaction except a few parks and community centers, completely disregarded them. The philosophy of both the social reformers and public housing officials was paternalistic. The residents were treated like children, and the tragedy is that for some it was the self-fulfilling prophecy—they acted like children and were satisfied to have public housing and welfare policies control their lives. Public housing thus tended to perpetuate a permanent class of dependent people, unable to fend for themselves.

The most basic fault in the concept of public housing was that it isolated poor families into enclaves containing only other poor families. Such limited exposure fails to provide the residents, especially the children, an opportunity for contact with people in a variety of circumstances, as is the case in more heterogeneous settings. Even in slum areas there is usually some better housing occupied by middle-class families, and often many who own their own homes. The ideal of making the extremely poor population upwardly mobile, that was part of the original philosophy of public housing, would have best been achieved by getting them out into the general population where there is some interaction across class lines, some exposure to how the economy and the business world operate, and some exposure to persons with substantial education.

Another major reason for the lack of success of family public housing in Chicago was simply that it had too many missions. In addition to providing housing for poor people, and providing jobs for construction workers, it was used as a major vehicle for slum clearance. This added tremendously to the cost of land acquisition, and required by definition that the projects be located in slum areas, where the only tenants who could be attracted would be those on the very bottom of the income scale, usually with large families, who simply could not afford to go elsewhere. The slum clearance itself also displaced thousands of families, many of whom were relocated to existing CHA projects under special priorities. A de facto purpose of public housing in Chicago, at least after Elizabeth Wood left CHA in 1954, was to isolate the poor and especially the black population away from the white middle-class areas of the city. Although CHA is nominally an independent agency, in reality it has operated as an arm of city government, because its commissioners are appointed by the mayor, because much of its planning is done by city agencies, and because its sites have had to be approved by the City Council.

Public housing construction in Chicago during the 1950s and most of the 1960s involved almost exclusively high-rise buildings. This type of housing was viewed by CHA as involving a certain inevitability. As has been demonstrated, they could have constructed the same number of units in low-rise buildings, on the same sites where the high-rise projects are located. Also, throughout the period there were available numerous small vacant lots and large vacant tracts of land in Chicago, both in the inner city and in the outlying areas. Other major cities including Cleveland, Pittsburgh, and Los Angeles built no elevator family public housing whatsoever. The high-rise projects in Chicago are ironically anti-urban in their planning. With 80 percent or more of the sites left vacant, they lack the characteristics that differentiate a city from a suburb: intensity of land use, a variety of building types, the presence of small shops and other businesses, churches and institutions of various types.

The attempts to develop moderate-income subsidized housing in Chicago, like public housing, were not very successful, but not for the same reasons. The endeavors of the Chicago Dwellings Association, and later the Kate Maremont Foundation and the Community Renewal Foundation, involved smaller projects than those of CHA, better architecture, and some experiments with rehabilitation of existing housing. They were financial failures, however, because of inadequate subsidies and mismanagement. The Section 221 (d) (3) and 236 projects developed by community organizations were also a fiasco. In retrospect it is incredible that completely inexperienced groups were allowed to develop multimillion-dollar projects, with 100 percent financing. The input of such groups into planning housing is highly desirable, but it should have been recognized that the housing field is a highly complex and competitive one. To turn over such undertakings to amateurs is comparable to teaching a novice to fly an airplane by putting him in the cockpit and giving him the controls. The better course would have been to let the community groups start with small rehabilitation projects, and let only the ones which showed real proficiency get involved in the large undertakings.

According to HUD statistics as of mid-1976, in the City of Chicago fifty Section 221 (d) (3) and 236 projects, with 2,639 units, had been foreclosed or were in the process of foreclosure. This represents more than 13 percent of such units in Chicago.[15] The foreclosures were heavily concentrated in the projects developed by nonprofit sponsors. Some of the buildings rehabilitated under the two programs in Chicago had by 1976 actually been demolished, notably 56 of the 71 units rehabilitated by the Kate Maremont Foundation and the Lawndale Freedom Movement, and two buildings with a total of 36 units in Woodlawn. In addition there were 33 projects, with 4,620 units that had their mortgages in default as of August 1976.[16] Many of the mortgages in default were for new construction projects by profit-making developers. Some were only a few months behind in their mortgage payments, and some, like Woodlawn Gardens, had been in default since 1971, and were more than fifty months in arrears.[17] HUD does not want to take back the projects because it is not set up to own and manage housing, and the market values of the projects are considerably below the balances of the mortgages. Also, too many foreclosures are embarrassing to HUD, because it shows they financed nonviable projects. HUD thus strings along with the owners of many properties in default, especially if at least the interest on the mortgages is being paid. If the Chicago foreclosure and default figures as of 1976 are combined, they comprise 83 projects, with 7,259 units, or 36.4 percent of all 221 (d) (3) and 236 projects built in the city, a dismal record. HUD hires private real estate companies to manage the properties it forecloses, and eventually hopes to sell them to new buyers. Many are in bad locations, and some are in terrible physical condition. It is questionable whether they can be sold without HUD rehabilitating them, and this is unlikely in light of the losses HUD has already taken on the properties. Many of them may thus be demolished.

Even with the high delinquency and foreclosure rates, some of the 221 (d) (3) and 236 developments in Chicago have been financially successful, especially those built by professional real estate developers. They were, on the whole, much more careful about the sites they selected than the nonprofit developers, and location has traditionally been considered the single most important factor in determining the value of residential property. A few of the private developers have achieved the full permissible return of 6 percent, and many others have made a profit of less than 6 percent. They have presumably all benefited also from the tax shelter afforded by the projects, and some have even contributed additional capital to help cover operating expenses in order to prevent a project with a negative cash flow from going under, to preserve the tax advantages, and their equity position.

In addition to selecting better locations, the private developers have tended to hire experienced managers or management companies for their properties, whereas some of the community organizations have not done so. Professional management has not guaranteed success, but has achieved a better record than that of community groups which managed their own properties, not only because the professionals were more experienced on the average, but because they were more insulated from local pressure, for example, to rent apartments to the friends and relatives of the leaders of community groups, regardless of their desirability as tenants. The professional managers tended to screen potential tenants more carefully, and to favor elderly tenants, who are more dependable than younger families and usually do not have children in the home, some of whom are prone to carelessness and vandalism. For many of the 221 (d) (3) and 236 developments, even those with good locations and management, the unexpectedly high taxes and sharply increasing operating expenses, and the limits on rent increases were simply too much of a liability and they failed to break even. For those projects the subsidies received were not enough to make the projects viable. There were those who benefited regardless of the viability of the projects, including the building contractors and mortgage lenders. Both groups lobbied aggressively for the programs, and saw to it that they were designed in such a way that they lost nothing even if the projects failed.

By 1976, with the virtual halt in the construction of CHA projects and the 221 (d) (3) and 236 programs, additional multi-family subsidized housing in Chicago was limited basically to projects with mortgages from the Illinois Housing Development Authority. In part because of the tremendous escalation of new construction costs, IHDA is financing a number of rehabilitation projects. Its rehabilitation projects have been successful, unlike the earlier CDA, Maremont, and Community Renewal Foundation ones, basically because those financed by IHDA have been in good locations, with realistic rents charged. The RESCORP New Vistas and other projects in South Shore, and the Near West Apartments rehabilitation are among the few promising recent experiments in subsidized housing in Chicago.

It must be remembered that the cost of IHDA projects is not free
to the taxpayers, as it might appear on the surface. In fact, the mechanism of tax-exempt bonds to finance mortgages is actually very
expensive when the drain on the federal treasury is considered.
Research on the subject has found the cost of mortgages financed by
tax-exempt bonds to be high, in relation to the benefits conferred.
Since most of the bonds issued by state housing finance agencies are
held by persons in the high income tax brackets, and by banks and
insurance companies, it has been estimated that the tax loss is equal
to 48 percent of the amount of interest paid on the bonds, because
the average bondholder is in the 48 percent tax bracket. The dollar
benefit conferred, in the form of lower interest rates on the
mortgages, is considerably less than 48 percent.[18] It would thus be
less expensive for the federal government simply to subsidize the
mortgages directly, rather than losing a greater amount of tax reve-
nue through tax-free bonds.

Future Chicago housing policy must be formulated in the context
of what is happening to the city generally, and can only be made
intelligently if the major demographic forces in the city are under-
stood. The most dramatic change in Chicago during the quarter
century from 1950 to 1975 was the accelerating loss of population.
The population of Chicago, as recorded by the census, reached its
peak in 1950, when it stood at 3,620,962. It declined to 3,550,404 in
1960, a drop of 70,558, or just under 2 percent. By 1970 the population had fallen another 181,045 to 3,369,359, or a decline of more
than 5 percent. It has been estimated that the 1975 population of the
city stood at 3,094,143, a decline of 275,216, or 8.2 percent in only
five years.[19] It is almost certain that the city's population will be
below 3,000,000 by 1980, for the first census year since 1920.

The decrease in the population of Chicago is due to the combination of the declining birthrate and a greater number of people moving out of the city than moving into it. As the total population of the
city has decreased, the black population has increased steadily, from
14 percent in the 1950 census, to 23 percent in 1960, 32 percent in
1970, and an estimated 38 percent in 1975.[20] The decline in population has been so great that according to estimates of the United
States Bureau of the Census, between 1973 and 1974 the entire
metropolitan area lost population, because the suburban growth was
less than the city's population loss. Specifically, in the six-county
Chicago Standard Metropolitan Statistical Area (SMSA), the population fell from 6,999,800 on July 1, 1973, to 6,971,200 a year later; the
1974 figure was actually 6,500 less than the 1970 Chicago SMSA
total.[21] These declines are part of the national phenomenon of mi-

gration to the "sunbelt" areas of the South and Southwest, especially Florida, Texas, and Arizona.

The housing stock of Chicago also shifted during the period. In 1950 there were 1,106,100 units in the city, and the total increased by 108,800 units, or 9.8 percent, to about 1,215,000 in 1960.[22] The housing supply in the city increased significantly during the decade, even though the population decreased somewhat, because of the ending of the postwar housing shortage, less doubling up of two or more families in a single unit, and creation of a vacancy reserve, which is normal in a market without an acute shortage of housing. Since 1960 the housing stock has fallen in Chicago. In 1970, according to the census, it stood at 1,209,200,[23] a decline of 5,800 units or about one-half of one percent during the decade. A special Census Bureau study, called Components of Inventory Change (CINCH) found a slightly smaller total of 1,197,300 units in the city in 1970, and found that there had been a decrease of 19,300 units during the 1960 to 1970 decade.[24]

During the years 1971 through 1975 building permits (excluding public housing) were issued for only 18,673 units in Chicago,[25] and demolition permits for 30,282 units,[26] meaning a net decline of at least 11,609 units. The actual decrease in housing units during the period was probably considerably greater, because of: 1) units demolished without permits; 2) the surplus of mergers of small apartments, over conversion to smaller units of large apartments, caused mainly by the banning of glass emergency fire doors opening into other apartments and 3) the withdrawal of marginal units from the market, for example, the city has been aggressive in forcing discontinuance of use of illegal basement and attic apartments. As the stock of housing has fallen in Chicago, and the suburban areas have grown, the city's proportion of the housing units in the metropolitan area has decreased from 66 percent in 1950, to 56 percent in 1960, to only 49 percent in 1970—the first year the suburbs had more units than the city.[27]

Even though the supply of housing has fallen in Chicago since 1960, the decrease has been much less than the population drop, and thus the housing market is nowhere near as tight as it was then. In fact available evidence indicates that by the 1970s there was no longer an overall housing shortage in Chicago although specific shortages remain, most notably sound housing for poor families, and lack of available rental units in specific areas such as Hyde Park, the North Side lakefront neighborhoods, and the Far Northwest Side. The best indication of the lack of an overall housing shortage is that the vacancy rate of housing units in the city increased from 4.7

percent in 1960 to 5.8 percent in 1970.[28] The 1970 Chicago vacancy rate was twice as high as New York City's 2.8 percent, and higher than the 4.6 percent rate in Los Angeles.[29]

Traditionally the greatest shortage of housing in Chicago has been that available to the black population. In the last three decades there has been such considerable white out-migration from the city, and racial change of vast areas in Chicago from virtually all-white to virtually all-black occupancy, that by 1976 there was not even a general shortage of housing units in the predominantly black sections of the city. As the black population of Chicago has become increasingly middle class, and moved to neighborhoods not previously occupied by blacks, the vacancy rate in the traditional ghetto areas has gone up, for example, Woodlawn and Lawndale became depopulated as many of their residents moved to South Shore and Austin respectively. The remaining shortage of sound housing for the poverty population of Chicago is more a function of the inability to pay rentals necessary to support such housing, rather than a physical shortage of housing units.

In the late 1960s and the 1970s a new phenomenon has come upon the scene in Chicago, and many other American cities—the large-scale abandonment of housing, where owners simply walk away from their buildings and leave them to be eventually demolished by the city. Housing abandonment has been most prevalent in Chicago in the old ghetto areas of the South and West sides, but is also occurring in Uptown, and the Near Northwest Side Humboldt Park area. The ultimate cause of housing abandonment is lack of demand for marginal and slum housing. Because of this lack of demand, rents in the late 1960s and the 1970s have stayed constant, or at least not gone up enough at the lowest end of the housing spectrum, to offset inflation of costs, especially heating costs, maintenance, repair of vandalism, and real estate taxes.

A 1973 study for HUD by Arthur D. Little, Incorporated, evaluated real estate taxes in ten cities and found that in Chicago tax rates were relatively higher in slum areas than in other sections of the city. The study isolated "Stable Neighborhoods" (Hyde Park and Norwood Park), "Upward Transitional" ones (Lincoln Park), "Downward Transitional" (Logan Square), and "Blighted" (Woodlawn). The effective real estate tax rates, that is, property tax as a percentage of owner-reported market value of the property, for the selected Chicago neighborhoods were as follows: Stable, 5.2 percent; Upward Transitional, 0.8 percent; Downward Transitional, 4.7 percent; and Blighted, 10.7 percent.[30] Thus the effective tax rate was

thirteen times higher in the Blighted neighborhoods, than in the
Upward Transitional ones.

The precise effect of real estate taxes on housing abandonment is
difficult to ascertain. The Arthur D. Little study also found that
when real estate taxes in Chicago were considered as a percentage of
rental receipts, the differences between types of neighborhoods were
not as great. The figures were: Stable, 20.7 percent; Upward Transitional, 9.9 percent; Downward Transitional, 17.4 percent and
Blighted, 19.9 percent.[31] The study may become obsolete by the late
1970s because of new assessment practices in Cook County. As each
of the four assessment districts are being reassessed, according to
the regular quadrennial pattern, there is greater input into the system than previously (by the use of computerized data) of recent sales
of comparable real estate in the area. Many properties in the inner
city of Chicago actually have had their assessments lowered for the
first time in many years. Also, it is difficult to evaluate real estate
taxes and housing abandonment because taxes have in fact usually
not been paid for several years prior to the abandonment.

As demand for housing in the worst areas of the city has decreased, the nature of slum ownership has changed. Multiple ownership of buildings in such areas by real estate companies and investors has been reduced, because of their declining profitability. The
buildings are increasingly individually owned, or at least being
bought on contract, by people who live in the buildings themselves,
or in the area. If there were still high demand for housing in the
inner-city areas, the rents there would be bid up, and there would be
an incentive to maintain the buildings at least at the minimum level
necessary to avoid a demolition suit by the city.

An important factor for the future of Chicago is whether the city
will be able to maintain its existing middle-class population, both
black and white. In recent years there has been some middle-class
relocation from the suburbs to Chicago, but of course a much greater
out-migration of middle-class families to the suburbs. Chicago has
always had very strong neighborhood identification, especially by its
middle-class population, which was originally based to a high degree
on ethnicity. In light of this fact it is unrealistic for the city to try to
attract middle-class families in any great numbers to the highly
blighted areas, even if attractive housing were made available there.
Because of its limited resources, the city seems to have no choice
but to limit large-scale expenditures in those areas. Possibly in
twenty years or more, when the cycle has been completed, there will
be the possibility of a revitalization there. If there is future interest

in redevelopment in such areas, it can be accomplished by a new wave of urban renewal, where the city sells the land it has accumulated by virtue of demolition liens and unpaid real estate taxes.

A controversial philosophy concerning the city's role in the current urban dilemma has been articulated by Anthony Downs, chairman of the board of the Real Estate Research Corporation, who has long been influential in Chicago and national housing policy. In recommending how cities should spend the limited funds available under the federal Community Development Program, he draws the analogy to the military medical technique called triage. Under it combat surgeons divide their patients into three categories: 1) those who will probably survive whether operated on or not, 2) those who are so badly injured they will probably die whether operated on or not, and 3) those for whom an operation would probably make the difference between life or death. Like the surgeon, Downs advocates that cities should devote their major resources to neighborhoods in the third category, which he calls "in-between areas," as opposed to the "healthy areas" or "very deteriorated" ones.[32] Although such a policy is unpopular with many people, it seems the only rational course at the present time with the federal funding of housing and urban programs at a very low level. If cities tried to spread the funds out to all problem areas, they would probably have no discernible effect, as has been the case with many urban programs in the past.

The economic and social forces affecting housing in Chicago are so vast it is certain the city government itself is unable to have any major impact on them, and it is questionable whether even the present programs of the federal government, unless funded at a very high level, would have much effect. It is clear that modest programs, such as those of Sections 221 (d) (3) and 236, have not been very important in the overall recent history of the city. Rather than trying to provide housing by programs such as these, the ultimate solution to the problem of low-income housing is to provide the poverty population as a group with the necessary funds to compete adequately in the private market.

The main housing problem of the poor is simply that they do not have the funds to secure adequate housing. There are two major ways this could be remedied: by a guaranteed annual income, or by a system of housing allowances. The guaranteed annual income would be the most comprehensive solution to the problem, and the one that would promote maximum freedom. It would allow poor families to afford sound housing in the private market, but would also permit them, if they chose, to live very modestly and spend a small proportion of their income on housing, and the rest for other things. Although the idea of a guaranteed annual income had been widely discussed for a decade by 1976, support for it did not seem to be increasing, because of the high projected cost, and the unknown effect such a system would have on employed persons with marginal incomes just above the level of the guarantee figure.

Sections 501 and 504 of the Housing Act of 1970 directed HUD to set up an experimental program to determine the feasibility of a system of housing allowances. The Experimental Housing Allowance Program was launched in 1971 by HUD's Office of Policy Development and Research. Among the major institutions participating in various aspects of the experiments are the Urban Institute, Stanford Research Institution, Rand Corporation, the National Opinion Research Center, and the M.I.T.–Harvard University Joint Center for Urban Studies. The project is actually composed of three major studies. The first is a three-year consumer or demand experiment, to measure the effect on low-income recipients of different types and levels of allowances. It is being conducted in Allegheny County, Pennsylvania (Pittsburgh), and Maricopa County, Arizona (Phoenix), and is scheduled to be completed by the end of 1977. Over 1,700 households at each location are being provided with seventeen different forms of housing allowances, for comparison to each other and with a control group not receiving any allowances.

The second major experiment is a market one, called the Housing Assistance Supply Experiment, to determine what effect housing allowances have on the supply of housing. Major questions being considered are: will the allowances merely bid up rents in poverty neighborhoods, or enable the poor to move out of them? Will housing allowances cause an increase in the supply of sound housing by encouraging rehabilitation and new construction? This experiment, which is to last five years, is being conducted in Brown County, Wisconsin (Green Bay), and St. Joseph County, Indiana (South Bend). It started in 1974, and ultimately will involve about 15,000 households. The program is open to all families (but not to single people under sixty-two years old, unless handicapped) unable to afford standard housing using one-quarter of their adjusted gross incomes. Each such household receives monthly cash payments, to bring it up to that level, provided each resides in safe and sanitary housing. The study includes both renters and homeowners. As of the end of September 1975 the median income of those enrolled in Green Bay was $3,480, and the median monthly housing allowance was $59. In South Bend the median income was lower, only $2,730, and thus the median allowance of $74 per month was higher.[33] The final experiment, to run for two years, is to evaluate administrative methods and costs. It involves eight public agencies administering small housing allowance programs of 400 to 900 families each in various urban and rural locations around the country.

By the early 1980s the studies should be finished and evaluated, and there may then be an effort to enact a housing allowance program. Such a system, unlike earlier federal housing policies that were funded at such a relatively low level that they failed to touch most of the poor, would be based on universal entitlement, and would thus be a major income transfer program. Like other such programs, public aid, food stamps, and Medicaid, it would be aimed at a specific national goal. It could be funded at any level, but to be effective the cost would be large. Very early estimates have ranged from $5 to $7 billion per year.[34] A realistic estimate for the cost during the 1980s, would be $10 billion annually. That amount could theoretically be raised simply by cutting back the $2.38 billion direct federal budget outlay for subsidized housing, and eliminating the indirect federal housing subsidy now in existence, based on the income tax deductibility of real estate taxes and mortgage interest, which totals more than $9 billion per year.[35] These indirect federal housing subsidies accrue overwhelmingly to families with incomes of $10,000 or more per year.[36]

If a national housing allowance system were enacted it would cause a large inflow of resources into the Chicago housing market, and might well provide sufficient demand to stimulate the maintenance and rehabilitation of a considerable amount of existing housing. In the past United States housing policy has experimented with several subsidized housing programs, in an attempt to find solutions to the problem of adequate housing for poor people. The programs have not made a decisive impact, at least not in Chicago. The potential of a housing allowance program is that it would involve large-scale resources, and that it would work through the private housing market, which has efficiently produced a tremendous supply of largely well-designed and constructed housing. The housing allowance remains the best hope for a solution to the low-income housing problem, and perhaps for the future viability of the housing stock of Chicago.

Notes
Index

Notes

1. PHILANTHROPIC HOUSING PROJECTS

1. For an architectural description of the building see Grant Manson, *Frank Lloyd Wright to 1910: The First Golden Age* (New York: Reinhold, 1958), pp. 80–83.
2. Thomas H. Hines, *Burnham of Chicago: Architect and Planner* (New York: Oxford University Press, 1974), pp. 270–71.
3. This and other information about Francisco Terrace is contained in a 1971 letter from Mary Waller Langhorne, last surviving child of Edward Waller, in the possession of the author.
4. Stanley Buder, *Pullman: An Experiment In Industrial Order and Community Planning 1880–1930* (New York: Oxford University Press, 1967), p. 89.
5. Benjamin J. Rosenthal, *Reconstructing America: Sociologically and Economically* (Attica, Ind.: Arcadia Book Company, 1919), p. 5.
6. Daniel H. Burnham and Edward H. Bennett, *Plan of Chicago* (Chicago: The Commercial Club, 1909), pp. 108–9.
7. Harold M. Mayer and Richard C. Wade, *Chicago: Growth of a Metropolis* (Chicago: University of Chicago Press, 1969), p. 326.
8. These figures come from documents in the files of the Estate of Benjamin J. Rosenthal, which in 1976 still maintained offices in the North America Building at 36 South State Street.
9. This information was obtained from tax stamps on deeds for the properties filed with the office of the Cook County Recorder of Deeds.
10. Carl W. Condit, *Chicago 1910–29: Building, Planning and Urban Technology* (Chicago: University of Chicago Press, 1973), Table 3.
11. M. R. Werner, *Julius Rosenwald: The Life of a Practical Humanitarian* (New York and London: Harper and Brothers, 1939), pp. 127–33.
12. Allan H. Spear, *Black Chicago: The Making of a Negro Ghetto 1890–1920* (Chicago: University of Chicago Press, 1967), Table 1.
13. Werner, *Julius Rosenwald: The Life of a Practical Humanitarian*, p. 278.
14. Condit, *Chicago 1910–29: Building, Planning and Urban Technology*, p. 166.
15. "Garden Apartments Provide School and Recreation Activities," *Architectural Record* 76 (August 1934): 110–12.
16. Undated Marshall Field Gardens rental brochure, in the library of the Chicago Historical Society.
17. Stephen Becker, *Marshall Field III* (New York: Simon & Schuster, 1964), pp. 113, 114.

2. EARLY PUBLIC HOUSING

1. Carl W. Condit, *Chicago 1930–70: Building, Planning, and Urban Technology* (Chicago: University of Chicago Press, 1974), Table 3.
2. *The Chicago Housing Authority, Manager and Builder of Low-Rent Communities* (Chicago Housing Authority, 1940), pp. 7–9.
3. Wayne McMillen, "Public Housing in Chicago, 1946," *Social Service Review* 20, no. 2 (June 1946): 151.
4. Edith Abbott, *The Tenements of Chicago: 1908–1935* (Chicago: University of Chicago Press, 1936), p. 442. The book also appears in a reprint edition—New York: Arno Press and the *New York Times*, 1970.
5. Ibid, p. 488.
6. *Survey of Tenants of Trumbull Park, Julia C. Lathrop and Jane Addams Houses* (Chicago Housing Authority, 1949), p. 29.
7. *The Chicago Housing Authority, Manager and Builder of Low-Rent Communities*, p. 17.
8. Martin Meyerson and Edward C. Banfield, *Politics, Planning and the Public Interest: The Case of Public Housing in Chicago* (Glencoe, Ill.: The Free Press, 1955), p. 20.
9. Ibid, pp. 121–22.
10. *Information in Regard to the Proposed South Park Gardens Housing Project* (Chicago Housing Authority, 1938), p. 27. The Ida B. Wells Homes was called the South Park Gardens Project in the planning stages.

3. CHICAGO HOUSING AUTHORITY: THE WAR YEARS

1. Wayne McMillen, "Public Housing in Chicago, 1946," *Social Service Review* 20, no. 2 (June 1946): 150.
2. See F. A. Hayek, *Verdict on Rent Control: Essays on the Economic Consequences of Political Action to Restrict Rents in Five Countries* (London: Institute of Economic Affairs, 1972) and Ernest M. Fisher, "Twenty Years of Rent Control in New York City," *Essays in Land Economics* (Los Angeles: University of California Real Estate Research Program, 1966).
3. McMillen, "Public Housing in Chicago, 1946," p. 153.
4. *Report to the Mayor: 1941* (Chicago Housing Authority) p. 21.
5. Martin Meyerson and Edward C. Banfield, *Politics, Planning and the Public Interest: The Case of Public Housing in Chicago* (Glencoe, Ill.: The Free Press, 1955), p. 123.
6. *Report to the Mayor: 1945* (Chicago Housing Authority), p. 8.
7. Meyerson and Banfield, *Politics, Planning and the Public Interest*, p. 125.
8. Ibid, p. 128.

4. CHICAGO HOUSING AUTHORITY: THE MIDDLE YEARS

1. Carl W. Condit, *Chicago 1930–70: Building, Planning, and Urban Technology* (Chicago: University of Chicago Press, 1974), Table 3.
2. 334 U.S. 1 (1948).
3. Rose Helper, *Racial Policies and Practices of Real Estate Brokers* (Minneapolis: University of Minnesota Press, 1969), p. 225.
4. *The Livability of Low-Rent Public Housing: A Pilot Survey of Five CHA Projects* (Chicago Housing Authority, 1950).
5. J. S. Fuerst, "Public Housing Measured—3 Criteria for Success," *American City*, February 1949, pp. 97–98. J. S. Fuerst and Rosalyn Kaplan, "Chicago Public Housing Program Helps Save Babies' Lives: Better Living Conditions Plus Health Services Reduce Infant Mortality Rate," *The Child* 15, no. 10 (June–July 1951): 178–81.
6. John P. Dean, "The Myths of Housing Reform," *American Sociological Review* 14, no. 2 (April 1949): 281.
7. *The Chicago Housing Authority Report for 1948*, p. 20.
8. See *Memorandum on Relocation: Chicago Housing Authority Experience* (Chicago Housing Authority, 1948).
9. Elizabeth Wood, "Realities of Urban Redevelopment," *Journal of Housing* 3, no. 1 (December 1945–January 1946): 12–14.
10. Elizabeth Wood, *Housing Design: A Social Theory* (New York: Citizen's Housing and Planning Council of New York, 1961), pp. 3–4.
11. *Chicago Housing Facts: Supplement to the 1951 Annual Report of the Chicago Housing Authority*, Table IV–8.
12. *Illinois Revised Statutes* (1949), Ch. 67½, Sec. 9, as amended.
13. Martin Meyerson and Edward C. Banfield, *Politics, Planning and the Public Interest: The Case of Public Housing in Chicago* (Glencoe, Ill.: The Free Press, 1955), pp. 129–31, 134.
14. "The Dreary Deadlock of Public Housing—How to Break It," *Architectural Forum*, June 1957, pp. 222–23.
15. "Experiment in Multi-Story Housing," *Journal of Housing* 8, no. 10 (October 1951): 367.
16. For an architectural discussion of these five projects, plus Prairie Avenue Courts, see Julian Whittlesly, "New Dimensions in Housing Design," *Progressive Architecture* 32 (April 1951): 57–68.

5. CHICAGO HOUSING AUTHORITY: YEARS OF TURMOIL

1. Chicago's Housing Need: An Interim Measurement (Chicago Housing Authority, July 1949).
2. *Housing Today, Key to Chicago's Tomorrow: Annual Report of the Chicago Housing Authority to the Mayor of Chicago, 1950*, p. 1.
3. Glencoe, Ill.: The Free Press, 1955. The book has been reprinted in a paperback edition—New York: Macmillan, Free Press, 1964.
4. Martin Meyerson and Edward C. Banfield, *Politics, Planning and the*

Public Interest: The Case of Public Housing in Chicago (Glencoe, Ill.: The Free Press, 1955), pp. 136–37.

5. Ibid, pp. 199–200.
6. *The Trumbull Park Homes Disturbances: A Chronological Report, August 4, 1953 to June 30, 1955* (Chicago Commission on Human Relations, n.d.), p. 24.
7. Ibid, p. 41.
8. Ibid, pp. 61–63.
9. Robert Gruenberg, "Chicago Fiddles While Trumbull Park Burns," *Nation* 178, no. 21 (May 22, 1954): 441.
10. *Report to the Mayor and to the City Council of the Committee on Racial Tensions in Housing Projects* (Chicago Commission On Human Relations, January 15, 1954).
11. *Trumbull Park: A Progress Report* (Chicago: Housing Opportunities Program, American Friends Service Committee, March 1957), p. 5.
12. Robert Gruenberg, "Trumbull Park: Act II, Elizabeth Wood Story," *Nation* 179, no. 12 (September 18, 1954): 231.
13. J. S. Fuerst, *Public Housing In Europe and America* (New York: John Wiley and Sons, Halsted Press, 1974), pp. 159–61.
14. New York: Macmillan Publishing Co., Collier Books, 1973.
15. New York: Random House, 1961.

6. CHICAGO DWELLINGS ASSOCIATION

1. "Chicago Provides Middle Income Housing: Small Project Replaces Former Slum," *American City*, March 1956, pp. 199, 201.
2. *Low-Cost Single Family Dwelling Units for the Chicago Dwellings Association* (Chicago: Holabird and Root and Burgee, Commission Number 8397, April 25, 1949).
3. Rob Cuscaden, "A Simple, Direct, Quiet Approach to a Low-Cost, Inner-City Home," *Inland Architect*, July 1969, p. 16.
4. Carl W. Condit, *Chicago 1930–70: Building, Planning, and Urban Technology* (Chicago: University of Chicago Press, 1974), p. 163.
5. Chicago Dwellings Association, *Annual Report 1966* (n. pag.).
6. Ibid.
7. Chicago Dwellings Association, *Annual Report 1967*.
8. *Chicago Dwellings Association Quarterly Report to the City Council Planning and Housing Committee: For Period Ending December 31, 1972.*
9. *Chicago Dwellings Association Lawndale Properties: Project Nos. 665, 666, 667, 680, 681, 682, 683.*

7. CHICAGO HOUSING AUTHORITY: THE HIGH-RISE YEARS

1. *A Report by the Chicago Community Inventory, University of Chicago, to the Department of City Planning, City of Chicago* (February 1960), p. 1.

2. Chesley Manly, "Public Housing Really Houses Few In Chicago. Here's the Record After 20 Years," *Chicago Tribune*, September 9, 1956.

3. *Annual Report of the Chicago Housing Authority. 1956—A Year of Progress* (n. pag.).

4. *Chicago's Investment in Public Housing: Highlights of the Twenty Years and 1955. Annual Report of the Chicago Housing Authority* (n. pag.).

5. *Chicago Housing Authority Annual Report. Year Ended June 30, 1959*, Table 13.

6. Chicago Housing Authority, *CHA Monthly Report*, December 1951, pp. 3–4.

7. Carl W. Condit, *Chicago 1930–70: Building, Planning, and Urban Technology*, (Chicago: University of Chicago Press, 1974), p. 158.

8. *Rockwell Gardens: The Chicago Housing Authority's Plan for Saving An Old Neighborhood From Blight* (Chicago Housing Authority, 1956).

9. Ruth Moore, "PHA Can't Pin Down High Building Costs Here," *Chicago Sun-Times*, June 2, 1959.

10. M. W. Newman, "Chicago's $70 Million Ghetto," *Chicago Daily News*, April 10, 1965.

11. M. W. Newman, "Irony of the Taylor Homes Mess—It Was Planned," *Chicago Daily News*, April 15, 1965.

12. Ruth Moore, "Architects Propose CHA Build Low-Rise Apartments," *Chicago Sun-Times*, May 14, 1964.

13. Chicago Housing Authority, *Memorandum to Commissioners*, March 9, 1976.

14. Letter From Charles R. Swibel, chairman, Board of Commissioners, Chicago Housing Authority, to Larry S. Fanning, executive editor, *Chicago Daily News*, April 26, 1965, p. 7.

15. Catherine Bauer, "The Dreary Deadlock of Public Housing," *Architectural Forum*, May 1957, p. 221.

16. *Chicago Public Housing Today* 6, no. 2 (June 1, 1957): 1–2.

17. Ruth Moore, "Seek Delay In CHA Plan for High-Rises," *Chicago Sun-Times*, October 20, 1964.

18. Chicago Housing Authority, *Statistical Report 1974* (May 1975), Table 12.

19. "CHA Has a Vacancy Problem—On Its Board, Not in Housing," *Chicago Daily News*, June 26, 1963.

20. Edward T. Pound and Scott Jacobs, "Swibel Fined For Failing to Clean Up Skid Row Flophouse," *Chicago Sun-Times*, August 10, 1975.

21. Edward T. Pound and Scott Jacobs, "Tell Swibel Ties to Bank Holding CHA Accounts," *Chicago Sun-Times*, July 20, 1975.
Edward T. Pound and Scott Jacobs, "Asks State Probe on Ousting Swibel," *Chicago Sun-Times*, July 23, 1965.

22. Ruth Moore, "Hyde Park–Kenwood Area to Get Varied Homes," *Chicago Sun-Times*, April 26, 1965.

23. Peter H. Rossi and Robert A. Dentler, *The Politics of Urban Renewal:*

The Chicago Findings (New York: Macmillan, Free Press, 1961), pp. 225–39. Julia Abrahamson, *A Neighborhood Finds Itself* (New York: Harper and Brothers, 1959), pp. 270–71.

24. Condit, *Chicago 1930–70: Building, Planning, and Urban Technology*, pp. 151, 200n21. "Chicago to Sell Public Project as Co-op," *Cooperative Housing* 5, no. 2 (Spring 1968): 8.

25. *Chicago Housing Authority Times*, April 1968, p. 1.

26. *The Chicago Housing Authority Year Ended June 30, 1963: Highlights of the Operation*, p. 5.

8. THE COMMUNITY RENEWAL FOUNDATION AND THE KATE MAREMONT FOUNDATION

1. Building Permit Application 323847, City of Chicago, Department of Buildings (1944).

2. Letter of June 14, 1975, from Bertrand Goldberg to the author.

3. *The Community Renewal Foundation: A History in Review* (Chicago: Community Renewal Foundation, November 1972), p. 10.

4. Ibid.

5. Ibid, p. 11.

6. Ibid, p. 12.

7. Ibid, p. 21.

8. Ibid, pp. 20, 21.

9. Ibid, p. 25.

10. *Demonstration Project Report on Low Income Housing* (Demonstration Grant Project No. I111. LIHD-2, Sponsored by Community Renewal Foundation, Inc.), p. 1.

11. See *The Kate Maremont Foundation: Urban Housing Program* (Chicago: Kate Maremont Foundation, n.d.), n. pag. The figures also include the Michigan Boulevard Garden Apartments, omitted from that report.

12. From interview with Michael Maremont, vice-president of the Kate Maremont Foundation, conducted by the author May 18, 1976.

13. *The Kate Maremont Foundation: Urban Housing Program*.

14. Susan Boie, "Tenants Object to Converting to Condominium," *Chicago Tribune*, May 14, 1967.

15. Interview with Michael Maremont.

16. Ruth Moore, "Remaking of a City—Foundation Rescues Slums," *Chicago Sun-Times*, April 11, 1965.

17. Interview with Michael Maremont.

18. Ibid.

19. Ruth Moore, "Better Housing Foundation Hit By W. Side Rent Strike," *Chicago Sun-Times*, February 10,1968.

20. Cornelia Honchar, "Ex-Prof Says He Helped Start Maremont Projects," *Chicago Tribune*, December 10, 1971.

21. Cornelia Honchar, "FBI to Be Asked to Look into Housing Failures," *Chicago Tribune*, December 6, 1971.

22. Cornelia Honchar, "Maremont Project Files Put under Tight Security," *Chicago Tribune*, December 7, 1971.

23. Thomas M. Gray, "Deny Mismanagement in 2 Housing Rehabilitation Failures," *Chicago Sun-Times*, December 8, 1971.

24. Cornelia Honchar, "Audit Showed Maremont Shaky Before New Projects," *Chicago Tribune*, December 20, 1971.

25. Interview with Michael Maremont.

9. FEDERALLY SUBSIDIZED, PRIVATELY SPONSORED HOUSING

1. U.S. Department of Housing and Urban Development, *Occupancy Report Control List, As of June 30, 1976*; and *Roster of Private Sponsors of Low and Moderate Income Housing: Number 4* (City of Chicago Department of Development and Planning, December 1972).

2. "What's a Nice PUD Doing in a Former Slum?" *House and Home*, July 1970, p. 48.

3. For a description of the Near South Side urban renewal area, see Gerald D. Suttles, *The Social Construction of Communities* (Chicago: University of Chicago Press, 1972), pp. 82–107.

4. "What's a Nice PUD Doing in a Former Slum?"

5. Deborah Pellow, *The New Urban Community: Mutual Relevance of the Social and Physical Environments* (Chicago: Council for Community Services in Metropolitan Chicago, 1975), p. 25.

6. From interview with Elaine Soloway (resident of South Commons who studied the population for a Master's thesis in preparation for the University of Illinois at Chicago Circle) conducted by the author October 19, 1976.

7. New York: Random House, p. 318.

8. Mort Kaplan Press Release for The Woodlawn Organization and the Kate Maremont Foundation, March 24, 1974.

9. Thomas M. Gray, "TWO Officials Probe High Costs of Housing Development," *Chicago Sun-Times*, December 7, 1971.

10. Cornelia Honchar, "Maremont Foundation Group Fired As Manager of Woodlawn Project," *Chicago Tribune*, December 8, 1971.

11. Cornelia Honchar, "Maremont Project Funds $45,000 Short," *Chicago Tribune*, December 9, 1971.

12. Gary Washburn, "Woodlawn Gardens Moving Toward a Bright Future," *Chicago Tribune*, February 23, 1975.

13. U.S. Department of Housing and Urban Development, *Multifamily Default Analysis* (August 1976).

14. Washburn, "Woodlawn Gardens Moving Toward a Bright Future."

15. M. W. Newman, "Instant Myth and All That Thing vs. Real Low-Income Housing," *Inland Architect*, October 1970, p. 12.

16. Department of Housing and Urban Development, *Multifamily Default Analysis*.

17. David Lowe, *Lost Chicago* (Boston: Houghton Mifflin Company, 1975), p. 211.

18. Constance M. Greiff, *Lost America: From the Atlantic to the Missis-sippi* (Princeton: The Pyne Press, 1971), p. 210.

19. Much of the information about Parkway Gardens came from an interview with Joseph M. Deas, Jr., longtime resident, board member, and manager of the development, conducted by the author, October 12, 1976.

20. *Douglas-Lawndale Amended Urban Renewal Plan* (City of Chicago, Department of Urban Renewal, April 1968), Exhibit No. 1.

21. *Report of the Hearing Examiner on the Public Hearings Held by the Assessor of Cook County to Determine a Differential Taxation Policy for Real Property in Cook County* (n.d.), pp. 22, 36–37.

22. *Special Study: Assessment Practices Regarding Subsidized Housing, Cook County, Illinois* (Appraisal Research Counselors, Ltd., Real Estate Appraisal Company of Chicago, May 1974), Sec. 12-6.

23. Report of William J. Townsley, appraisal consultant, to the Cook County Assessor's Office (November 18, 1974), pp. 1, 2, 100.

24. *Leased Housing Program* (Chicago Housing Authority, November 1975).

25. Scott Jacobs, "Rent Subsidies for Middle Class—Dawn of an Era," *Chicago Sun-Times*, December 14, 1975.

10. CHICAGO HOUSING AUTHORITY: THE FOURTH DECADE

1. Chicago Housing Authority, *CHA Monthly Report*, November 1951, p. 7.

2. *Year ended December 31, 1965: Highlights of the Operation* (Chicago Housing Authority), p. 6.

3. *CHA Facts 1974* (Chicago Housing Authority), p. 13.

4. The "Summit Agreement" (Chicago: Leadership Council for Metropolitan Open Communities, August 25, 1966), par. 3.

5. Gautreaux v. Chicago Housing Authority, 66 C 1459 (N.D. Ill. 1966), Complaint, par. 16.

6. *Gautreaux v. Chicago Housing Authority*, Deposition of C. E. Humphrey, pp. 97–100.

7. Hills v. Gautreaux, 425 U.S. 284 (1976).

8. Scott Jacobs, "Lovely CHA Flats Pleasant Surprise to Many Neighbors," *Chicago Sun-Times*, December 13, 1975.

9. *Human Needs In Public Housing: A Summary of Social Welfare and Health Services and Needs of Residents In Public Housing Developments Serving Families in Chicago* (Welfare Council of Metropolitan Chicago, 1970). Note: the Welfare Council was later renamed the Council for Community Services in Metropolitan Chicago.

10. *Impact of Federal, State and Local Policies on Chicago Housing Authority Residents in Model Neighborhoods* (Chicago: Social Planning Associates, 1970).

11. *Comprehensive Security Program for the Cabrini-Green Homes* (Mayor's Office and Chicago Housing Authority, 1972), p. 10.

12. Scott Jacobs and Edward T. Pound, "CHA To Put $21 million into Cabrini," *Chicago Sun-Times*, July 28, 1975.

13. Unpublished figures from the Chicago Housing Authority Division of Information and Statistics.

14. Andy Shaw, "Gardens—and Hope—Sprout at Cabrini," *Chicago Sun-Times*, August 1, 1976.

15. *Chicago Housing Authority Year Ended December 31, 1966: Highlights of the Operation*, p. 7.

16. *CHA Facts 1974* (Chicago Housing Authority), p. B.

17. Ibid, p. 8.

18. Chicago Housing Authority Division of Information and Statistics.

11. THE ILLINOIS HOUSING DEVELOPMENT AUTHORITY

1. *For Better Housing in Illinois: Report of the Legislative Commission on Low Income Housing* (1967), pp. 6–7.

2. Nathan Sherman Betnun, "State Housing Finance Agencies and Public Purpose Housing Development" (Ph.D. diss. for the Department of Urban Studies and Planning, Massachusetts Institute of Technology, 1975), pp. 9, 22.

3. Ibid, p. 269.

4. Illinois Housing Development Authority Act, *Illinois Revised Statutes* (1967), Ch. 67½, Secs. 301–4.

5. Betnun, "State Housing Finance Agencies," p. 28.

6. See pp. 1–9.

7. Betnun, "State Housing Finance Agencies," p. 122, Table 11.

8. *Housing Development Status Report as of April 30, 1976: Summary of Mortgage Loans to Date* (Illinois Housing Development Authority), p. 2.

9. See Irving M. Gerick, *Critical Issues in Property Management: Report to U.S. Department of Housing and Urban Development* (Nonprofit Housing Center, Inc., as consultants to Arthur D. Little, Inc., 1972), p. 1.

10. Figures From the Illinois Housing Development Authority.

11. Betnun, "State Housing Finance Agencies," p. 148.

12. Illinois Housing Development Authority, *Annual Report 1972*, p. 13.

13. Illinois Housing Development Authority, *Annual Report 1975* (n. pag.).

14. Betnun, "State Housing Finance Agencies," p. 50.

15. *Progress Report of Housing Production* (Illinois Housing Development Authority, 1975), p. 24.

16. Betnun, "State Housing Finance Agencies," pp. 2, 15.

17. Ibid, p. 15.

18. *Progress Report of Housing Production*, p. 7.

19. *Housing Development Status Report as of April 30, 1976: Summary of Mortgage Loans to Date* (Illinois Housing Development Authority), p. 1.

12. OVERVIEW

1. Chicago Housing Authority, *Statistical Report 1975* (November 1976), Table 2.
2. Ibid, Table 5.
3. Chicago Housing Authority, *Statistical Report 1974* (May 1975), Table 5.
4. *Statistical Report 1975*, Table 5.
5. Ibid, Table 9.
6. Ibid, Table 10.
7. Ibid, Table 12.
8. Chicago Housing Authority, *Summary Statement of Receipts and Expenditures CHA-Owned Developments Under Management, For Period Ended December 31, 1975* (1976).
9. For a full description of the Brooke Amendment see Daniel R. Mandelker, *Housing Subsidies in the United States and England* (Indianapolis: Bobbs-Merrill Company, 1973), pp. 81–112.
10. *CHA Facts 1975* (Chicago Housing Authority), p. H.
11. *Chicago Housing Authority Times*, June 1976, n. pag.
12. Letter dated December 30, 1971 from C. E. Humphrey, CHA executive director, to Lewis W. Hill, commissioner of City of Chicago Department of Development and Planning.
13. Letter dated January 20, 1976, from G. W. Master, CHA acting executive director, to Lewis W. Hill, commissioner of City of Chicago Department of Development and Planning.
14. Chicago Housing Authority, *Summary Statement.*
15. *Properties Foreclosed or in Foreclosure, and Properties Closed, Previously Foreclosed* (lists provided the author by HUD in October 1976, pursuant to the Freedom of Information Act).
16. U.S. Department of Housing and Urban Development, *Multifamily Default Analysis* (August 1976).
17. Ibid.
18. Nathan Sherman Betnun, "State Housing Finance Agencies and Public Purpose Housing Development" (Ph.D. diss. for the Department of Urban Studies and Planning, Massachusetts Institute of Technology, 1975), pp. 265–69.
19. Unpublished estimate the Chicago Area Geographic Information Study, University of Illinois at Chicago Circle (December 1976).
20. Irving Cutler, *Chicago: Metropolis of the Mid-Continent* (Dubuque, Iowa: The Geographical Society of Chicago and Kendall-Hunt Publishing Company, 1976), p. 47.
21. "Estimates of the Population of Metropolitan Areas, 1973 and 1974, and Components of Change Since 1970," *Current Population Reports: Population Estimates and Projections* (U.S. Department of Commerce, Bureau of the Census, Series P-25, No. 618, January 1976), Table 1.
22. *Housing and Households: Chicago–1970* (Department of Development and Planning, City of Chicago, June 1975), p. 1.

23. Ibid.

24. Ibid, p. 48.

25. *Survey of Building* (Bell Federal Savings and Loan Association, January 1972, 1973, 1974, 1975, 1976).

26. *Summary of Work Classification Permits* (City of Chicago, December 1971, 1972, 1973, 1974, 1975).

27. *Housing and Households*, p. 1.

28. Ibid.

29. Ibid, p. 6.

30. *A Study of Property Taxes and Urban Blight* (Report to U.S. Department of Housing and Urban Development, H-1299, January 1973), Table 11.4.

31. Ibid, Table 11.5.

32. Anthony Downs, "Using the Lessons of Experience to Allocate Resources in the Community Development Program," *Recommendations for Community Development Planning* (Chicago: Real Estate Research Corporation, n.d.), pp. 18–24.

33. *Second Annual Report of the Housing Assistance Supply Experiment: October 1974–September 1975* (U.S. Department of Housing and Urban Development, Office of Policy Development and Research, R-1959- HUD, May 1976), p. xviii.

34. Al Hirshen and Richard R. LeGates, "Neglected Dimensions in Low-Income Housing and Development Programs," *Urban Law Journal* 9, no. 3 (1975): 11.

35. Kenneth F. Phillips and Michael B. Teitz, "Central-City Housing Conservation: A Mortgage Insurance Approach," *California Management Review* 18, no. 3 (Spring 1976): 86.

36. Henry A. Aaron, *Federal Housing Subsidies: History, Problems and Alternatives* (Washington: The Brookings Institution, Reprint 261, 1973), p. 276.

Index

DATE DUE

DEC 12 2002		
ell 20/4		

Demco, Inc. 38-293

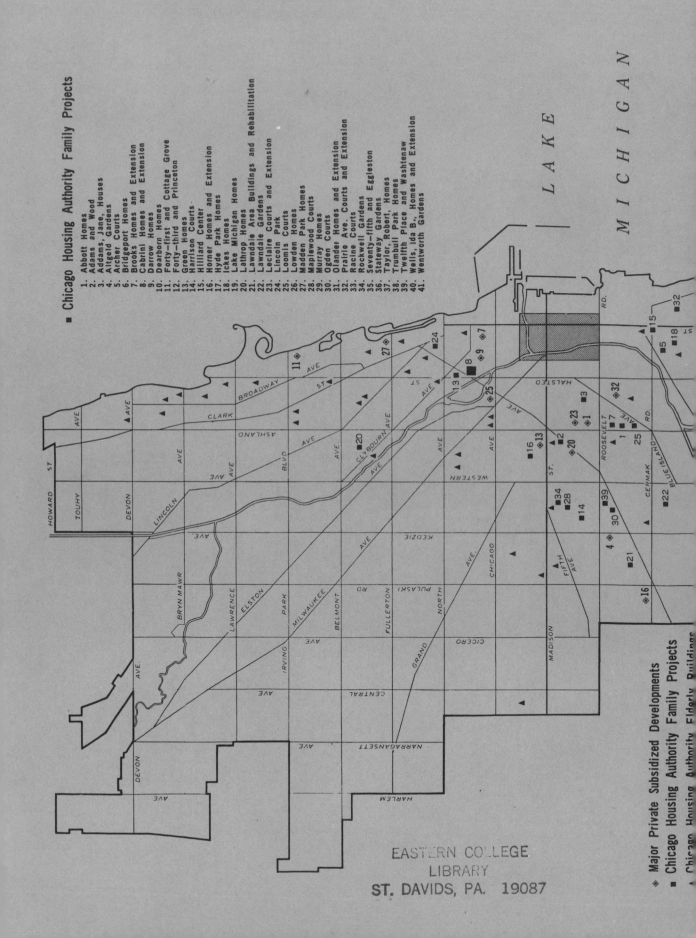

■ Chicago Housing Authority Family Projects

1. Abbott Homes
2. Adams and Wood
3. Addams, Jane, Houses
4. Altgeld Gardens
5. Archer Courts
6. Bridgeport Homes
7. Brooks Homes and Extension
8. Cabrini Homes and Extension
9. Darrow Homes
10. Dearborn Homes
11. Forty-first and Cottage Grove
12. Forty-third and Princeton
13. Green Homes
14. Harrison Courts
15. Hilliard Center
16. Horner Homes and Extension
17. Hyde Park Homes
18. Ickes Homes
19. Lake Michigan Homes
20. Lathrop Homes
21. Lawndale Area Buildings and Rehabilitation
22. Lawndale Gardens
23. Leclaire Courts and Extension
24. Lincoln Park
25. Loomis Courts
26. Lowden Homes
27. Madden Park Homes
28. Maplewood Courts
29. Murray Homes
30. Ogden Courts
31. Olander Homes and Extension
32. Prairie Ave. Courts and Extension
33. Racine Courts
34. Rockwell Gardens
35. Seventy-fifth and Eggleston
36. Stateway Gardens
37. Taylor, Robert, Homes
38. Trumbull Park Homes
39. Twelfth Place and Washtenaw
40. Wells, Ida B., Homes and Extension
41. Wentworth Gardens

◆ Major Private Subsidized Developments

■ Chicago Housing Authority Family Projects

▲ Chicago Housing Authority Elderly Buildings